SO-BQX-031

Moving Working Families Forward

Moving Working Families Forward

Third Way Policies That Can Work

Robert Cherry with Robert Lerman

NEW YORK UNIVERSITY PRESS
New York and London

NEW YORK UNIVERSITY PRESS
New York and London
www.nyupress.org

References to Internet websites (URLs) were accurate at the time of writing.
Neither the author nor New York University Press is responsible for URLs
that may have expired or changed since the manuscript was prepared.

Library of Congress Cataloging-in-Publication Data
Cherry, Robert D., 1944–
Moving working families forward : third way policies that can work /
Robert Cherry with Robert Lerman.
p. cm. Includes bibliographical references and index.
ISBN 978-0-8147-1718-9 (cl : alk. paper) —
ISBN 978-0-8147-9000-7 (pb : alk. paper) —
ISBN 978-0-8147-7299-7 (ebook)
1. Working class families—Government policy—United States.
2. Working poor—Government policy—United States.
3. United States—Economic policy.   4. United States—Social policy.
I. Lerman, Robert I.   II. Title.
HD8072.5.C474   2011
331.12'042—dc23   2011018448

New York University Press books are printed on acid-free paper,
and their binding materials are chosen for strength and durability.
We strive to use environmentally responsible suppliers and materials
to the greatest extent possible in publishing our books.

Manufactured in the United States of America
10 9 8 7 6 5 4 3 2 1

To my grandchildren:
Jacob, Gita, Kentaro, and Daniela

Contents

Acknowledgments

Over the last decade, I had become increasingly cynical concerning public policies. As partisanship has grown, it has become difficult to find support for centrist policies. While they may be acceptable to some Democrats and some Republicans, these policies can never be a priority, since they do not meet the needs of the polarized core constituencies. While I think Republican politicians are most responsible, Democrats are not blameless.

My attitude was colored by the continued unwillingness of Democrats to take ownership of the welfare reform legislation that may well have been the crowning achievement of the Clinton administration. Despite protests from liberals, President Clinton steadfastly pursued this legislation. Aided by favorable economic circumstances, this legislation dramatically transformed for the better the lives of single mothers. But rather than pointing to this legislative success, most Democrats have erased its memory. Indeed, when Hillary Clinton ran for president in the 2008 Democratic primaries, neither she nor her opponent, Barack Obama, mentioned this legislation.

Not surprisingly, I was particularly disheartened when my book *Welfare Transformed: Universalize Social Policies That Work* was pretty much ignored. When the 2008 presidential cycle began, however, my children, Sara and Joshua, convinced me that I should make one more try at putting forward a set of centrist policies. After all, both Democratic candidates were pretty centrist so that despite some necessary leftist rhetoric, they and their advisers would be sympathetic to the kinds of policies I would advocate. So, reluctantly, I began on the journey that led to this book.

As I began working on this project, I became less cynical. First, I was buoyed by the enthusiasm I received at NYU Press, particularly from my editor, Ilene Kalish. Next, I was most fortunate to enlist the efforts of Bob Lerman, someone I had met during my welfare project. He was cajoled into preparing two of the policy chapters: on housing and strengthening partnerships. These chapters added substantial value to the book. Just as important, his general counsel and suggestions clarified my thoughts and improved substantially many other sections of the book.

I also gladly acknowledge many individuals who read book chapters: Alex Vitale, Carolina Bank-Munoz, Veronica Manlow, Herve Queneau, Sumitra Shah, Sanford Schram, Myra Kogen, Mary Gatta, Marc Fox, and Paul Moses.

1

A Third Way Perspective

Deep conflicts over public policy persist not simply between Republicans and Democrats but also within the Democratic Party. This book highlights these intra-Democratic differences. It points to a "Third Way" between the left-liberal wing of the Democratic Party and conservatives who dominate the Republican Party. These policies are crucial given the current economic malaise that persists, and the divided Congress that must find common ground.

With persistent near-double-digit official unemployment rates, with record levels of long-term joblessness, more must be done to aid working families. But almost from the start, the Obama administration has had to struggle with Congress. In the middle of 2010, almost a year after the recession was officially over and economic growth had begun, there were almost five unemployed workers for every job opening. This was almost double the ratio during the worst of the economic slowdown at the beginning of the decade. Despite this, Republican senators balked at extending unemployment insurance. As a result, over 2 million of the more than 5.5 million unemployed workers who qualified for unemployment insurance had their benefits temporarily halted. Thankfully, Democrats were able to successfully extend benefits for another four months.[1]

But even when President Obama has been successful at extending federal benefits, state and local officials did not follow suit. While the number of families receiving federally funded food stamps increased substantially at the beginning of the recession, states minimally increased the number of families collecting cash assistance. "There is ample reason to be concerned here," said Ron Haskins, a former Republican congressional aide who helped write the 1996 law overhauling the welfare system. "The overall structure is not working the way it was designed to work. We would expect, just on the face it, that when a deep recession happens, people could go back on welfare. When we started this, Democratic and Republican governors alike said, 'We know what's best for our state; we're not going to let people starve,'" said Mr.

Haskins, who is now a researcher at the Brookings Institution in Washington. "And now that the chips are down, and unemployment is going up, most states are not doing enough to help families get back on the rolls."[2]

Much of this resistance reflects a conservative ideology that emphasizes individual responsibility. This was most clear when some state and local officials refused to adjust policies even when the cost would be picked up by the federal government. Texas and South Carolina governors rejected federal stimulus funds that required them to relax unemployment compensation rules that would have allowed more unemployment workers to qualify for benefits. These proposed procedures were already in place in twenty states and were helping many lower-waged workers.

Even the more moderate Mayor Michael Bloomberg of New York City refused federal funds for a food stamp expansion because it conflicted with his notion of encouraging self-sufficiency. Cognizant of the economic downturn, the federal stimulus plan entitled able-bodied single adults without dependents to remain eligible to receive food stamps until September 2010. This overturned present law, which limited these recipients to a guaranteed food stamp entitlement of only three months in a three-year period. Mr. Bloomberg would extend benefits beyond three months only if these adults enrolled in the city's workfare program, which offers some training, some internships, and some low-level work. A *New York Times* editorial lamented, "We can understand the mayor's ideal of 'work, not welfare,' but this is not a time to be stingy with food, especially if Washington is picking up the tab."[3]

These conservative responses to the problems faced by the less fortunate can be callous, but some left-liberal responses are also questionable. In our view, they overly emphasize the need for more government spending and too often minimize the importance of influencing individual behavior. As a result, we believe that the necessary policies to advance the economic well-being of working families must reflect a Third Way.

There are three important parameters that distinguish the Third Way: the importance of personal responsibility, structural impediments, and financial incentives. On one end of the political spectrum are conservatives. They emphasize the importance of personal responsibility and believe that individuals should rely on and will benefit from a competitive free-market system.

At the other end of the political spectrum are left liberals. While there are certainly variations among them, most left liberals generally minimize any notion of personal responsibility, which they characterize as "blaming the victims," and instead see profit-seeking motives as the source of problems.

They focus on examples of market exploitation: underpayment of workers, overcharging of consumers, and predatory lending in low-income areas.

The Third Way navigates an intermediate position between these two poles. While supporting policies to limit market excesses, Third Way proponents also find opportunities to use market incentives to aid working people. While personal responsibility should be encouraged, Third Way proponents believe that the government must provide significant supports that enable working people to move forward—supports that require substantial government resources.

Third Way proponents also identify important structural impediments that will hold back personal advancement in the absence of government initiatives. Most important has been the potentially damaging impact that poverty has on the long-term outlook for children, especially those living in single-parent households. As a result, Third Way proponents support a range of policies to strengthen low-income families.

Third Way proponents also contend that technological changes have created important impediments to the upward mobility of many working people. These changes have made most manufactured goods cheaper to produce in suburban industrial parks or abroad rather than in central cities, where most low-income families still live. In addition, technological innovation, by increasing the sophistication of machines, has increased the educational requirements for even those who are employed in traditional blue-collar vocations. Thus, these skill and locational changes have added to employment difficulties, particularly those faced by less educated central-city workers.

More generally, the Third Way has a left-liberal commitment to government funding that enhances the incomes of working families while at the same time recognizing that conservative concerns for program effectiveness and individual responsibility are sometimes justified. Government must be both compassionate and competent. In addition, including conservative recommendations can avoid some of the contentious distractions that reliance on ideological purity often causes, something that is particularly important with a divided Congress.

New York Times columnist David Brooks noted that the conservative perspective, which rejects the role of government, has lost its hold on the American populace. He wrote, "The emphasis on freedom and individual choice may work in the sparsely populated parts of the country. People there naturally want to do whatever they want on their own land. But it doesn't work in the densely populated parts of the country: the cities and suburbs where

Republicans are getting slaughtered. People in these areas understand that their lives are profoundly influenced by other people's individual choices."

He then pointed out that there are two relevant visions of the role of government within the Democratic Party. One vision—what we have labeled left liberalism—rejects reliance on the market and instead has "teams of experts draw up plans to engineer order wherever problems arise. And there is the more centrist vision in which government sets certain rules, but mostly empowers the complex web of institutions in which the market is embedded."[4]

In each of the policy areas to be discussed the Third Way approach will contrast with the recommendations made by most conservatives and left liberals. Our recommendations will rely heavily on research findings. Let us simply state here some of these differences so that the reader can better understand the Third Way perspective. For example, we reject the nativist if not racist sentiment that energizes many within the anti-immigration movement. We are also uncomfortable, however, with left liberals who dismiss the legitimate grievances against legalizing and expanding *low-wage* immigration. We take seriously the unintended harmful effects that this pattern of immigration has on state and local budgets and on the employment of less educated native-born workers.

Similarly, we reject conservative attempts to stifle government-funded educational programs that would help many blacks and women gain a foothold in the middle class. We believe, however, that some of the initiatives emphasized by left liberals are inconsistent with benefit-cost assessments: too much money will be spent with few positive results. In particular, we believe that four-year college degree goals have been overly emphasized at the expense of occupational training at community colleges. We find that many students who fail out of academic programs could have succeeded at occupational ones.

One final example is the workings of the labor market. Conservatives believe that competition forces firms to pay workers fairly. If one employer seeks to underpay his workers, other less exploitive firms will bid these workers away. They believe that wage disparities reflect solely differences in skills and motivation. As a result, they reject government interference with employment decisions, such as through Equal Employment Opportunity (EEO) regulations or legislation to facilitate unionization.

By contrast, most left liberals believe that race and gender wage gaps are dominantly the result of direct and indirect discrimination so that they focus on strengthening government antidiscrimination efforts. In addition, many believe that wages are determined by a struggle between capital and labor so that unions and government-mandated wage policies, including living-wage and minimum-wage legislation, are the most important ways to raise the economic well-being of working people.

The Third Way certainly believes that EEO policies have been an important vehicle for limiting discriminatory labor market behavior and should be strengthened in labor markets for less educated workers. And unions and government-mandated wage policies have played a positive role. But Third Way advocates also believe that in large part race and gender wage gaps reflect behavioral and structural factors. In particular, improving both soft and hard skills among black men can substantially reduce racial earnings disparities among men with less than four-year degrees. Similarly, Third Way advocates focus on policies that enable working-class women to better balance work and family. These policies include better child care arrangements and strengthening partnerships relationships to encourage marriage or long-term cohabitation.

Most important, Third Way advocates believe that there has been too great an emphasis on maximizing the number of four-year college graduates. In pursuit of this goal, left liberals discourage occupational training in high schools and community colleges. They fear that providing attractive occupational programs will inevitably track low-income students into low-wage, dead-end jobs, reproducing poverty in another generation. They ignore evidence that weakly prepared high school graduates do not have the academic skills necessary to pursue college-level work, resulting in very low college graduation rates. They ignore evidence that when community colleges do not provide these programs, many low-income blacks and Latinos seek them at private, for-profit schools that often saddle students with loans and problematic employment credentials.

Finally, Third Way advocates believe that left liberals focus too much on raising wages through either government mandates or union efforts. By contrast, Third Way advocates believe that because of firm mobility and the skill deficiency of workers, government supplements like the Earned Income Tax Credit (EITC) may be a more effective way to raise incomes of struggling working families.

Targeting Working Families

Now that we have given some sense of the perspective that will underpin the policy recommendations to be proposed in this book, some understanding of the target population will be useful. Every politician espouses concern for working families, but few explicitly identify whom they exclude. For example, President Obama's working families only exclude those making more than $250,000—less than 5 percent of all families. This book identifies a much smaller subset of families: those that have annual incomes below $70,000. This subset includes the officially poor—those with incomes below $20,000; the near-poor—those with incomes between $20,000 and $40,000; and the lower middle class—those with incomes above $40,000 but no higher than $70,000.

In 2007, 55 percent of all families but only 46 percent of married-couple families had incomes below $70,000 so that this threshold reflects a rough calculation of the median income of all families nationally. The $20,000 figure closely matches the current government income threshold for judging the official poverty rate. In 2009, families with one adult and two children were officially poor if their income was below $17,285; for families with two adults and two children, the poverty-line threshold was $21,756.[5]

In 2009, 43.6 million people, or 14.3 percent of all U.S. residents, were classified as poor. Virtually all researchers believe that the official poverty-line thresholds are outmoded. Indeed, the Census Bureau calculates poverty rates for a number of alternative measures, all of which are higher than the official cutoffs. Depending upon how out-of-pocket medical expenses and adjustments for geographic location are treated, alternative poverty measures can be significantly higher than the official rate.

It should also be noted that the government's measure of family income may be too low. Specifically, it does not include current refundable tax benefits like the EITC and child credit that add substantially to the purchasing power of low-income families. If the government used a measure of *disposable* income, with its current income cutoffs, poverty rates would decline by about 25 percent.[6]

According to a range of studies, the share of families that experience material hardships declines as income increases. Material hardships persist, however, in a significant share of families until income rises above twice the poverty-line thresholds.[7] These material hardships include going without a meal because of lack of income at least once in the past month or having some utility turned off for lack of payment during the last year. Thus, the $40,000 threshold was chosen to identify near-poor households whose incomes are above the poverty cutoffs but less than what is necessary to fully escape material hardships.

Not surprisingly, the distribution of income is different for families headed by a married couple and those headed by a woman with no husband present. In 2007, 34.3 percent of female-headed families but only 6.6 percent of married-couple families were poor (figure 1.1). By contrast, 32.6 percent of married-couple families but only 6.3 percent of female-headed families are in the upper middle class: those families with incomes over $100,000. Indeed, only 15.2 percent of female-headed families had incomes above $70,000.[8]

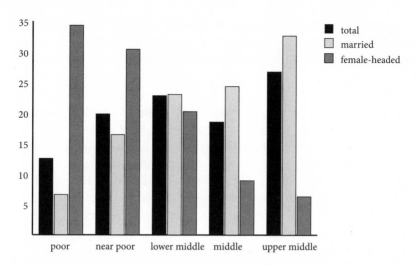

Figure 1.1. The share of each family type across income groups, 2007

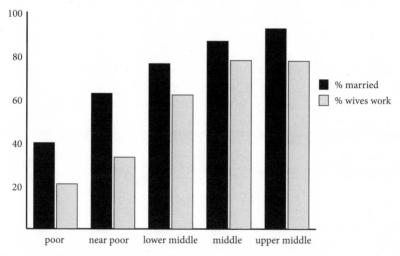

Figure 1.2. Characteristics of married families across income groups, 2007

Married couple families constitute 39.6 percent of all poor households and 62.4 percent of all near-poor households (figure 1.2). These low-income married-couple families are characterized by very low employment of wives. In poor and near-poor married-couple families, the share of wives who are employed is 20.6 and 33.0 percent, respectively. By contrast, for lower-middle-class and middle-class married-couple families, the share is 61.7 and 77.6 percent, respectively.

For many of these married couples, the low income that they are experiencing may reflect the years in which wives shift out of the labor market to care for their young children. As their children age, most of these families are likely to move into the lower middle class when mothers return to the paid workforce. Thus, many married-couple families that are classified as poor or near-poor at some point in time are unlikely to suffer persistent long-term material hardships.

The families that are most at risk to experience persistent *long-term* material hardships are those that are female-headed. As indicated in figure 1.1, very few are in the upper half of the income distribution. They constitute 50.8 percent and 28.4 percent, respectively, of poor and near-poor families. As we go up the income ladder, the share within each income group that is female headed continues to decline. Less than 5 percent of upper-middle-class households are female-headed.[9] This suggests that it will be important to have policies that specifically target female-headed households if we want to reduce the number of families that are at risk for experiencing *persistent* material hardships.

Lessons from the Clinton Administration

When he took office, President Clinton faced an economic climate that had important similarities with those facing President Obama. Though to a much milder degree, then too working families were having difficulties after three years of economic stagnation. Then, too, working families were facing declining standards of living, the specter of widespread underemployment, and a declining set of expectations. These difficulties were particularly severe in central-city neighborhoods where the loss of manufacturing jobs and the crack cocaine culture had created havoc.

President Clinton's thinking on welfare reform was strongly influenced by Third Way advocates associated with the Democratic Leadership Council, which he chaired from 1990 to 1991, especially its publication, *Mandate for Change*.[10] For his chief domestic policy adviser, Clinton selected one of its founders, Bruce Reed. This Third Way approach was signaled by two pronouncements Governor Clinton made during his 1992 presidential campaign: his campaign slogan to "end welfare as we know it," and his condemnation of those who believed that racist practices were so pervasive that any criticism of black Americans was "blaming the victim." Each of these pronouncements has been perceived as examples of his political savvy, of his ability to triangulate conservative opposition and mistrust. By contrast, this book will argue that they were driven by his decision to find a Third Way to confront problems of low income and racial disparities.

After being stable for more than a decade at 3.8 million families, welfare rolls increased beginning in 1989, reaching 5.1 million families by 1992. Most left-liberal policy makers considered these increases responses to an economic downturn: to the lack of available jobs and the low wages offered to less educated workers. Indeed, they pointed to evidence that for many mothers, a shift from welfare to paid employment would lower family income.[11] As a result, left liberals suggested that a more robust economy, by providing more jobs and better pay, would lead to a natural reduction of the welfare rolls so that no changes in welfare policies were warranted. By contrast, President Clinton believed that welfare policies must change: single mothers must take responsibility by participating in employment-enhancing activities as a condition for receiving cash assistance.

President Clinton also rejected the antidiscrimination stance that many left liberals advocated. While he did undertake expansionary policies that raised incomes for the lowest-paid workers, there were no *targeted* policies undertaken to reduce racist practices. This approach was consistent with the way he responded to the urban unrest in Los Angeles after the Rodney King incident.

In 1992, Rodney King was brutally beaten by the police after being stopped for a traffic violation just outside Los Angeles. Outraged by this incident, large sections of the Los Angeles black community rioted, inflicting substantial property and personal damages. Defenders of this protest focused on deeply imbedded racist practices. One of the most vocal advocates for retaliatory violence was the rap singer Sister Souljah. After interviewing her, *Washington Post* reporter David Mills claimed, "[Her] empathy for the rioters reached a chilling extreme. Forget the statistics emerging on the racial variety of looters and people who died. Forget the economic motives of those who plundered stores. To Souljah, this was a black-on-white 'rebellion,' plain and simple and righteous."[12]

A month later, Souljah was an invited speaker at Jesse Jackson Sr.'s Rainbow Coalition. The following day, Governor Clinton addressed the same gathering and condemned her rhetoric and questioned why she had been invited. "Her comments before and after Los Angeles," Clinton said, "were filled with a kind of hatred that you [the Rainbow Coalition] do not honor."

This criticism infuriated Jackson. He said afterward that Sister Souljah "represents the feelings and hopes of a whole generation of people," and that she said she had been misquoted in the *Post*. Roger Wilkins, one of the most respected voices of the black community, was deeply distressed by what Governor Clinton had done. Wilkins said, "At the panel the night before, Jackson stood up to Sister Souljah, insisting that you can and must work within the system. And she finally agreed with him. . . . In that context Clinton's speech was arrogant, and it was cheap. He came there to show suburban whites that he can stand up to blacks. It was contrived."[13]

When he assumed office, Clinton did not combat attempts like California's Proposition 209 to terminate preferential admissions programs. The journalist Katha Pollitt pointed out that "President Clinton was silent on Proposition 209 throughout the election season, when his leadership—and his party's money and muscle—might have made a difference."[14] Nor did he seek to enhance the economic safety nets available to the poor. Instead, he championed legislation to replace welfare with work and focused on class rather than race when formulating economic policies.

President Clinton's welfare policies reflected the synthesis that is a hallmark of Third Way policies. Under the slogan "Make Work Pay," Clinton supported left liberals who believed that the government must do more to support working mothers: raising their earnings through increases in the minimum wage and EITC; and easing their family burden by making child care accessible and affordable. President Clinton also embraced conservative concerns that there were behavioral impediments that must be confronted. With prodding from Bruce Reed, Clinton supported requirements that mothers had to engage in work-enhancing activities in order to receive cash assistance.

Left liberals within the Democratic Party forcefully opposed President Clinton's welfare proposals, initially forestalling their approval. They criticized the requirements imposed on recipients: replacing an entitlement with policies that distinguish between the deserving and undeserving poor. Left liberals decried the focus on the alleged dysfunctional behaviors of the poor rather than the discriminatory barriers they faced. Highlighting the long and recent history of racial discrimination, they claimed that President Clinton was capitulating to regressive policies, ones that would inflict untold miseries on the most destitute and defenseless families.

The left-liberal position was most dramatically articulated by a longtime Clinton ally and friend, Marianne Wright Edelman, president of the Children's Defense Fund. During the congressional deliberations she implored: "The Old Testament prophets and the New Testament Messiah made plain God's mandate to protect the poor and the weak and the young. The Senate and House welfare bills do not meet this test."[15] Responding to the lifetime limits included in the proposed legislation, Senator Patrick Moynihan charged, "To drop 2,414,000 children in our central cities from life support would be the most brutal act of social policy we have known since Reconstruction."[16]

When President Clinton chose to sign off on welfare legislation, three senior Health and Human Services (HHS) officials—Wendell Primus, Peter Edelman, and Mary Jo Bane—chose to resign. Wright Edelman wrote:

This legislation is the biggest betrayal of children and the poor since the Children's Defense Fund began. President Clinton's signature on this pernicious bill makes a mockery of his pledge not to hurt children. . . . This act will leave a moral blot on his presidency and on our nation that will never be forgotten. Today marks a tragic end to our nation's legacy of commitment to our most vulnerable children—this is truly a moment of shame for all Americans.[17]

As promised, the "Make Work Pay" legislation provided welfare recipients with substantial aid in their transition to work. First, the welfare bill called for a dramatic expansion of federal funding for child care and nonprofit organizations that helped leavers find jobs and sustain employment. Between 1997 and 2003, federal funding of child care increased from $4.1 to $12.3 billion.[18] Just as important, Clinton raised the minimum wage from $3.25 to $5.15 per hour and doubled the Earned Income Tax Credit, a federal supplement to wage income providing working mothers with two children as much as $4,000; if they lived in one of fifteen states that have their own EITC program, they received up to an additional $1,000. As a result, even full-time work at the minimum wage would yield sufficient income to escape official poverty.

Anxieties when welfare reform was initiated were understandable. By 2000, however, evidence had accumulated that a very large share of welfare leavers had improved their economic situation and only a very small share had moved backward. As the welfare rolls plummeted, so too did poverty

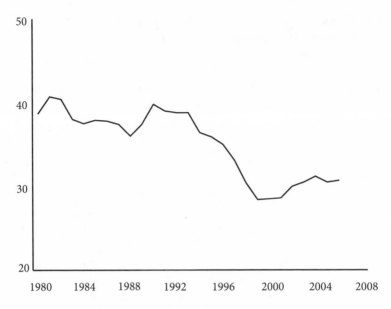

Figure 1.3. Povertty rate for female headed families, 1981–2007

rates. For the fifteen years prior to welfare legislation, poverty rates among female-headed households fluctuated between 36 and 41 percent. Between 1994 and 2000, the rate fell by more than one-quarter—from 38.6 to 28.5 percent (figure 1.3).

Another goal of welfare reform was to reduce teen pregnancy. During the late 1980s teen pregnancy rates, especially among young black women, had begun to increase. By 1991, the birthrate for black women aged fifteen to seventeen was 8.3 percent, 18 percent higher than it was five years earlier. Left liberals were unsure how to respond. While some believed that contraceptives and abortions should be stressed, this ran counter to the attitudes of many within the black community.[19]

Other left liberals claimed that young motherhood was a rational decision, given the bleak circumstances these women faced. Given their disadvantaged circumstances, delaying childbearing would not raise their annual incomes. It was even beneficial to have children at a young age when these women were healthier and had more access to familial support.[20] Once more, a fear of "blaming the victim" led many left liberals to be uncomfortable pursuing government policies that would lower teen birthrates.

Fortunately, when changes in state welfare policies began to be implemented in the early 1990s, teen pregnancy rates began to decline, and the decline accelerated later in the decade. By 2000, birthrates for fifteen- to seventeen-year-old black women were halved; for comparable-aged white women they fell by one-third. For all teenage women, the birthrate fell by more than 25 percent.

Evidence also indicated that the material hardships experienced by welfare leavers were lowered substantially. It was this evidence that convinced early critics, including Jason DeParle and Christopher Jencks, to change their views.[21] Indeed, when Congress was considering reauthorization, Jencks recommended that since "welfare reform has succeeded in its present form, in our view legislators should now leave it alone, rather than trying to fix what is not broken."[22]

Declining poverty rates and material hardships were the result of the successful transition to work for the vast majority of welfare leavers. The employment rate of single mothers living in the largest urban areas increased from 59 percent to 73 percent, with even larger increases for black and Latino never-married women—the population most impacted by welfare reform.[23] Studies consistently found that it was primarily the new welfare regulations that prodded (or forced) mothers to leave cash assistance, not the strong labor market.[24] Thus, together with the government supports to welfare leavers, the "Make Work Pay" philosophy was responsible for the dramatic declines in poverty rates.

Despite this mounting evidence, many left-liberal analysts continued to paint a dismal picture of welfare reform.[25] The most venomous criticisms came from left-liberal academicians. A 2002 book sponsored by the Academy of Political and Social Science, *Lost Ground*, exemplifies this attitude. Its coeditor Randy Albelda claimed, "As currently implemented, the welfare to work solution is a match made in hell" (80). Gwendolyn Mink believed that "TANF's foremost objective is to restore the patriarchal family" and that it "exploits women of color to suffocate single mothers' independence" (96, 99). In denouncing the reforms, Kenneth Neubeck wrote, "The passage and signing of [TANF legislation] demonstrates how well welfare racism functions [so that] welfare reform is best viewed as an effort at racial control" (116, 118). A leading social work educator, Mimi Abramovitz, along with Kenneth Neubeck and Noel Cazenave, helped popularize the term "welfare racism" to signify the disproportionately perceived adverse consequences the legislation had on black women.[26]

Left-liberal criticisms of President Clinton's lack of targeted initiatives to combat racial discrimination were much more defendable. For many academicians, like myself, weaned on late 1960s writings by William Ryan (*Blam-*

ing the Victim) and Frances Fox Piven and Richard Cloward (*Regulating the Poor*), racism was considered the fundamental reason for racial disparities, and the continued prevalence of racist stereotypes in the blue-collar working population—the so-called Reagan Democrats—explained why they rejected progressive policies such as affirmative action.

These attitudes informed our teaching and writings. They continued to do so even after William Julius Wilson (*The Declining Significance of Race*) argued in the mid-1980s that white racist attitudes and practices were no longer compelling explanations for racial disparities. Thus, it was not surprising that there would be a negative reaction to Clinton's decision to rebuke Sister Souljah, a negative reaction that I shared at the time.

Combating racist practices should have been a more important part of President Clinton's agenda. Certainly federal officials should have responded to the racist implementation of welfare policies in a number of localities. More recently, racist police incidents, the government's indifference to the victims of Hurricane Katrina, the racial component of the housing crisis, and the racist backlash to President Obama have made clear that we are far from a postracial society.

The problem with the left-liberal perspective, however, is its unwillingness to *balance* efforts to combat racist practices with other policies that attempt to counter behavioral and social impediments. For most left liberals, white racism is still the *core* explanation for economic disparities—blacks are still victims of an unrepentant racist system where only cosmetic changes have been made.[27] Thus, accepting any policy that does not confront racism will only strengthen the "blaming the victim" mentality, a perspective, they believe, that still dominates white America.

These arguments discount important evidence concerning the reduction of labor market racial discrimination. Among those African Americans who gain a four-year college degree, the racial earnings gaps among men and among women are caused by factors other than racist labor market policies. While on average for each gender, a black college graduate earns less than a white college graduate, virtually all of these differences are the result of black college graduates living disproportionately in the South where wages are lower, having fewer years of work experience, and having weaker academic skills than white graduates as measured by either basic skills tests or class rank.[28]

Conservatives incorrectly seize on these findings to claim that labor markets are unbiased so that hirings are based solely on merit, and that *all* aspects of affirmative action should be abandoned. They minimize the need for equal employment laws to maintain a level playing field for college graduates. Maybe even more important, they ignore the workings of the labor markets for non–college graduates. In these markets, there is still a modest wage gap—probably more than 10 percent—even after making adjustments for differences in skill-related factors.

These studies, however, only compare the wages of *employed* black and white men. As significant as these persistent wage disparities are, much more severe are the racial employment rate disparities. In 1996, just as welfare reform was initiated—and before the Clinton-era economic boom created very tight labor markets—the inability of black Americans to gain employment was quite striking, especially in the Midwest. In that region, 74 percent of white men but only 57 percent of black men were employed; 59 percent of white women but only 53 percent of black women were employed. While the economic boom decreased these employment gaps, they still remain substantial among men.

It would be a mistake, however, to focus primarily on reducing discriminatory barriers. In 1999, national unemployment had fallen below 4 percent. In many cities, firms were forced to employ virtually any workers available. As labor markets tightened, employers were much less likely to use exclusionary advertising and rely on racial stereotypes when choosing among applicants.[29] The employment rate for black men did rise relative to the rate for whites, but the racial gap remained substantial. This suggests that factors beyond discriminatory hiring practices are important in understanding why black men have such poor employment records.

One such factor is the impact of the great postwar migration to the North that began when cotton production was fully mechanized. Black men were still excluded from the better-paying craft occupations. Economic growth and low national unemployment rates, however, allowed substantial mobility for white workers, freeing up positions in manufacturing for black workers. By 1975, the share of young black men employed in manufacturing in midwestern cities reached 40 percent.

While this migrating generation was generally able to secure stable employment, their children—the postmigration generation—were less fortunate. The economy began to fizzle in the mid-1970s just when the ending of the Vietnam War brought many young men back into the labor force. At the same time, manufacturing firms began closing their northern and midwestern *urban* factories, moving from central-city to suburban sites and from the older industrial areas to the South.[30]

Part of this strategy was to limit investment in their older urban plants so that by the mid-1970s many of these facilities were obsolete and economically no longer viable production sites. Employment prospects for young black men living in central cities were further weakened by the shift of manufacturing to suburban industrial parks. The newly built interstate highway system enabled trucking to replace railroads. To avoid traffic congestion, many manufacturing firms relocated to suburban sites adjacent to a highway. And new assembly-line techniques required sprawling suburban factories rather than multifloor central-city locations.

Young black men living in central cities found it increasingly difficult to follow the manufacturing jobs to the suburbs. There is also some evidence that Latino immigrants were able to replace black workers at jobs that remained in the central city.[31] By 1989, the share of young midwestern black men employed in durable manufacturing fell to 12 percent.[32] This was the backdrop against which the postmigration generation struggled to find gainful employment and why the racial employment gap was so large in that region.

By the mid-1980s, crack cocaine had become a further plague on black communities. Congress and state legislatures dramatically increased the penalties for crack cocaine possession, more than doubling the prison population. Nearly 90 percent of those sentenced to prison for its use and distribution were black. As a result, interaction with the criminal justice system became a common occurrence in poor black communities. For example, in Baltimore, at any point during the early 1990s, the majority of black men aged eighteen to thirty were in prison, on probation, or had a hearing pending within the criminal justice system. Black men born in the late 1960s had a 20.5 percent probability of being in prison by age thirty to thirty-four; if they were high school dropouts, the probability rose to 58.3 percent.[33]

These social and economic problems had profound effects. They help explain the substantial intimate violence poor black women experience and the instability of the relationship between fathers and their children. During the early 1990s, the intimate violence rate was 43 percent higher for black than for white women.[34] Even after adjusting for economic differences, the rate was still substantially higher for black than white women. Welfare dependency also increased as violent partners sought to limit the ability of teen mothers to gain additional education or outside employment.[35]

Left liberals were uncomfortable with policies to reduce the intimate violence experienced by poor women, fearing that they would undermine efforts to reduce the structural and socioeconomic causes of the ills of the poor.[36] Only after welfare reform was legislated did left liberals mobilize efforts to confront the significant intimate violence that plagued the lives of welfare recipients. Their important efforts led Senator Paul Wellstone (D-MN) to place provisions within the implementation guidelines that required domestic violence to be a component of recipient evaluations.

Left liberals were less responsive to the need for stronger legal provisions to enforce child support payments from absent fathers.[37] When the Clinton administration proposed new regulations, left liberals balked. Cynthia Newbille, director of the National Black Women's Health Project, and members of the Congressional Black Caucus cautioned that without a comprehensive job creation strategy, measures such as wage garnishment would be largely ineffective within the African American community. Many left liberals suggested that it was just blaming black men who themselves were victims of the racist system that would not allow them to obtain meaningful employment that was necessary to support their children.

Despite these protests, federal efforts to increase child support payments moved forward in 1994. At the time, only 18 percent of families in the child support program received any child support. During the subsequent decade, these payments increased fourfold, not only providing needed funds for families but also having a positive effect on the relationship between fathers and their children. By 2004, the collection rate had risen to 51 percent. Studies also indicated social benefits beyond financial gains: stringent child support reduced marital disruptions and out-of-wedlock childbearing.[38]

In summary, Third Way advocates enacted a number of policies during the Clinton presidency that proved helpful in moving working families forward. President Clinton went too far in slighting policies that directly confronted discriminatory practices. His overall efforts, however, did substantially aid black families and counter the pervasive hopelessness that the 1980s structural changes had created.

Left liberals continued to believe that racial discrimination was the *core* explanation for the persistence of black economic and social difficulties. As a result, they were unprepared for the substantial changes in racial attitudes that enabled Barack Obama to win the presidency with as large a share of the white electorate as other Democratic candidates had garnered in any of the previous eight presidential elections. Yes, there has been a racist backlash, and it should be confronted, but an overreaction can be counterproductive. One example was the rush by many left liberals to judge the arrest of Harvard professor Henry Louis Gates Jr. as racially motivated. As more evidence of the incident became known, it became increasingly difficult to sustain the claim of racial motivation.[39] Unfortunately, President Obama's perceived support for this claim may have caused a decline in his popularity among white

Americans.[40] Most important, there must be a multifaceted policy approach to raising the living standards of black families.

Many left liberals also reject some Third Way policies because they have a particular feminist view: women must be able to earn a *middle-class* income by *themselves* so that they can be free of economic dependence on men. From this perspective, child support payments are not a viable solution, since they continue to keep mothers dependent on their former male partners' income. Indeed, the substantial employment expansion experienced by these women was not considered a "success" because the low-waged jobs they obtained did not allow them to escape completely from material hardships without reliance on additional sources of income.

This perspective led many left liberals to reject President George W. Bush's initiatives to strengthen partner relationships because they would inevitably reinforce patriarchy. Left liberals also rejected state regulations that do not allow welfare recipients to maintain college enrollment beyond vocational programs because only four-year degrees would enable single mothers to earn enough income to escape material hardships. This position on educational attainment is summed up eloquently by Katha Pollitt: "The problem with welfare reform is its basic structure. It throws women off the rolls into jobs that are too ill paid and too unstable to support a family, while denying them the education and support they need to advance. It creates a permanent class of low-skilled, low-wage workers—a kind of reserve army of the semi-employed."[41]

By contrast, Third Way proponents are more open to these policies. Certainly, it would be ideal if, with modest support, many more single mothers could attain four-year college degrees. Given their often weak educational backgrounds and family circumstances, however, this direction is not viable for most of these women. Instead, it may be much more effective to encourage many of them to pursue occupational programs and credentials. This direction would not consign these mothers to dead-end low-wage employment because many of these occupations pay well above poverty-level wages. To the extent these jobs pay inadequate wages, Third Way advocates support income enhancements. These enhancements, which include food stamps, the EITC, housing and child care subsidies, and the refundable child credit, are a reasonable way of closing the gap between their earnings and what is necessary for families to avoid material hardships.

Just as important, Third Way advocates support policies that enable these single mothers to rely more on financial and emotional support from the father of their children. Child support is only one of these policies. These advocates also favor government support for programs that strengthen relationships between fathers and their children. These programs help fathers and mothers overcome attitudes and behavior that play a destructive role.

The government must be careful not to promote marriage as the key to moving these mothers and their children into the middle class. It must, however, make clear that children benefit from the emotional and financial support provided by their fathers, and so it is in the children's interest that partnerships be strengthened where possible. In addition, the government should make a concerted effort to eliminate the substantial financial penalty working single mothers face if they marry a working partner.

The Book's Structure

In subsequent chapters, the book will present targeted policies that can move working families forward. Before delving into these policy areas, however, it is important to gain a firmer understanding of why there is a need for targeted policies and how we should evaluate them. In particular, one might argue there is no need for targeted policies, since a high-employment economy would enable working families to prosper: "A rising tide lifts all boats." The Clinton-era economic boom, with the national unemployment rate reaching below 4 percent, was a real-world laboratory that should enable us to judge this thesis.

Chapter 2 will identify the wage and employment benefits to working families from a high-employment economy and identify its inadequacies. Unfortunately, the primary lesson from the Clinton administration will not be from its last years, when the economy approached full employment. With the persistence of near-double-digit official unemployment rates, and even higher for at-risk groups, particularly teenagers, it will be many years before we have a high-employment economy. Instead, we might learn more from the Clinton administration's first five years, when the economy was coming out of the 1990–91 recession. During that period, black employment grew less than declining unemployment rates suggested, and the lessening of gender wage gaps hid the different experiences of working-class and professional women. These experiences point to the need for policies that target working-class women and black Americans.

Once we judge that there is a need for some targeted policies, chapter 3 will provide a necessary framework to judge their effectiveness. We must certainly judge the merits of any proposed policy by asking, "How well does it focus benefits on the targeted population?" For example, Democrats and some Republicans, including John McCain, opposed the 2001 Bush tax cuts because they did not sufficiently target working families and instead provided a disproportionate share of benefits to wealthy taxpayers.

Even if we judge that a policy sufficiently targets benefits, we must make sure that it does not have serious unintended consequences: harmful effects on other groups. For example, suspending clean-coal regulations may keep energy costs low for many midwestern families and manufacturers but would generate pollution that substantially adversely affects northeastern communities. If these spillover effects are substantial enough, then the targeted policies would be hard to defend from a national perspective.

Sometimes policies that appear to target benefits to a particular group may actually harm them when the full impact is understood. This was certainly the claim made by conservatives when they opposed welfare as an entitlement. Though welfare gave immediate aid to needy families, conservatives claimed that it trapped many in long-term dependency that doomed them to a lifetime of poverty and social isolation. Similarly, conservatives traditionally argued—before data decisively undermined their claims—that the minimum wage harmed the least skilled workers by raising the wage rate above the level at which they could be profitably employed. As a result, conservatives claimed, the minimum wage increased unemployment rates of the most vulnerable workers. These and other issues related to targeting will be explored in chapter 3.

With this background, each of the next seven chapters focuses on a particular policy area, generating recommendations to enhance the well-being of working families. Chapters 4 and 5 look more closely at factors that influence race and gender income disparities and suggest corrective policies. For black workers negative stereotypes persist, limiting their access to employment, particularly in informal labor markets. The use of employee referrals to fill vacancies exacerbates these problems. In addition, the impact that background checks, educational credentials, and testing procedures have on employment decisions will be assessed.

For female workers, particularly single mothers, the lack of sustained employment has a significant impact on gender wage differentials. For this reason, access to affordable child care is crucial for not only employment but also wage advancements. Child care arrangements are particularly critical if women seek employment in traditional male-dominated occupations that require longer workweeks and for training and educational programs while they are employed. Chapter 5 will also assess the degree to which women have been entering male-dominated industries and will look at two areas where women have gained a substantial representation: IT occupations and the telecommunication industry. Finally, it will discuss the possibility of raising wages in female-dominated industries.

Both chapters 4 and 5 include material on teenage employment. With high and persistent unemployment, there is a real danger than many youth will become disconnected from work and school. The collapse of teen employment during the current economic slowdown only increases the likelihood of this occurring. These chapters examine the importance of teen employment for black and female youth, and policies to counter the current situation.

Chapter 6 assesses general education policies at the community colleges. Left liberals emphasize providing access to four-year degree programs for all. They fear that shorter occupational programs will track students into low-wage dead-end jobs. Unfortunately, left liberals often ignore important unintended consequences: if public colleges do not provide these occupational programs, many students will choose instead to attend for-profit proprietary schools that load students with loans and often do not provide sufficient training for them to obtain certification or employment. Left liberals also often ignore the data that indicate many young adults do not have the basic skills necessary to be successful in academic programs so that their dropout rate is high. For these reasons, there may be justification in directing a substantial share of students into occupational and credential programs provided by the community colleges.

Starting in 2001, the federal government began funding programs to strengthen the relationship between fathers and mothers. Left-liberal critics decried President Bush's initiative to promote marriage, convinced that it would reinforce patriarchal relationships by increasing women's dependence on men. Evidence from pilot programs, however, suggested that these policies had a modestly positive effect on improving interpersonal discourse and did not have the unhealthy aspects that left liberals most feared.

Chapter 7 counters the notion that marriage has substantial benefits only for middle-class individuals. It documents the positive effects that marriage has on family well-being, particularly for the health and development of children, for even poorer, less educated individuals.[42] Fatherhood programs not only enforce financial support requirements but also enhance the employment potential of these men.[43] Chapter 7 concludes that policies to increase the earnings of less educated fathers and the strengthening of relationship skills can be successful in raising economic and noneconomic well-being, whether or not marriage rates are increased.

Many of these chapters indicate a link between economic well-being and tax policies targeted to working families. Chapter 8 explores ways to improve two of these policies: the EITC and child care tax policies. The EITC is effective at lifting families out of poverty but is less effective at enabling the near-poor to move forward. In particular, the phasing out of credits reduces the income gains to these families when their income grows, especially if near-poor families are gaining benefits from other means-tested programs such as Section 8 or public housing and food stamps. In addition, the phasing out of benefits from means-tested programs also creates a substantial marriage penalty to working mothers. Combined incomes cause these families to have a substantial drop in benefits, making marriage costly. Finally, child care tax policies are particularly important for near-poor families who have incomes too high to receive substantial subsidies from government-funded programs. While states have aided these families through refundable child care tax credits, chapter 8 will explore ways to improve the coordination between federal and state programs to further aid them.

The economic well-being of working families may also be impacted by immigration policies. Chapter 9 will assess immigration's impact on wages, employment, and tax burden. This chapter will recommend moving to a Canadian-style admissions system that would reduce the share of less educated workers and their families that could legally enter the United States.

Economic well-being is also influenced by the availability of affordable housing. Government housing policies reflect sharp ideological differences. Conservatives generally reject government intervention into the housing market. They suggest that the normal workings of the market—building new housing units for the better off—inevitably leads to a "filtering down" of acceptable housing to the less fortunate. More extreme, some conservatives reject housing code regulations, claiming they impose unnecessary cost on landlords who are then forced to raise rents to their poor tenants. By contrast, left liberals fear the market and so want the government to constrain it by imposing rent control on private-sector housing units and by sustaining as many government-owned low-income housing units as possible.

Chapter 10 presents Third Way policies that rely on private markets to provide housing to meet the needs of the working poor. It recommends expanding government rent subsidies to more families by reducing maximum grants and delinking them from dedicated units, including public housing projects. It also finds that, as a result of housing price declines coupled with rental increases, government housing subsidies in many cities may be used more effectively to purchase affordable housing rather than subsidizing for rental units.

2

Employment Growth

Its Strengths and Limitations

The Obama administration initially focused its efforts on limiting the economic contraction, and by the third quarter of 2009, production increased at an annual 3.5 percent rate. Production increases continued through 2010, with modest employment growth. A "rising tide lifts all boats," so that all groups of workers are benefiting from the employment expansion. Once unemployment begins to fall rapidly, *wage* growth should improve for workers, including those at the bottom of the economic ladder. We should not, however, rely on employment growth alone to solve the problems of working families, particularly those at risk. Even at the peak of the Clinton-era economic boom—when national unemployment rates fell below 4 percent—at-risk groups were not fully benefiting.

While it is important to understand the limitations of robust employment growth, at issue today is how to respond to the substantial employment shortfalls that will continue for some time. This chapter will focus on the most prominent at-risk groups—black men, single mothers, and teenagers. We will assess the previous employment slowdown (2000–2004) to judge its disparate impacts. These findings will be compared with the current, much more severe employment contraction. We will also explore the impact of the first six years of the 1990s economic boom as it may mirror what we can anticipate over the next few years.

Benefits of a High-Employment Economy

In a talk given in New York City in 1997, Joseph Stiglitz recounted his experience the previous year at a meeting of world economic leaders. As chair of the Council of Economic Advisors, he had boasted of the employment achievements of the Clinton administration compared with many European countries that were experiencing double-digit unemployment rates. In disgust, a French adviser retorted, "You have only created crummy jobs. If we had created jobs, they would have been good jobs!" At the talk, Stiglitz claimed that many good jobs had been created. However, the "crummy" jobs were exactly the employment opportunities that most suited job seekers who had limited education and work experience.

Chapter 1 documented how these "nickel-and-dime" jobs helped increase dramatically the employment rates of single mothers, many of whom were leaving cash assistance. They also aided the employment rate of less educated black men.[1] In a study conducted in Boston during 1994, economists Barry Bluestone and Mary Stevenson found that black and white men with no more than a high school education were just as likely to have worked sometime in the previous twelve months. However, the number of hours worked differed dramatically; black men averaged 1,327 hours, whereas white men averaged 2,020 hours.[2]

National data also show similar disparities. In 1994, among those with no more than a high school degree, only 31.6 percent of black men were employed full-time, compared with 50.2 percent of white men. As the economic boom tightened labor markets, the share of these less educated black and white men who worked full-time rose. The increase was more substantial for black men so that, by the end of 1999, 43.8 percent of less educated black men and 60.4 percent of less educated white men were employed full-time.

When confronted with this evidence, left-liberal critics retreat to the retort of the French minister: these were low-wage, dead-end jobs that would consign workers to a life of poverty. Two leading education scholars, W. Norton Grubb and Marvin Lazerson, summarized this position nicely: "While the booming economy after 1996 allowed many welfare recipients to find jobs, these were largely unskilled positions vulnerable to economic business cycles."[3]

Critics also ignored the broad social benefits from low-wage work. Typical was the response of social critic Barbara Ehrenreich when encountering Wal-Mart workers who liked their jobs. In disbelief, she claimed that they had been brainwashed during their orientation sessions.[4] By contrast, in her excellent book on Wal-Mart, Liza Featherstone found that many women welcomed the opportunity after years of housewifery. Moreover, they liked dealing with the public; even workers who did not like working for Wal-Mart nonetheless liked helping customers. Featherstone concluded, "That's one of the attractions of retail, despite the low pay."[5]

These workers are not alone. Labor researchers find that low-wage workers in the health care industry often find their work rewarding.[6] In *American*

Dream, Jason DeParle pointed out that welfare leaver Angie's perseverance as a nurse's aide reflected the intrinsic value she gained from her efforts: her job "tapped a vein of energy and imagination dormant in other parts of her life. She certainly had more patience for her patients than she did for her kids."[7]

David Shipler also found nonfinancial benefits for the low-waged workers he interviewed. He noted, "Contact with new, more successful people has been a boon of going to work, say many who have moved off welfare and out of the stifling circle of indigence. Encounters with achieving colleagues can revive, broaden, and educate." For Shipler's interviewee Peaches, work provided a healthy social environment where "I can enjoy myself and be a real person and have something to talk about besides who screwed who, who shot who, so and so's dead."[8]

I found this attitude in the women I interviewed when studying welfare reform. MiShonda completed the STRIVE welfare-to-work program in Chicago and was hired by Avon to package their products. She felt good about her ability to raise her wages from seven to eleven dollars per hour and about two small financial awards she received for her efforts. Her face brightened when discussing the pleasure her job brought her: "Okay, while I am only working at Avon, I am making products people like to use. I'm helping them be beautiful, feel comfortable, and making them smell good. And I've done it. Gives you something to look forward to. You're doing your part to make someone else happy."[9]

In another study, Katherine Newman followed the lives of black and Hispanic minimum-wage fast-food workers in a poor neighborhood in New York City in 1993. She found that for many inner-city poor, work was a haven away from troubled personal lives, and it helped individuals build constructive social relations and improved self-worth.[10] In a follow-up study, Newman and Chauncy Lennon found that for most of those working in 1997, "the high flyers and low riders alike, expectations remain[ed] positive and a sense of personal responsibility for their fate strong, even in the face of recognized inequalities along the lines of race and gender" and even among women who "had *not* become astounding success stories . . . they still see themselves as moving toward a set of goals, not as stagnating in the face of impossible obstacles."[11]

Critics feared that welfare reform would flood the low-wage market, making wage growth unlikely. The actual experience was otherwise. For groups of Philadelphia and Cleveland welfare leavers, between 1998 and 1999, their average income increased by 23 percent.[12] Over a thirty-month-period among employed welfare leavers in New Jersey, monthly earnings grew by

33 percent.[13] More than 40 percent of those workers whose first job paid less than $6 per hour had a wage increase of at least 50 percent. For Work First participants in Washington, the average hourly wage rate increased from $7.50 to $8.91 two years later.[14] Thus, the concern that welfare leavers would depress wages was unfounded during the Clinton-era economic boom.

More generally, wage increases were particularly robust in areas with low unemployment rates.[15] One example of this striking improvement was Brian Bennett, who graduated from an inner-city high school in Raleigh, North Carolina, in June 1997. After working at a series of temporary jobs for a year, he landed a full-time position as a front-desk clerk at an Embassy Hotel. Planning to study hotel management part-time with tuition help from his employer, Bennett said, "The sky is the limit, no one can hold me back but me."[16]

The manager of the Raleigh Employment Security Commission office said, "Employers are hiring people that two, three, five years ago they weren't hiring." In the early 1990s, 400 black men between the ages of nineteen and twenty-five from the local area used to take part in a midnight basketball league where networking and interviewing tips were as much on the agenda as foul shots. However, by 1999, there was increasing "difficulty getting enough people to play because they [were] in the job market."[17]

More generally, the late 1990s witnessed the first time in twenty years that the average wage grew faster than the inflation rate, and this growth was most robust for those at the bottom of the labor market. Indeed, between 1991 and 2006, the earnings of the lowest-paid quintile of workers "increased more in percentage terms than incomes of any of the other groups: The bottom fifth increased its earnings by 80 percent, compared with around 50 percent for the highest-income group and around 20 percent for each of the other three groups."[18] Thus, tight labor markets were most helpful for two of the most at-risk groups: former welfare recipients and less educated young black men.

Black Men Left Behind

While these benefits from tight labor markets are undeniable, they did not lift everyone. Many black workers gained, but many others were left behind. In particular, the gains were concentrated among those black men who had a foot in the labor market in the early 1990s. Tight labor markets were not so helpful to those who had been distant from the paid labor force.

This distinction is clearly found in the New York City study. Newman and Lennon estimated that 81 percent of those who were employed in 1993 were still working in 1997. For those employed in 1997, measured in 1993 dollars, average hourly wages increased from $4.37 to $7.24; 28 percent had wage increases of at least $5 per hour. This outcome contrasted dramatically with the work experience of the ninety-three workers they followed who had been unemployed in 1993. In 1997, 43 percent of this group were unemployed, with most working only intermittently in the previous four years.[19]

More generally, when we look at all adult men, large racial disparities remained even at the peak of the economic boom. In 2000, the unemployment rate of black men aged twenty and older was 6.9 percent—much lower than the 13.5 percent rate in 1992 but well above the 2.8 percent rate for comparably aged white men.

But even this measure understates the *employment* gap at the peak of the Clinton-era economic boom. In 2000, 72.8 percent of adult black men were in the active labor force, compared with 77.1 percent of adult white men. At least a portion of this difference reflected black men who were not in the active labor force because they either used informal job search activities or had become so discouraged that they had given up looking for work. And if they were not in the active labor force, they were not included in the official count of the unemployed.

In addition, official unemployment statistics include only those in the noninstitutionalized population. In 2004, within the Asian, Latino, and white communities, there were approximately an equal number of men and women aged twenty to thirty-five in the noninstitutionalized population. By contrast, as a result of the high incarceration rate of black men, there were 119 black women for every 100 black men in that age-group in the noninstitutionalized population. This disparity has important ramifications for black social relationships and family structure that will be discussed in subsequent chapters; it also has implications for judging racial labor market disparities. Most incarcerated black men have weak job skills and work histories and so would not be employed if they had not been arrested.

If we look at *young* black workers at the peak of the Clinton-era economic boom, the situation was even bleaker. At any point during 1999, 22.8 percent of all black men between the ages of sixteen and twenty-four were neither in school nor at work; a full 10.7 percent had been idle for at least one year. These rates rise to 28.5 and 17.1 percent, respectively, if we include those black men in this age-group who were in prison.[20]

Equally troubling, black teenagers and students continued to have extreme difficulty obtaining employment. Only about one-quarter of black teenagers were employed, compared with one-half of white teenagers. Among sixteen-

TABLE 2.1

Employment Rate for Less Educated Black Men Not in School
by Education and Age, 1979–2000

Group	1979	1989	1999/2000
16- to 24-year-old high school dropouts	53.4	45.7	37.0
16- to 24-year-old high school degree only	72.7	68.8	63.8
25- to 34-year-old high school dropouts	74.0	65.3	59.5
25- to 34-year-old high school degree only	86.7	79.4	79.9

to twenty-four-year-olds, 50.7 percent of white students but only 28.6 percent of black students were employed.[21]

The improvements for less educated young black men brought about by the Clinton-era economic boom also paled when looked at historically. Table 2.1 presents employment rates at the peak of the last three business cycles. Employment rates at the peak of the Clinton-era economic boom for all four groups were below their 1979 rates and, for all except twenty-five to thirty-four-year-olds with a high school degree, below their 1989 rates.[22]

These employment trends reflect the adverse consequences that the decline in central city manufacturing jobs and negative stereotypes have had on the employment of less educated black men. Between 1979 and 1999/2000, the blue-collar share of their total employment fell continuously from 34.3 to 24.6 percent. This decline was particularly severe in older central cities where jobs were lost to suburban industrial locations.[23]

With funding from the New York City Council, the Community Service Society of New York undertook a large-scale study of the joblessness of black men. The director of the study, Mark Levitan, told me, "We identified a large group of black men in their thirties and forties who had virtually never held a full-time job." Though most had at sometime in the past been involved with the drug trade, these men had avoided significant jail time; the vast majority of them now survived by cobbling together part-time, informal jobs.

When interviewed, these men did not see themselves as victims of a racist society but instead faulted themselves for bad choices they had made. Few even considered the possibility of applying for full-time jobs. They seemed to understand that their lifestyle and personal behaviors were not compatible with the soft skills necessary for sustaining formal employment. Instead, they were resigned to continuing their current informal employment arrangements. For a significant number, this included a role as "inspirational" speakers. Government agencies and nonprofits would hire them to go to schools and youth organizations, where they would tell about their lives. Hearing about the downside of street life from these authentic sources would hopefully keep more disillusioned youth from going down the same path.

Tight labor markets were especially inadequate for black men with prison records. Devah Pager conducted an audit study in Milwaukee to determine the impact of incarceration on employment. Male applicants were given a matched employment history and educational background, with the only difference being that one had been incarcerated for a nonviolent crime for eighteen months while the other had never been incarcerated. She found that applicants with a prison record were less than one-half as likely to be called back for a second interview as their matched counterpart. Her study was conducted in 2001, when Milwaukee's unemployment rate was still relatively low, forcing employers to be more flexible in their hiring practices than they would have been if applicants were more plentiful.[24]

Pager's findings are quite consistent with those of employer surveys conducted during the 1990s, which found that only around 40 percent of employers in the four urban areas studied were very likely to hire an otherwise qualified job applicant who had a criminal record compared with more than 80 percent that would be likely to hire a former welfare recipient. The percentage that would probably hire an applicant with a criminal record was lowest among those employers that did background checks. During the 1990s, the share of firms doing these checks seemed to increase, a change that may explain why the share of firms willing to hire workers with criminal records did not increase significantly even when labor markets tightened at the peak of the economic boom.[25]

Impact of an Economic Downturn

The fact that even when labor markets became tight, at-risk groups continued to experience employment problems is not particularly relevant today. With unemployment rates tracking near double digits, it is important to respond to the disparate impacts of a *weak* job market. To understand the problems created by an underemployed economy, we must first clear up a confusion caused by the particular definition used to measure recessions: a period in which, after adjusting for inflation, the value of total *production*—real gross domestic product (GDP)—is declining.

Unemployment rates can increase for a substantial period of time even after real GDP begins to increase due to ongoing increases in labor productivity and the size of the workforce. In particular, labor productivity has been increasing at about 2 percent annually. As a result, total production must grow at 2 percent just to keep the same number of workers employed. In addition, the labor force has grown by about 1 percent each year, reflecting the shift to the paid labor market among married women with children and substantial immigration to the United States. Thus, just to keep the unemployment rate constant, real GDP must increase by about 3 percent annually.

Using the accepted definition, the recessions of 1990–91 and 2001 were quite short—each less than twelve months. In each case, however, subsequent real GDP growth was initially below 3 percent. As a result, unemployment kept increasing. Indeed, the unemployment rate increased during the first thirty months of the *employment* slowdown that began in 2001.[26] Let us look at its effects so that we can better judge the distinctive aspects of the current employment slowdown.

Impact on Female Workers

During the early stages of the economic slowdown that began in 2001, analysts feared that women would be disproportionately adversely affected because employment losses seemed to be concentrated in industries dominated by female employment. For example, employment in personal supply services and hotels and lodging saw heavy employment losses during the recession; in the immediate aftermath of 9/11, employment in the usually recession-proof bar, restaurant, and general merchandising sectors fell substantially.[27]

The harsher job market experienced by women during the *initial* stages of the employment contraction, however, was more than offset in subsequent years. Many of the private female-dominated sectors rebounded much more than the sectors in which male employment dominates. In addition, both government and health care—sectors in which female employment is high—experienced steady growth. As a result, between 2000 and 2004, the employment rate declined by 1.5 and 2.7 percent, respectively, for women and men.[28]

Even if, on average, the job losses women experienced were not so severe, single mothers might be expected to face worse prospects. Heather Boushey and David Rosnick identified nine industries in which 62 percent of welfare leavers were employed.[29] During the three-year period from the start of the recession in February 2001, private-sector employment declined by 3.1 percent, while the estimated employment decline of welfare leavers employed in these nine industries was only 2.0 percent.[30] This strongly suggests that a favorable industrial concentration may have enabled single mothers to avoid as steep an employment loss as the overall economy.

Just as important, employment declines were disproportionately larger in relatively highly paid male employment sectors and smallest in professional areas populated by women. After adjusting for inflation, the average real weekly wage of women working full-time *rose* by 1.8 percent annually between 2000 and 2004. As a result, the usual weekly wage of female workers rose from 76.4 percent of the male wage in 2000 to 80.4 percent in 2004.[31]

In past economic slowdowns, wages for those at the bottom did not keep pace with inflation, so that it was actually quite surprising how well the wages of single mothers held up. Nevertheless, this was still a pretty grim picture. For single mothers raising their families on $8 an hour in 2001, adjusting for inflation, they were able to earn $8.16 an hour in 2004.

This wage stagnation was particularly alarming for the directors at the New Hope and STRIVE welfare-to-work programs when I interviewed them in November 2004. Both programs had been successful by impressing on welfare leavers the need to consider their first job as only the starting point in their employment trajectory. This worked well during the 1990s boom: work effort translated into promotions and substantial wage increases for many welfare leavers.

After three years of slow growth, however, these administrators could no longer instill such hope in the welfare leavers they were counseling. Without a strong business expansion, the number of promotions shrank alongside the likelihood of a robust wage trajectory. Welfare leavers became frustrated with their flat paychecks, unable to secure a significant raise despite their best efforts.

These administrators had to fight against the instinct of some welfare leavers to quit one job before they had another. Indeed, as STRIVE director, Nina Hernandez, lamented, "We could no longer feel confident placing our clients in better jobs after they had gained work experience. We have to constantly tell them, 'Stay at your current job until you have been offered a better one.'" Gone was the substantial upward mobility, along with a strong belief that "work pays," which had marked the 1990s boom.

Work, however, still was much more beneficial than welfare. Despite the substantial decline in their employment rates, the share of single mothers moving backward was quite modest. Among all single parents, food hardships declined between 1999 and 2002 whereas it increased for married parents. Even among low-income single parents, food hardships increased only slightly.[32]

These findings are also consistent with the very modest increase in poverty rates of single mothers. Between 2000 and 2004, the poverty rate for female-headed households rose by only 6.7 percent, in contrast to a 13.2 percent increase in the national poverty rate.[33] Indeed, the growth in poverty rates among female-headed households was much less than during the previous prereform economic slowdown ten years earlier.

One final piece of evidence comes from a study done by Federal Reserve Bank economists Mary Daly and Joyce Kwok, who measured the distribution of household income of young single mothers at the low employment point of the last three business cycles: 1982, 1993, and 2004 (figure 2.1). In 1982 and 1993, young single mothers were heavily clustered at the low end of the income distribution curve. But by 2004, income distribution had moved upward significantly, and young single mothers were less likely to have incomes below the poverty threshold.[34] Thus, welfare-to-work efforts seem to have limited the adverse impact of economic slowdowns on the economic well-being of young single mothers and their children.

Impact on Black Men

In 2000, employment rates were 72.8 percent and 67.7 percent, respectively, for adult white and black men—a racial employment rate gap of 5.1 percentage points. Over the next four years, more black than white men dropped out of the active labor force, and among those who remained, black

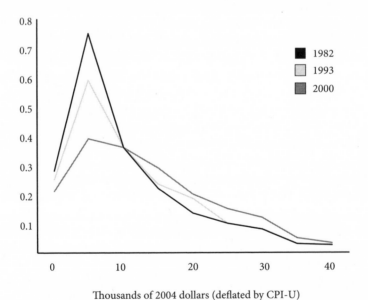

Thousands of 2004 dollars (deflated by CPI-U)

Figure 2.1. Distribution of household income of single mothers, 18 to 24 years old

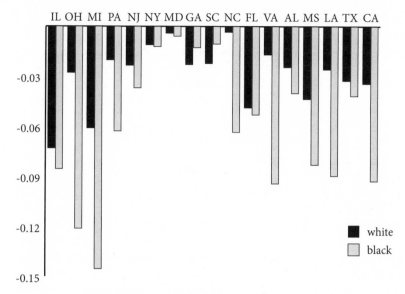

IL OH MI PA NJ NY MD GA SC NC FL VA AL MS LA TX CA

-0.03

-0.06

-0.09

-0.12

-0.15

■ white
□ black

Figure 2.2. Percentage change in male employment, 2000/01 to 2004

unemployment grew more rapidly than white unemployment. As a result, the racial employment rate gap increased to 8.9 percentage points.[35]

The disproportionate decline in black employment rates was fairly uniform throughout the country. Figure 2.2 measures the percentage change in the male employment rate between the 2000–2001 average rate and the 2004 rate in the seventeen states that have the largest number of black workers. In the states that were hit significantly by the slowdown, the black rate declined more substantially than the white rate. These states included California and those in the old manufacturing heartland and the Deep South. Only in some of the Mid-Atlantic and South Atlantic states, where employment declines were small, did black men not fare any worse than white men.

The differential racial impact undoubtedly reflected the negative stereotypes of black men held by many employers. Studies have consistently found that when job applicants are plentiful, employers are much more reluctant to hire qualified black workers.[36] In addition, these racial disparities also reflected the differences in the characteristics of the jobs held by black and white workers, particularly in the noncollege job market. Recently hired whites were much more likely than blacks to be in jobs that required a high school diploma (60.3 percent versus 45.3 percent), prior related experience (45.5 percent versus 26.4 percent), or previous training or certification (30.3

percent versus 23.3 percent). Three-quarters of white workers but only one-half of black workers were in entry-level jobs for which these three factors were required or extremely important. In addition, only 24.8 percent of less educated black workers were employed in jobs that required computational skills, compared with 47.5 percent of less educated white workers.[37] As firms contracted their employment, these differences were likely to cause employers to lay off black workers first.

Current Economic Downturn

The current economic downturn is not only more severe for men than the one at the beginning of the decade but started from a weaker employment situation. That is, employment rates before the current downturn began were lower for both adult black and white men than just before the 2001 downturn (figure 2.3). Employment rates were lower for white men in all of the seventeen states with the highest black employment; they were lower for black men in all but two of the states: New York and Virginia.

Starting from these lower employment rates, the current economic downturn was particularly harsh for black and Latino men (see figure 2.3). Whereas the employment rate between 2007 and 2009 fell by 6.0 percent

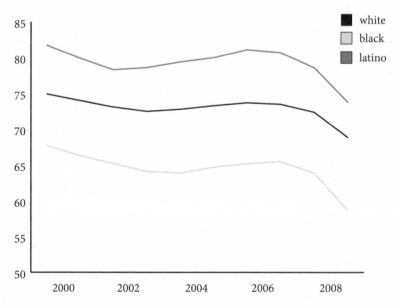

Figure 2.3. Adult male employment rates by race and ethnicity, 2000–2009

TABLE 2.2

Employment by Industry, Age, and Gender

Selective Industries	Employment Levels (000)		Employment Changes
	2006	2009, IV	2009/2006
Education and health	17,823	19,316	+8.38 %
Government	21,971	22,501	+2.41
Leisure	13,108	13,020	−0.67
Manufacturing	14,148	11,552	−18.35
Construction	7,692	5,724	−25.59
Total	144,164	138,138	−4.71
Women, 20 and older	63,579	63,133	−0.70
Men, 20 and older	74,422	70,572	−5.17
Teenagers, 16–19	6,163	4,433	-28.08

Sources: For industry employment: *Employment and Earnings;* for total employment: *Current Population Survey*

for white men, it declined by 8.6 percent and 10.4 percent, respectively, for Latino and black men. Indeed, by the end of 2009, the employment rate for black men twenty years and older had fallen to below 58 percent nationally.

The weakening employment position of men reflected their concentration in construction and manufacturing. Employment in these two sectors peaked in 2006 and by the last quarter of 2009 had declined by 25.59 and 18.35 percent, respectively (table 2.2). By contrast, for 2009, employment in female-dominated sectors—education and health care, government, and leisure—was almost the same as, if not higher than, in 2006. As a result, whereas adult male employment had fallen by more than 5 percent since 2006, it had fallen by less than 1 percent for adult women. Just as important, the concentration of employment losses in the relatively high-waged manufacturing and construction industries indicates that this downturn impacted more on middle-class families than the previous downturn.

Teen Employment Crisis

During this period of slow growth, there is an urgent, crucial need for targeted policies to relieve the desperate situations that currently afflict a large share of working families. Maybe most important, we should watch carefully the behavior of teenagers, given their precipitous employment decline by 28.08 percent since 2006 (see table 2.2). Drops in high school graduation rates or rising teen pregnancy rates, particularly in poor neighborhoods, would signal a growth in the hopelessness and fatalism that so victimized many of the postmigration generation in the 1980s.

While the government stimulus package has enabled the economy to begin to rise, teenage employment rates are at all-time low levels. For white youth sixteen to nineteen years old, the employment rate declined from 36.4 percent to 26.9 percent from first quarter 2007 to first quarter 2010. For comparable-aged black youth, the rate declined 19.3 percent to an anemic 14.5 percent over the same time period. These rates might be manageable if summer employment was robust, but it is the exact opposite. In summer 2000, 52.8 percent of U.S.-born teenagers were employed. By summer 2009, this rate had plummeted to 33.5 percent—39.6 percent for white teenagers and only 19.4 percent for black teenagers.

Evidence from the mid-1990s indicated that job growth primarily aided those who had a foot in the labor market and not those who had drifted away from paid employment. To the extent that young people become disconnected from paid employment and school, it will make it difficult for them to reconnect when the economy improves. These targeted programs, then, are not necessarily those that enhance productivity and income—the focus of this book—but rather those that will forestall the inevitable pessimism that will threaten the long-term outlook and prospects of many young people if they become disconnected from *both* work and school.

With so many people competing for so few jobs, unemployed youth "are the silent victims of the economy," said Adele McKeon, career specialist with the Boston Private Industry Council, who counsels students on matters such as workplace etiquette, professionalism, and résumé writing. Getting the first job "is an accomplishment, and it's independence," McKeon said. "If you don't have it, where are you going to learn that stuff?"[38]

Fearing an even worse employment situation in summer 2010, Democratic lawmakers proposed adding $1.2 billion to the stimulus package, which would translate into about 320,000 additional jobs. Given the more than 5 million employed teens in summer 2009, this will have only a modest impact, but for Chicago students like Anthony Roberts and Deandre Briber, the federal money offers some hope.

Briber said he had applied at T. J. Maxx, Target, Kmart, and a local docking company, with no luck. Having an income would help ease the burden on his mother. He also said, "I feel like I do need to get a job because I'm kind of a handful. I want things, clothes, and to take care of myself. I just want to be on my own, to help with the bills."[39]

Roberts said he had been searching for a job for a year and a half. Everywhere he goes, there are other teenagers ahead of him. "It bothers me, but at the same time," he said, "I try not to let it bother me."[40]

Clinton-Era Employment Boom

During the first three decades of the postwar era, recessions were quickly followed by robust expansions. This pattern reflected a quick and dramatic expansion of manufacturing employment. Beginning with the early 1990s recession, however, the initial expansions became quite tepid, reflecting the declining significance of manufacturing employment.

It is certainly possible that the current expansion could follow the earlier pattern. Green technology could spur manufacturing, a falling value of the dollar could spur exports, or pent-up demand could spur new automobile sales. However, given the lack of hard evidence that any of these outcomes will materialize, and given the continued overhang of the housing market, it is more likely that the current expansion will continue the recent pattern of an extended period of weak economic growth. For this reason, we believe that the anticipated expansion over the next couple of years may very well mirror the experience during the first portion of the 1990s economic boom.

While the official recession ended in early 1991, GDP growth was not sufficiently robust to begin lowering unemployment rates until eighteen months later. Unemployment rates did decline thereafter, but at the end of 1997 there was still substantial slackness in the labor market. Only afterward did the continued Clinton-era economic boom create tight labor markets where jobs were plentiful compared with the number of job seekers. We have already looked at the final stage of the expansion—1998 through 2000—when tight labor markets helped those at the bottom of the economic ladder. Here, let us look more closely at the earlier stages of the business expansion, which can help us anticipate the labor market dynamics that are likely to unfold over the next few years.

As data have consistently shown, female workers have been insulated from the worst of economic downturns because they are situated in industries that are less sensitive to the business cycle. Between 1991 and 1994, the overhang of high employment in male-dominated industries enabled female wages to increase at a more rapid pace. As a result, in eight of the nine national regions, the female-to-male earnings ratio increased substantially. By con-

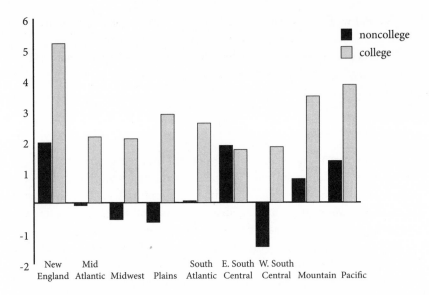

Figure 2.4. Changes in the gender earnings ratio by occupational sector, 1991-1997

trast, as the expansion gained steam in the succeeding three years, wages for males rose substantially, outpacing wage gains for females in seven national regions, constituting 85 percent of national employment.

This past experience suggests that during the coming period of economic expansion, the advancement of female workers may stall. Further exploration of the Clinton-era labor data allows us to pinpoint the source of this problem: the experience of women in occupations that do not require a four-year college degree. During the first six years of the expansion, 1991–97, there was a robust increase in female wages in occupations that require a four-year college degree. In every one of the nine national regions, the female-to-male wage ratio in college-required occupations increased by at least 1.7 percentage points (figure 2.4). By contrast, in five regions, the female-to-male wage ratio in non-college-required occupations was either unchanged or declined.[41]

The advances that women are making and will be making in professional labor markets may enable the *national* female-to-male wage ratio to continue to increase. This overall improvement should not lead us to ignore the persistent inequities that less educated female workers face. This is what occurred during the slow-growth period earlier in this decade: the female-to-male earnings ratio increased while working single mothers, particularly those who had been on welfare, experienced below-average wage increases.

We believe that these impediments to the economic advancement of working-class women can be overcome by targeted policies. We should explore ways to better enforce antidiscrimination procedures in these blue-collar occupations and to increase female representation in higher-paying fields. Specific policies will be discussed in subsequent chapters.

There is similar evidence that during the Clinton-era economic boom, until labor markets were substantially tightened, black male employment gains were limited. The difficulties are not apparent when one looks only at unemployment rates of black men, which decreased substantially throughout the expansion. The benefits seem much more problematic if one looks at labor force participation rates.

As already mentioned, one problem with the official unemployment rate is that it measures only those members of the labor force who are unemployed. If unemployed individuals do not meet certain job search criteria, they are not considered members of the labor force and are not included in unemployment statistics. Beginning during the Reagan era, unemployed black men increasingly withdrew from the labor force in response to the dismal employment prospects they faced.

The withdrawal of black men continued during the early years of the Clinton-era economic expansion (figure 2.5). As a result, almost the entire

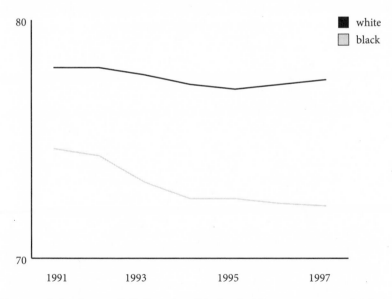

Figure 2.5. Labor force participation rates of black and white men, 20 years and older, 1991–1997

improvement in official black unemployment rates during this period was the result of the withdrawal of unemployed black men from the labor force rather than their movement into gainful employment. This evidence further indicates the employment problems black men will face in the coming years.

Conclusion

Between January 2008 and January 2010, the private sector lost 8.84 million jobs. While all men were disproportionately adversely affected, the sharpest declines were among black men. Most troubling, economic growth over the next twelve months increased private sector employment by only 1.26 million, or only 14 percent of the previous job losses.[42] As a result, it will be a number of years before the U.S. economy will again experience robust job markets. Evidence also indicates that, until labor markets are tight, working-class women are not likely to receive the wage increases obtained by professional women. As a result, improvements in the gender earnings ratio may disguise the continuing if not growing difficulties faced by working-class women. Finally, data highlight the growing employment problems faced by teenagers. For those teenagers who are disconnected from work *and* school, disillusion and despair will likely grow. Thus, targeted policies to aid adult black men, working-class women, and teenagers are crucial if we want working families to move forward in these troubling times.

3

Evaluating Targeted Policies

Society cannot rely solely on macroeconomic expansions to solve problems of underemployment of at-risk populations or to lift families out of near poverty. Some targeted policies are required. Subsequent chapters will present the targeted policies that we believe can be most effective in raising the material living standards of those who could be left behind. In this chapter, some general guidelines will be developed for judging program effectiveness. Here is where conservative, market-oriented analysts *sometimes* have something important to offer: well-intentioned policies recommended by left liberals may not be well targeted enough and may have unintended consequences or other defects that undermine their effectiveness.

Benefit-Cost Analysis

The hallmark of rational behavior is the weighing of benefits against costs. In most cases, consumers should purchase goods and services only when the benefits outweigh the price they must pay. Similarly, businesses should produce only if the price at which they can sell units is higher than their cost of producing them.

There are, of course, exceptions to this rule. Individuals and companies can certainly be altruistic. Consumers might buy products from higher-priced stores because they have a positive feeling toward the sellers, and firms might sell at below cost to certain consumers because they have positive feelings toward them. That is, individuals and firms may be "charitable" in their market transactions.

There is a broader set of situations in which individuals reject rational calculations: when they have *obligations*. Most often these obligations are culturally imbedded, justifying familial or communal responsibilities to others that cannot be easily negated. We may give unconditional love to our children (and maybe even our spouse) and do not condition our behavior toward them on rational calculations. We often have religious values that oblige us to contribute to the welfare of a larger community. In many cases, these obligations dictate *entitlements* for others.

Not surprisingly, many religious leaders have had an uncomfortable relationship with the impersonal logic of market capitalism: the production and distribution of goods and services based on rational calculations.[1] This distaste was most apparent in the attitude of many Populists during the latter part of the nineteenth century when they witnessed the harmful effects that the market system had on family farmers and factory workers. One of the leaders, Charles Sheldon, was outraged by "the horrible blunder and stupidity of our whole industrial system that doesn't work according to any well established plan of a Brotherhood of men, but is driven by forces that revolve around some pagan rule of life called supply and demand."[2]

While generally not motivated by religious tenets, most left liberals are also uncomfortable with using the cold calculus of benefit-cost analysis and notions of efficiency in determining government social policies. After all, much of the need for government is due to the *failures* of the market so, left liberals often reason, how can these failures be corrected if government intervention relies on the same framework of analysis? Indeed, this antimarket bias may have led many charities to shy away from using more effective for-profit consulting firms rather than nonprofits when devising fund-raising strategies.[3]

More important, many government regulations and programs should provide equity and entitlements that society demands without regard to costs. For example, we provide the disabled with access, regardless of its costs and the limited number of individuals who benefit. In my campus building there are two entrances: on one side, the entrance leads to elevators; on the other side, the elevators are half a landing up or down. Because this arrangement restricted the disabled to only one entrance, the college decided to close down one flight of one of the two stairways in order to install a lift so that the disabled could use either entrance. Though this lift is not used more than a handful of times during the year, it was warranted because, as a nation, we have decided that the disabled have certain entitlements to equal access and that benefit-cost calculations should not be used to justify their implementation.

Protection against bodily harm is another situation in which we generally believe that the public has an entitlement that cannot be negated by benefit-cost considerations. For example, a rational model would say that after some point, additional police officers should not be employed, since their meager reduction in crime would not justify the added expenditures. That is, there would be an "optimal" crime rate based on this benefit-cost analysis. Any decision to lower the crime rate further would be considered suboptimal because it would raise costs more than the safety benefits provided.

Do you think a politician could get elected after announcing this approach? Of course not. The American public expects personal safety to be an entitlement and thus expects additional police officers to be hired as long as they can reduce the crime rate. Citizens expect government to *minimize* the crime rate, not *optimize* it!

These "ideals," however, cannot always be practiced when proposed expenditures are substantial. This is particularly true at the state level, where budgets must be balanced. When money is not "free," trade-offs are unavoidable. Higher expenditures in one area necessarily require lower expenditures in other areas and/or increased tax revenues. Unfortunately, judging these trade-offs is not something most individuals, indeed most legislators, wish to articulate.

In the 1960s, kidney dialysis was not automatically available to all regardless of age. State welfare boards often had the task of deciding who was worthy of receiving state support and who was not. Those rejected for treatment were almost certain to die. One board member, Marion Hilger, confronted Senator Vance Hartke of Indiana at a party, who later recalled: "She just put her head on my shoulder and cried. She said I had to do something for all those people who were dying because they couldn't pay for dialysis. She told me she was tired of playing God."

After gathering information, Hartke successfully sponsored 1972 federal legislation to provide insurance for all those with renal failure. On the floor of Congress, Hartke stated: "How do we explain that the difference between life and death is a matter of dollars. How do we explain that those who are wealthy have a greater chance to enjoy a longer life than those who are not?"[4] Today, the federal government spends more than $3 billion annually to provide dialysis to more than 150,000 individuals who would die without this treatment.[5]

Absent federal government funding, however, states are forced to make trade-offs. In 1987, seven-year-old Coby Howard contracted acute lymphocytic leukemia and needed a bone marrow transplant. Earlier that year, the Oregon legislature had discontinued Medicaid coverage for organ transplants so that amid much publicity, Coby died. In response, Oregon set out to address two problems: lack of insurance among low-income people and denial of lifesaving treatment despite coverage of less effective therapies for less serious conditions. Thus, Oregon decided to make more explicit its rationing of medical services.

In its Medicaid program, the Oregon Health Services Commission listed more than 700 distinct treatments and then categorized the procedures from the most necessary to the least necessary. To increase Medicaid coverage to a substantial portion of the uninsured, the Oregon legislature decided to eliminate from coverage all procedures considered the least necessary, reducing medical expenses by 10 percent for all those previously insured. This savings allowed the legislature to extend coverage so that in a few years, the number of Medicaid recipients rose by 39 percent, covering 150,000 previously uninsured individuals.

Many critics feared that the explicit rationing of services, based on financial considerations, set a dangerous precedent. They noted that in order to further save expenses, the number of covered procedures has been slowly decreasing from 606 to 574. Others even questioned whether the expansion of health services to the poor was primarily due to the restricting of services.[6]

While we may question the use of benefit-cost analysis by the government when it is making life-and-death decisions with taxpayer money, in our daily lives we often take such choices for granted. For example, most of us are quite willing to have higher speed limits that cost a modest number of additional serious traffic accidents. We are unwilling to expend the additional travel time that lower speed limits would entail. Many of us are unwilling to spend the extra funds to have antilock brakes installed in our cars even though they would lower the probability of serious injuries. Many of us do not purchase home alarm systems and other safety devices because we do not judge the gains to be worth the additional cost. Thus, benefit-cost calculations are unavoidable though we are often uncomfortable admitting how they significantly impact our personal safety decisions.

Indeed, benefit-cost analysis is of value even when we agree that the government has the obligation to provide an entitlement. For example, few question that in the United States every citizen has a right to shelter. There are, however, two conceptual issues involved in determining the delivery of housing to the needy. Society must decide whether it is a pure entitlement or instead is influenced by the behavior of the recipient. That is, do we make the housing provided conditional on recipients' behavior, such as chores they must perform or classes they must attend?

Second, how do we deliver the housing to the intended recipients? Beginning in 1937, the federal government started building public housing projects. In 1974, Congress passed the Housing and Community Development Act to create the Section 8 program, under which tenants can rent apartments in the private sector as long as the monthly rent is no higher than an approved rate. Tenants must pay about 30 percent of their income for rent; the remainder is paid with government vouchers. More recently, the federal government has given subsidies to builders who are willing to include affordable housing among the units they are constructing.

How do we judge how much money should be allocated to each of these methods of housing delivery? One of the factors is an assessment based on benefit-cost analysis. In each community, we could calculate the cost of delivery of housing units through each of the methods to maximize the total number provided from a given government expenditure. In some circumstances public housing may be most efficient whereas in others the Section 8 program would be most cost effective. Thus, benefit-cost analysis can be used to maximize the effectiveness of the government's expenditure on the desired entitlement. Indeed, this approach will be central to our housing recommendations.

In sum, whatever the difficulties and dangers it entails, government must not formulate policies strictly on the basis of moral obligations and social entitlements. We should be very careful to limit these obligations and entitlements because they often leave unstated and unmeasured the adverse impact they have on other policies. Government must be compassionate *and* competent, and competency requires recognition that weighing of benefits against costs is a necessary component of most policy decisions.

How Well Are Policies Targeted?

All kinds of policies are promoted with claims that they will help a specific group: small businesses, the poor, struggling workers, women, youth, and so on. Evidence often indicates, however, that the targeted groups are not the main beneficiaries of these policies and sometimes are only marginally helped. For example, farm aid is almost always justified by citing the needs of the family farmer. Isn't that what John Mellencamp, Willie Nelson, and other artists projected with the numerous "Farm Aid" concerts they supported? Government payments, however, do not go primarily to family farmers but to large agribusiness concerns, like Archer Daniels Midland (ADM) and Cargill. This is why critics often characterize farm aid as "welfare for the rich" and why the Obama administration sought to "slash about $5 billion in the coming year for direct payments to agribusinesses and farmers with more than $500,000 in annual revenue."[7]

Minimum Wage

Another case where effective targeting has been questioned is the minimum wage. Through most of the 1980s, the main criticism of the minimum wage was that it created unemployment. Conservative critics maintained that in high-employment economies, individual firms must compete for workers. If an individual employer attempted to pay applicants significantly less than their productive worth, these workers would find other less greedy employers who would hire them at fairer wages. In this case, all those who are unemployed must have too low a productivity level to be profitably hired at the going wage rate.

According to this perspective, each time the minimum-wage legislation raises wages, employers fire their least productive workers: those whose productivity is now below the firm's new higher wage. In addition, the higher wages force firms to raise prices, which reduce the demand for their products. In turn, production cutbacks cause further layoffs.

A number of studies in the 1990s decisively undermined these conservative claims by demonstrating that raising the minimum wage did *not* result in layoffs. In particular, David Card and Alan Krueger assessed the effect when New Jersey raised its minimum wage above the national minimum wage that covered Pennsylvania workers. Because firms would have lower production costs in Pennsylvania, they could charge their customers less and so, according to the conservative analysis, should have more robust growth than similar New Jersey firms. The growth differential should be especially large for industries where low-wage workers make up a significant share of their workforce.

To test this hypothesis, Card and Krueger compared employment growth in fast-food restaurants in Pennsylvania counties on one side of the Delaware River to employment growth in fast-food restaurants in New Jersey counties on the other side. The data did not support the conservative hypothesis. The New Jersey restaurants expanded their employment by *more* than their neighboring Pennsylvania restaurants.[8]

Similar results were obtained when comparing employment growth along the Washington-Idaho border. In 2007, Washington employers faced a minimum wage almost three dollars an hour higher than Idaho employers. Despite this disparity, firms experienced more employment growth and less worker turnover in Liberty Lake, Washington, than eight miles away in Post Falls, Idaho.[9]

This evidence made it impossible for conservatives to sustain their claims that minimum-wage increases adversely affected employment. Conservatives then shifted their criticism of the minimum wage and began arguing that if the justification for the minimum wage is to reduce poverty, it is not well targeted to poor families.

Data do consistently show that less than one-half of those who work at or near the minimum wage live in families that by the government's definition are considered poor or near-poor. The explanation is simple: the overwhelming majority of minimum-wage workers are teenagers and adult women living in multi-wage-earning households. Once households have more than one wage earner, it is not surprising that the total household income is above $40,000.

Conservatives have used these data to argue against raising the minimum wage and instead favored more targeted policies like the Earned Income Tax Credit, a credit that goes only to those workers who live in households with incomes of less than $40,000.[10] We should not, however, necessarily accept this conservative claim and alternative policy recommendation. First of all, unlike the conservative vision, low-wage labor markets do not generally experience high employment. The unemployment and underemployment rates for these workers are always substantially higher than the national average. In the absence of the minimum wage, workers would be underpaid because of the competition for scarce employment. In this case, the minimum wage would be necessary for workers to obtain a fairer wage.

In addition, two-thirds of minimum-wage workers are adult women. We may therefore consider raising the minimum wage as part of a program to bring about more gender equity, since it reduces the male-female earnings gap. Thus, by expanding our objectives, the minimum wage might be well targeted. In this case, we should support the EITC not as a substitute for minimum-wage legislation but as a supplement.

College Admissions Policies

Race-based college admissions programs do not simply give a leg up to the original target group: lower-income black and Latino students who had attended underfunded public schools. These programs have evolved to include a larger group by refocusing their mission to promoting diversity. As a result, all black and Latino students qualify regardless of their family's income or the schools they attended. Indeed, President Obama's two daughters would qualify.

In particular, 60 percent of black and Latino students who benefit from these programs come from families who are in the top quartile of the income distribution, while only about 10 percent come from families in the lowest quartile. In addition, these admissions programs make no distinction between native- and foreign-born applicants. For example, only about one-third of Harvard's black undergraduates have four grandparents who were descendants of U.S. slaves. Thus, there is substantial evidence that the benefits of these programs are no longer well targeted to lower-income native-born black and Latino students.[11]

Government Tax Benefits

Tax benefits should also be assessed for how well they target intended populations. For example, traditional tax benefit policies enable households to reduce their taxable income when they itemize deductions. When households contribute to a recognized charity, the government allows them to deduct that contribution from their taxable income; when households make home mortgage payments, the interest paid can be deducted from their taxable income.

This approach targets families that can itemize their deductions and, most important, those that have taxable income. Over the last twenty years, legislation has eliminated all federal income tax liability for the vast majority of families with children having annual incomes below $25,000. Because these households pay no federal income tax, they receive no tax benefits from the interest paid on their mortgage or the charitable donations they give. As a result, a number of tax benefits have little value to low-income families.

One of these traditional tax benefit programs is the federal child and dependent care (CADC) tax credit. Because it benefits only those families with taxable income, it provides virtually no benefits to poor and near-poor families who need it the most. In response, a number of states, including New York and California, legislated generous CADC tax credits that are *refundable*: if the family has qualifying credits above its tax liability, the state will send the family a refund check equal to the difference. The federal government also has a refundable child credit and EITC that enable these programs to aid poor families.

Unintended Consequences

Often well-intentioned policies have harmful unintended consequences. A depressing example of unintended consequences was the way New Deal policies impacted on the southern black population. Between 1927 and 1932, cotton prices fell from twenty cents to five cents per bushel. In response, the

Roosevelt administration enacted the Agricultural Adjustment Act (AAA) under which the government paid cotton producers to keep some land out of production so that supplies were reduced, enabling the market price to rise. Landowners used the government's funds to mechanize, reducing substantially their labor needs. As a result, when cotton production increased, planting could be done by a smaller group of workers using the newly purchased capital equipment. Indeed, many landowners no longer needed their black sharecroppers and employed only a modest number of hired laborers during the harvest season. Thus, the cotton support program had a devastating impact on black agricultural workers.

In 1938, national minimum-wage legislation was enacted. Starting at twenty-five cents per hour, the minimum wage increased by five cents per hour in each of the next three years. This policy was intended to aid underpaid southern factory workers, but it had serious unintended consequences for *black* factory workers. The vast majority of southern industrial jobs became high-paying jobs. Once these jobs were desired by white workers, black workers were excluded. In the tobacco industry, whereas in 1930 two-thirds of the workers were black, by 1960 the labor force was only one-fourth black.[12] Thus, once again, the unintended consequences of New Deal legislation proved harmful to black Americans.[13]

Ethanol Policies

More recently, the expansion of ethanol production has been promoted as a means of improving the environment. Ethanol's energy benefits are meager. Because corn is a very energy-intensive crop to produce, the amount of energy required to produce and transport it to refineries is substantial; thus the net energy savings are quite small.[14] And because ethanol yields fewer miles per gallon in automobiles, it may not be very cost-effective for drivers despite the substantial government subsidy provided.

While ethanol production may modestly improve the environment and our energy independence, it has substantial unintended consequences. As ethanol production has expanded, it has caused corn prices to more than double. From a stable price of about two dollars per bushel from 1998 through 2005, it increased to almost eight dollars per bushel in 2008. While the drop in oil prices in 2009 caused the price of corn to drop, it rose again to over eight dollars per bushel by 2011.

The rise in corn prices has been one factor in the doubling of the price of wheat and soybeans since 2005. Richard Perrin estimated that about 30 to

40 percent of the rise in these grain prices could be attributed to the expansion of ethanol production. Because corn is the principal animal feed, pigs and poultry prices have also been substantially impacted. For American consumers, these rising prices have had only a small impact. By contrast, in less developed countries, where grains are a more central component of diets, the expansion of ethanol production might be responsible for a 15 percent increase in food cost.[15]

These rising food prices have reduced food consumption. The World Bank estimates that for each 2 percent rise in food prices, caloric intake among the poor drops by 1 percent. High food prices have also been linked to civil disobedience. Since the North Atlantic Free Trade Agreement (NAFTA) was legislated, Mexico has imported most of its corn from the United States. When corn prices doubled, so did the price of corn tortillas, setting off large protest marches in Mexico City in 2007. Protests linked to higher food prices have occurred in Pakistan, Indonesia, and China. Thus, the meager environmental benefits from ethanol in the United States may be dwarfed by the unintended consequences experienced by the world's poor.[16]

Other Policy Areas

Unintended consequences impact on a number of the policy areas that will be explored. One of the unintended consequences of seeking more child support from noncustodial fathers has been its impact on these men's employment decisions. Rather than seeking paid jobs where their wages can be garnished, some of these men may choose instead to work in informal labor markets. Their behavior not only keeps money away from their children but also limits the men's upward mobility.[17]

There are also unintended consequences when benefits programs are *too* well targeted. As income increases beyond the poverty level, near-poor families have benefits reduced. With higher incomes, families receive fewer food stamps, and their child care subsidies, housing subsidies, and EITCs are also reduced. As a result, for many near-poor families another $100 of wage income results in a loss of benefits of at least $75. These unintended consequences became more apparent with the increased employment of single mothers.

Moreover, most of these benefits are based on total family income. In this case, if a working female household head marries a working man, the resulting rise in family income will adversely impact on their economic well-being. There will be a reduction in the EITC, rent and child care subsidies, food stamps, and other means-tested benefits the couple were receiving before they married. Thus, some families will refuse additional work, and some female household heads will reject marriage because of the adverse consequences of these actions on the family's benefits.

Harms the Targeted Population

Some well-intentioned left-liberal policies might actually harm the targeted group. Today, many left liberals protest against the number of sweatshops in countries that export products to the United States. They demand that these exports be blocked if producing countries are unwilling to enforce higher labor standards. While the intention is to help workers in these countries, the actual impact of higher standards is not so straightforward.

In many of the *least* developed countries, requirements to improve labor standards might cause many firms to shift production to other developing countries that have better infrastructures. As a result, factory workers would be laid off, forcing them to shift to even less desirable employment endeavors. In this case, demanding stricter labor standards in these countries, no matter how well-intentioned, may harm the intended beneficiaries. These are the reasons that Nicholas Kristof, Paul Krugman, and many economists contend that sweatshops can be an important part of a poor country's developmental strategy.[18]

Welfare Dependency

Starting in the 1970s, conservatives claimed that when welfare was allowed to remain an entitlement, welfare dependency grew, causing long-term harm to recipients. Some conservatives pointed to statistics that consistently found that at *any point in time*, the majority of recipients were on welfare for many years.

Left liberals countered that this was an inappropriate way of judging whether or not welfare programs fostered welfare dependency. They noted that the vast majority of welfare recipients *over time* consist of short-term users. A simplified numerical example illustrates the left-liberal claim.

Suppose we have two groups of recipients within a ten-year period. One group consists of 200 long-term-dependent recipients who are on welfare for every one of the ten years. The second group consists of 800 short-term users who are on welfare for only one year: 80 different onetime receipts in each of the ten years. In any year, there are 200 long-term users but only 80 short-term recipients, just what conservatives point to. Over the ten-year period, however, only 20 percent of the total of 1,000 recipients consist of long-term users, just what liberals emphasize.

These illustrative data were fairly consistent with the actual data through the 1980s. In a widely referenced study, for the twenty-one-year period 1968 though 1989, 46.5 percent of all welfare users were on welfare for three years or less during their lifetime, while only 22.1 percent were on welfare for ten years or more.[19] Thus, up through the mid-1980s, left liberals were correct in rejecting the claim that dependency was a serious unintended consequence of the prereform welfare system.

The problem with using this study, however, was that the situation changed substantially after the mid-1980s, a period in which the loss of central-city manufacturing jobs and the crack cocaine epidemic caused havoc in many low-income communities. Just as teen birthrates spiked, so did long-term welfare dependency. In a study conducted in Baltimore, researchers found that between 1986 and 1996, welfare dependency increased from 31 to 51 percent. Similar results were reported for Milwaukee.[20] Thus, liberals were wrong about the size of the welfare-dependent population on the eve of welfare reform.[21]

The booming job market, welfare regulations, and "Make Work Pay" policies reduced the number of adults on welfare from more than 4 million in the mid-1990s to about 1 million ten years later. Despite these dramatic changes, conservatives remain vigilant, fearing that any backsliding by the government will again generate a welfare-dependent population. This attitude is reflected in the conservative response to attempts by President Obama to ease the burden of the current economic downturn on the least fortunate members of society.

One section of the stimulus package attempts to ease the difficulties faced by single mothers who have lost their jobs. It provides additional funds to states to pay for the expected increase in applicants for cash assistance. To further limit state expenditures, the federal government suspended requirements that a fixed percentage of recipients must be enrolled in work-related programs. Conservatives have attacked this initiative because it brings back the specter of entitlements into the welfare system. The civil libertarian Cato Institute immediately reacted. One of its senior fellows, Michael Tanner, stated,

> This is radical change. States that succeed in getting people off welfare would lose the opportunity for increased federal funding. And states that make it easier to stay on welfare (by, say, raising the time limit from two

years to five) would get rewarded with more taxpayer cash. The bill would even let states with rising welfare rolls still collect their "case-load reduction" bonuses. In short, the measure will erode all the barriers to long-term welfare dependency that were at the heart of the 1996 reform.[22]

Thus, welfare dependency concerns might have been valid at the time of welfare reform but they were not prior to the 1990s and are certainly inappropriate during the current national recession.

College Admissions Policies

Another area where it is important to judge the effects on intended beneficiaries is race-based affirmative action. In particular, what if a large share of black and Latino students who are able to enroll in more selective schools because of these programs are overwhelmed and fail out? It would be hard to then argue that these students were helped simply because the policies gave them an opportunity that they otherwise would not have had.

This situation seemed to be the case at the University of Michigan. In an effort to increase the university's black and Latino enrollment to 15 percent of its student population, admissions procedures did not significantly penalize students with low SAT scores and gave a significant bonus to minority applicants. As a result, whereas 98 percent of admitted white students had at least a 3.20 high school GPA and combined SAT scores of at least 1,000, only 44 percent of admitted black and Latino students did so.[23]

These lower admissions standards translated into lower performance. In particular, for the University of Michigan's entering class of 1999, the median GPA attained while at the university was 2.41 for black students, whereas three-quarters of white students had a GPA of 3.05 or higher. More than one-half of black students had been on academic probation at some point during their stay, and one-quarter had a GPA of 1.88 or lower. Such poor performance makes it difficult to claim that the University of Michigan's admissions policies helped their intended beneficiaries.[24]

Political Considerations

There may be situations in which targeting benefits too narrowly creates a political weakness for programs: too few families benefit so that supporters are not strong enough to fight for program improvements. This issue can arise when lawmakers consider expanding program eligibility. On the one hand, if total funds remain fixed and eligibility is expanded, some resources are shifted away from the original targeted group. On the other hand, having a larger constituency may bring about significant increases in total funding over time.

Housing Subsidy Policies

During the 1970s, some members of New York City's congressional delegation wanted lower-middle-class families to qualify for a modest portion of Section 8 funding. Given local housing costs, they reasoned that these families needed a subsidy. Advocates for the poor, however, saw this as a zero-sum game: given a fixed federal allocation, the funds that would go to these lower-middle class families must reduce funding for poor and near-poor families.

Proponents for a shifting of allocation rejected the zero-sum framework. They suggested that expanding eligibility to lower-middle-class families would result in more political support for the program, which would translate into future government funding increases. The advocates for the poor won out, and the program remained targeted to only poor and near-poor families.

Child Health Care Subsidies

A similar situation arose in 2007 with federal funding of the State Children's Health Insurance Program (S-CHIP). At the time, federal aid could be used to support S-CHIP payments only to poor and near-poor families. Again some members of the New York City congressional delegation argued that in high-cost areas, coverage should be extended to lower-middle-class families. Because this was not a fixed allocation, it would not have affected the funding to others. As a result, advocates for the poor supported this proposal.

Now it was conservatives who resisted. As the number of recipients expanded, they reasoned, the program would gain political strength, enabling further program expansions. Once the majority of children were covered, political momentum would strengthen demands that all children should be covered. Thus, conservatives feared that this modest S-CHIP expansion would inevitably lead to universal child coverage through government health insurance programs.

College Admissions Policies

A final example reflects the shifting rationale of college affirmative action admissions policies. These policies were originally supported as compensation for the adverse effects of Jim Crow policies. Many affirmative action proponents reasoned that as overt discrimination and memory of the Jim Crow era receded, the original rationale for affirmative action admissions policies would have waning political support. By contrast, notions of diversity have a contemporary vitality that could strengthen support for these admissions policies. Thus, it was not surprising that when affirmative action admissions policies were threatened, the central justification offered by proponents was that the diversity brought about by these policies benefited *white* students. They became more comfortable interacting in diverse settings among people with diverse views, experiences that would make them better citizens, employers, and workers.[25]

Social Considerations

Besides political and efficiency considerations, social considerations can also influence the choice of delivery. As mentioned previously, housing can be provided through public housing projects, Section 8 vouchers, or subsidizing construction of affordable private-sector housing. In particular, not only have no new public housing projects been constructed in forty years, but a substantial number have been eliminated. Instead, the number of Section 8 vouchers has increased substantially.

It is unlikely that benefit-cost considerations alone explain this shift. Instead, there were social considerations, such as the perceived adverse effects of concentrating the poor in public housing projects. Many reformers became concerned in the 1980s that public housing projects undermined the ability of the poor to maintain proper behavioral traits. These reformers reasoned that the dysfunctional behavior of some would spread in an environment that segregated the poor. Moreover, the public housing stereotype made employers fearful of hiring *any* applicants who resided in housing projects. To avoid this debilitating environment and its stigmatizing effects, some public housing projects were imploded and displaced tenants were given Section 8 housing vouchers.

Social considerations can also influence the method by which benefits are received. In general, if we want to increase the level of individual satisfaction, it is best to simply give cash to recipients and let them decide how to use it. For example, we often choose to give newlyweds cash instead of household gifts, since they are then free to purchase the goods and services that are most valuable to them.

When government funds are given to the needy, however, we are not simply interested in improving their welfare; we also want to make sure that they spend the funds on the goods and services *we* judge they need. As a result, we tend to give *dedicated* vouchers, not cash. These vouchers cannot be transferred legally to other uses: Section 8 housing vouchers can be used only for rent while food stamps can be used only to purchase food. Making allocation decisions for others is the way parents treat their children. Thus, when we design government policies, we should judge whether or not paternalism is appropriate.

This paternalism reflects the decision not only to give dedicated funding but also to use funding to influence behavior. The emphasis on the Earned Income Tax Credit in the 1990s increased not simply because analysts thought it was a well-targeted program. Many analysts favored expanding the credit as a "carrot" to encourage single mothers to seek paid employment.

Market-oriented analysts have also suggested using economic incentives to influence family formation, with the goal being fewer out-of-wedlock children and more marriages. One such proposal was made in 1990 when the FDA approved Norplant, a surgically implanted device to provide birth control for five years. Almost immediately legislators in Kansas, Oklahoma, and Louisiana introduced bills offering modest financial rewards to welfare mothers who agreed to Norplant implants. Although none of these proposals passed, the appeal of Norplant as a way to control costly reproduction by poor women was obvious. In an editorial, the *Philadelphia Inquirer* praised Norplant as an answer to problems of welfare.[26]

Left liberal groups look favorably on government programs that provide services free to the poor, thereby increasing access. Not surprisingly, they favor policies that make contraceptive devices freely available to teenagers and low-income women. Most left-liberal groups recoiled, however, at the Norplant proposals, fearing that they would be coercive. Indeed, the furor surrounding the *Philadelphia Inquirer* editorial caused an immediate reversal. In a retraction, its editors stated, "It's rare that we regret publishing an editorial from almost the moment it appeared in print. And it's rarer still that we feel the need to apologize to our readers for a misguided and wrongheaded editorial opinion."[27]

More recently, Senator Sam Brownback (R-KS) proposed providing marriage bonuses of up to $9,000 to poor District of Columbia mothers who choose marriage. A similar West Virginia proposal was endorsed by Wade Horn when he was assistant secretary for the Administration for Children and Families in the George W. Bush administration. Along the same lines was a proposal by Robert Rector of the conservative Heritage Foundation that women at high risk of bearing a child out of wedlock should be given up to $5,000 if they bear their first child within marriage.[28]

In the case of childbearing and wedlock, it is contentious whether or not the goals are appropriate. Many do not believe that the government should encourage marriage or discourage out-of-wedlock childbearing. Material incentives may not be appropriate, however, even when the behavior encouraged is desirable. For example, in 2007 New York City launched Opportunity NYC–Family Rewards, which provides cash payments to reward low-income families that take positive steps to improve their lives, with the goal of reducing both immediate and long-term poverty.[29] The three-year-old pilot project, the first of its kind in the country, gave parents payments for making positive decisions like going to the dentist ($100) or holding down a full-time job ($150 per month). Children were rewarded for attending school regularly ($25 to $50 per month) or passing a high school Regents exam ($600).

An interim evaluation indicated a significant reduction in current poverty and economic hardship, and also found some modest successes in achieving the desired long-term outcomes of improving children's education. High school students who met basic proficiency standards before high school tended to increase their attendance, receive more class credits, and perform better on standardized tests; more families went to the dentist for regular checkups. But the elementary and middle school students who participated made no measurable educational or attendance gains. While everyone agrees that high attendance, handing in homework assignments on time, and improved test performance are desirable, many question whether providing financial incentives (and rewards) are an appropriate means of encouraging this behavior in young children, especially if the educational gains may be quite modest.[30]

Conclusion

This chapter has provided an overview on the ways we must judge targeted policies. Because the government must be both compassionate and competent, it should utilize benefit-cost analysis for most program decisions. Even when obligations justify government support, we must choose the form in which the support is delivered based at least partially on efficiency considerations. These efficiency considerations necessarily require us to judge how well policies target the intended population. They also require us to judge the nature and size of unintended consequences on other groups. Most important, we must make sure that the intended groups do benefit rather than becoming victims of well-intentioned policies. Finally, we should judge the appropriateness of incorporating political and social considerations into our policy decisions. This is especially important when we consider using financial incentives to encourage behavioral changes.

4

Combating Racial
Earnings Disparities

When President Lyndon Johnson signed the 1965 Civil Rights Act, he lamented that this would be the end of the Democratic Party in the South. Sure enough the Republicans developed their "Southern Strategy," which led to their dominance not only there but also in many northern areas where they won over the so-called Reagan Democrats. At the epicenter of this transformation were the white Detroit-area families whose lives were tied to U.S. automakers.

While these Reagan Democrats favored Hillary Clinton in the 2008 Democratic primaries, most voted for Barack Obama over John McCain in the general election. Indeed, except in Appalachia and areas in the Deep South, Obama carried these lapsed Democrats, suggesting that racist attitudes were not as deep or resistant to change as many left liberals had forecast. For some observers, this demonstrated that the United States had finally entered a post-racial era where racist practices have become more of a nuisance than roadblocks to black advancement.

Clint Eastwood's film *Gran Torino* (2008) captured this rehabilitation of Reagan Democrats. In the film, Walt, the character played by Eastwood, is a retired Detroit autoworker who, unlike almost all his white neighbors, has remained in the central city. He routinely spews racist epithets at his new Hmong neighbors but then, through a series of occurrences, befriends them, particularly the teenage brother and sister living next door. Indeed, he goes out of his way to find the young man a job and to avenge the gang-style brutalization of the sister. Thus, even a racist white worker has the ability to transform himself away from the regressive behavior that for many years had been a basic part of his life.

While *Gran Torino* highlights the ability of circumstance to change behaviors, it also depicts, if indirectly, the structural impediments to equitable treatment. In the funniest scene in the movie, we witness how, with

Walt's counsel, the Hmong teenage boy is able to obtain a construction job. First, it is clear that he would never have been able to interview for the job without Walt's intervention. The employer is typical of those in noncollege labor markets, for which personal recommendations are necessary. Also crucial are the correct "soft" skills: Walt and his barber friend coach the teenager in the appropriate discourse and speech patterns. Thus, the sister's observation that "Hmong girls go to college, Hmong men go to jail" is a cautionary tale that parallels the experience of many less educated black men who lack the personal contacts or the soft skills necessary to compete for employment in these informal labor markets.

Labor Market Discrimination

No one questions that large racial disparities in earnings persist among men with less than four-year college degrees. At issue is how much of these differences can be explained by variations in productivity. For example, compared with white men, black men have lower levels of educational attainment, are younger, and disproportionately live in the low-wage South. If we adjust for education, age, and region of residency, how much of the racial difference remains among college-educated men? More controversially, should we also adjust for either performance on standardized tests or school grades? Since black workers have lower test scores and course grades than white workers with comparable levels of education, estimates of racial discrimination are reduced if these measures are included.

Finally, we must choose the measure of earnings: annual earnings or usual weekly wages; all workers or only those who work full-time; workers of all ages or only those within a specific age range. Because black workers suffer more unemployment than comparably educated white workers, the racial earnings gap is larger if a measure of annual earnings is used rather than usual weekly wage. Similarly, because black workers generally work fewer hours than white workers, racial disparities are larger if all workers are included, not just those who work full-time. Because racial earning gaps reflect the lack of black advancement with age, disparities are smaller if we compare only younger workers—say those younger than thirty-five—rather than all workers aged eighteen through sixty-four.

As *Gran Torino* illustrates, the lack of social networks and soft skills may be prominent explanations for black-white male employment disparities within labor markets for non–college graduates. At any point during 2008, among twenty-five- to sixty-four-year-olds, 83.6 percent of white men but only 71.8 percent of black men were employed. Among those with only a high school degree, there was an 11.0 percentage point employment rate difference between black and white men aged twenty-five to sixty-four and an even larger racial gap among younger men.[1]

Racial employment disparities have also been documented by audit studies. These are controlled experiments in which two individuals, one black (or Latino) and one white, are matched for all the relevant personal characteristics, such as references, employment backgrounds, and communication skills. They each apply for the same advertised entry-level job openings. Using black and white testers, the Urban Institute conducted audit studies in Washington, D.C., and Chicago during 1990 and 1991. Equal outcomes occurred in 79.9 percent of the audits. However, when there was a difference, whites were almost three times as likely as blacks (14.8 versus 5.3 percent) to advance further in the hiring process.[2]

Racial wage differences remain substantial even if we look only at the initial wage rate at which men are hired. In 2007, the median hourly wage rates for black, white, and Latino newly hired, less educated men equaled $10.23, $13.08, and $11.46, respectively. After adjusting for age, educational attainment, and immigrant status, the Latino-white earnings gap is reduced to 6.6 percent and is not statistically significant. By contrast, these factors have little impact on the black-white earnings gap, which remained at 17.3 percent and was statistically significant.[3] These findings are consistent with surveys that find that 31 percent of black workers believe they were discriminated against in the last year, including being passed over for promotions.[4]

In chapter 2, it was noted that black workers tend to be employed at jobs that require less experience, less training, and fewer technical skills. Indeed, a comprehensive study of firm hiring decisions found that "almost every task requirement or credential is associated with the reduction of black . . . workers."[5] These job requirement differences not only cause black workers to be more vulnerable to layoffs but also result in lower hourly wages for blacks. Indeed, after adjusting for these factors, the black-white hourly earnings gap is reduced to 12.8 percent.[6]

These findings were reproduced by another study that looked at less educated workers aged thirty-five to forty-three. After adjusting for age, area of residency, and education, black and Latino men had hourly earnings that were 19.0 and 6.8 percent lower, respectively, than those for comparable white men. Instead of taking into account job skills by looking at the actual job requirements, this study used performance on the Air Force Qualifying Test (AFQT). Including test results completely eliminated the Latino-white gap, while the black-white gap was reduced to 7.5 percent. The black-white gap was further reduced to 1.9 percent when a measure of actual worker experience was included.[7]

These last results point to some of the most perplexing issues in understanding the source of racial earnings and employment disparities. The large employment disparities create large racial disparities in work experience among men of equal age. As *Gran Torino* vividly illustrates, an important reason for these disparities is the way informal labor markets operate: favoring those with social ties to employers and with the required soft skills. But an important part of the story is the high incarceration rate of black men that further weakens their employment experience. Their employment difficulties were documented in the audit study by Devah Pager that is described in chapter 2.

At least one-third of all black men aged thirty-five or younger have had some involvement with the criminal justice system. As a result, a large share of less educated black men will suffer from unstable employment given the group stereotyping that Pager's study documented. In this case, less educated black men in their thirties will have fewer years of employment than comparably aged white men. This outcome helps explain why employers pay black men less than white men of the same age and level of educational attainment. Thus, while current employers may be justified in paying them less, the limited work experience of black workers may be the result of factors outside their control: the stereotyping that caused them to have unstable employment histories and the "get-tough" policing policies that resulted in incarceration rather than treatment programs for low-level drug offenders.

Just as important, black men perform more poorly than white men on a range of standardized exams that measure general academic skills. This racial disparity is also found in course grades, whether in high school, college, or law school. In virtually all cases, lower black performance persists even after adjusting for social class and most other factors that could influence academic performance. To the extent these academic measures are used to predict performance, they result in lower wages for black workers. Therefore, it will be important to judge the relevance of these measures for predicting job performance and whether or not they unfairly penalize black workers.

Enhancing Employment and Earnings of Black Men

There are numerous public policy issues we must confront if we seek to reduce the employment and wage disparities black men experience. How can we minimize the adverse effects when employers rely on personal networks for new employees? To what extent are these networks used because employers seek to avoid hiring black men? How do we overcome the difficulties black ex-offenders face when seeking stable employment? Does the use of test results or school performance in the hiring process result in unfair assessments of black workers?

There is strong evidence that social networks influence employment decisions. Many firms simply find it much cheaper and more efficient to attract new workers through recommendations from their current workers. After all, current workers are not going to risk their reputation within the company unless they are pretty confident that those who are recommended can do the job. Reflecting the importance of social networking, one study looked at employment records and found that residing on the same versus nearby blocks increases the probability of working together by more than 33 percent. The study also found that this effect is stronger when individuals share similar sociodemographic characteristics (e.g., both have children of similar ages) and when at least one individual is well attached to the labor market.[8]

Neighborhood networking may be one explanation for the change in the racial composition of new hires when the race of the hiring manager changes. Using more than two years of personnel data from a large U.S. retail chain, one study found that when a black manager in a typical store was replaced by a white, Asian, or Hispanic manager, the share of newly hired blacks fell from 21 to 17 percent. The effect was even stronger for stores located in the South, where the replacement of a black manager caused the share of newly hired blacks to fall from 29 to 21 percent.[9]

The researchers offered some partial explanations for why these differences in hiring patterns exist. They found that both black and nonblack managers tended to hire people who lived close to them. So if black managers lived in predominantly black neighborhoods, their hiring network was also likely to be predominantly black.

Informal hiring networks dominate the hiring process in low-wage labor markets among small and intermediate-size firms. In the 1990s, they accounted for approximately 35 to 40 percent of all new hires in four major metropolitan areas surveyed. More than one-half of all new hires for low-skilled blue-collar jobs were filled through informal methods. By contrast, newspaper advertising accounted for less than 30 percent of new hires.[10]

Surveys of business owners during the 1990s also indicated a significant amount of trepidation with respect to hiring young, less educated black men. More than 60 percent of urban employers cited workforce quality problems when discussing black workers. Employers consistently deplored blacks' inadequate interactive skills, lack of motivation, and inappropriate attire. Indeed, about one-quarter of black managers surveyed agreed that black workers lacked motivation when compared with other workers.[11]

Not surprisingly, employers often develop recruitment methods that discourage black applicants. William Julius Wilson found that "roughly two-thirds of the city employers who placed ads in newspapers did so in ethnic, neighborhood, or suburban newspapers instead of or in addition to the metropolitan newspapers." He noted that these employers "averaged 16 percent black in their entry-level jobs, compared to an average of 32 percent black for those who placed ads in the metropolitan papers."[12]

After documenting this racial profiling, Wilson concluded:

> Employers make assumptions about the inner-city black workers in general and reach decisions based on those assumptions before they have had a chance to review systematically the qualifications of an individual applicant. The net effect is that many black inner-city applicants are never given the chance to prove their qualifications on an individual level because they are systematically screened out by the selective recruitment process.[13]

The strength of the informal networks through which immigrants gain so many jobs at least partly reflects employer encouragement of immigrant referrals from friends and relatives.[14] Harry Holzer notes that employers preferred Latino workers even though they tended to have less schooling and weaker language skills than black applicants. Holzer suggests that these preferences reflect employer perceptions that Latinos will work for lower wages and have a better work ethic. His view builds on the work of Joleen Kirschenman and Kathryn Neckerman, who found that employers perceive blacks to be more troublesome and less compliant than Mexican Americans.[15]

Even if employers remain reluctant to hire qualified black men, economic circumstances can change their behavior. In particular, when applicants are scarce during economic booms, the demand for new employees may overcome the reluctance to hire black men. This dynamic was certainly at work during the Clinton-era economic boom. At its peak, with national unemployment rates below 4 percent, expanding businesses began to hire many workers who never would have been considered in a weaker economy.

The Clinton-era economic boom was particularly beneficial for young, less educated black men who had only a fragile foothold in paid employment, those who had poverty-wage jobs and those unable to work full-time year-round. In the early 1990s, black underemployment was pervasive. As chapter 2 documented, the subsequent economic boom was beneficial for these workers, particularly those who had some labor force attachment. Unfortunately, it will be a long time before such robust labor markets will reappear.

Overcoming Negative Stereotypes

Of course, discriminatory behavior would be reduced if employers overcame their negative stereotypes. The most damaging stereotype concerns criminality. With one-third of young black men having criminal records, this negative stereotype can victimize *all* young, less educated black men when employers make hiring decisions without doing criminal checks. For example, in the early 1990s, a Chicago employer recounted how he was unwilling to hire *any* black applicant who lived in housing projects, areas that were considered havens for black criminality.[16]

This discriminatory behavior might be reduced if employers were able to access accurate information on the criminal records of their applicants. Harry Holzer, Steven Raphael, and Michael Stoll reported that employer willingness to hire black men actually rose when the employers did criminal background checks and can thus determine which men had criminal records and which did not. This evidence suggests that the employment of black men will increase if firms are provided access to accurate information on criminal records, replacing more problematic Internet searches.[17]

Even when black men without criminal records are treated fairly, those with criminal records will still have difficulties finding employment even if they have turned their lives around. Unless there is *strong* evidence that an ex-offender is likely to succeed, many firms will not employ those with criminal records as long as other applicants are available. This problem might be alleviated with greater government funding of transitional programs that provide the necessary certification that particular ex-offenders should be employed.

State and federal agencies could replicate the efforts of welfare-to-work programs. At the time of the 1996 welfare reform legislation, negative stereotypes of welfare mothers were pervasive among employers. Welfare-to-work programs improved the "soft skills" and "cultural competence" that were crucial to obtaining and sustaining employment. In some cases, these intermediaries provided transitional employment to improve work readiness and credentials. They also provided ongoing support that gave firms more confidence in hiring from this "at-risk" population.

One such program in New York City is run by STRIVE. Its nationally respected executive director, Rob Carmona discussed with me one of its prisoner reentry programs. He believes that soft skills are crucial to employment and advancement and has cited many instances where attitudinal training had gotten men into the back room of banks and other firms, leading to living-wage jobs. He mentioned skill tracks in construction and office operations, with certification programs leading to significant wage increases.

The reentry program for ex-offenders that we spoke about consists of a four-week attitudinal training program. The program begins with 100 ex-offenders. Based upon attendance and general behavior, after two weeks about sixty men are left. Many of those who were dropped had family situations that precluded steady attendance; others gained employment that led them to drop out. By the end of the four weeks, the successful graduates number about forty, and virtually all are admitted into a state training program linked to available jobs.

When I mentioned to Carmona the findings of a Community Service Society study that many black men in their thirties lacked the ability to sustain full-time employment, he pointed out a crucial difference between those men and the ex-offenders in his reentry program. "One thing prison teaches: patience and a disciplined routine," he noted. "This contrasts with those who had not much jail time but have been living on a street economy." Thus, Carmona believed that those who completed STRIVE's four-week program could adapt effectively to traditional work routines.

Many municipalities have changed their hiring practices to make sure that applicants with criminal records are treated fairly. These new procedures no longer ask individuals to list their criminal records on their initial application forms, except for jobs, including law enforcement and education, where all those with criminal records are excluded from employment. For other government jobs, the criminal background checks are delayed until the final stages of the hiring process, either once the applicant has been selected for an interview or the city has made a conditional offer of employment. This process not only encourages those with criminal records to apply—thereby increasing the applicant pool—but also lowers hiring costs substantially.

Minneapolis adopted this procedure, known as "ban the box," in 2007. When the old form, which asked all applicants about their criminal records, was used, less than 6 percent of those with criminal records were hired. By contrast, with the new procedure, Minneapolis hired 60 percent of those whose criminal record was reported at the last stages of the hiring process.

In addition, having to do less screening, Minneapolis estimated that the new procedure reduced hiring costs by 28 percent.[18]

As of 2010, twenty-two cities and counties, including Boston, Chicago, Jacksonville, Memphis, and Portland, Oregon, have adopted "ban the box" hiring procedures. Boston has even legislated that such procedures be used by all private vendors that enter into new contracts with the city and that city agencies "review the vendor's [hiring] policies . . . as part of the process of evaluating the vendor's performance under the contract."[19]

Improving Soft Skills

While there certainly has been a growing demand for technical skills, 75 percent of employers surveyed mention soft skills first. The way applicants dressed, their general demeanor, and, most important, their interactive skills were crucial determinants in the hiring process. As the *Gran Torino* case typified, this was especially true of employers who relied exclusively on personal interviews.

There is some statistical evidence of a strong, *negative* link between the importance of the interview as a screening device and the level of black male employment in a given firm. This evidence suggests that the interviewer may be attuned to dynamics within the interview that reinforce common stereotypes. In addition, others have suggested that black applicants may be less successful because they are more ill at ease than other applicants. Interviewee concerns about speech patterns, appearance, and past experiences may be sources of tension in interview situations to a greater degree for blacks than for other racial groups.[20]

Employment-support programs like those at STRIVE do their part, but the public school system should do more to prepare students for the world of work. Central-city schools are now seeking ways to increase their offerings of algebra and Advanced Placement courses, which help develop the foundational skills for those planning to obtain four-year college degrees. Major educational organizations applaud these changes and believe that they will benefit all high school students. A typical statement is one made in a report on the 2005 National Educational Summit of High Schools under the sponsorship of the National Governors Association: "*All* students—those attending a four-year college, those planning to earn a two-year degree or get some postsecondary training, and those seeking to enter the job market right away—need to have comparable preparation."[21]

Evidence indicates, however, that for the majority of high school students, these added requirements *decrease* the likelihood that they will graduate. Just as important, the math and academic skills increasingly stressed in the academic college-for-all vision are not the skills necessary for most work. Surveys find that only 19 percent of jobs require skills learned in algebra I, and only 9 percent require skills learned in algebra II, yet high schools are increasingly including both courses as part of their general graduation requirements. These courses have traditionally been touted as a means of increasing logical thinking skills. There are, however, more direct, less abstract ways of developing those skills.

One unintended consequence of these increased mathematics requirements is the lowering of high school graduation rates, especially for students from low-income backgrounds. Another less visible unintended consequence may be just as damaging: the displacement of educational initiatives that would enhance the soft skills that are required for employment success.

The crucial role of these soft skills was documented by a U.S. Labor Department study that identified the competency skills most important for today's workforce. These skills included many capabilities not directly taught in schools, including the ability to allocate time and resources, to acquire and evaluate information, to participate effectively as a member of a team, to teach others, to negotiate differences, to communicate with customers and supervisors, to understand the functioning of organizational systems, to select technology, and to apply technology to relevant tasks. While in theory these skills can be taught within academic courses, students and instructors are likely to be much more receptive and more effective if the skills are placed in an occupational context.

Academic and technical skills are often necessary for advancement, but increasingly corporations provide short-term training to prepare workers in these areas. For example, King Cullen is a large New York supermarket chain that promotes workers who have managerial potential. Because many of these workers have limited writing skills and technical deficiencies, King Cullen offers training sessions to improve these skills. As a result, for these workers, it was their soft skills that were primary to their advancement, since their employer helped them gain the necessary level of hard skills through on-the-job training.

A study by James Heckman and associates verifies the relative importance of soft skills for most jobs. They analyzed the schooling and job market experience of a national sample of young workers as they aged from fourteen through thirty and found that except for four-year college graduates, non-cognitive skills exert at least as high an impact on job market outcomes as cognitive skills. Using a large national data set, John Deke and Joshua Haimson found that for two-thirds of all high school students, a nonacademic skill is most predictive of future earnings.[22]

Strengthening Teen Employment and Training

High schools would do well to use workplaces as environments for learning and assessment. The workplaces could be incorporated through service learning, youth-run enterprises, youth jobs, co-op programs, and youth apprenticeships. Coaches could help students learn technical tasks by demonstrating them and explaining how to perform them. In the case of social and personal competencies, students learn at workplaces how to understand systems and their organization, adhere to professional norms, cooperate with others in a team, and communicate with clear messages.

One must also confront the legitimate fears that reintroducing and strengthening occupational training in the high school curriculum would reproduce the tracking that victimized racial groups in the past. After all, if occupational tracking begins in high schools, it could easily filter down to instructional decisions at lower grades. Many grade school and intermediate school teachers, relying on stereotypes, may give up on students with difficulties, directing them into less demanding curricula because of an expectation that they will end up in occupational tracks. Many students may also be mistakenly drawn to these occupational tracks because of the potential to earn money more quickly compared with the uncertain outcomes from pursuing four-year college degrees.

These concerns certainly indicate that school systems must be vigilant in ensuring that the same tracking problems that victimized so many in the past do not reemerge. They must make sure that these occupational programs provide sufficient academic skills that these students would still be able to enter community colleges in the future if their career aspirations lead them to desire further training. Indeed, the best high school occupational programs would be those that had direct links to occupational programs at the community colleges. Ideally, there could be automatic acceptance into the community college program for those who successfully completed a portion of the training while in high school.

Many states have instituted College Now programs that link high school students with college credit courses. Unfortunately, the overwhelming emphasis has been on academic rather than occupational links, which have stifled the development of tech-prep collaborations. Recently, however, evidence of the efficacy of these links has been documented. In particular, studies have found that career and technical education (CTE) programs in Florida and New York have enhanced educational advancement.

Compared with other students in vocational high schools, Florida students who had direct links to college programs were 8.6 percent more likely to enroll in a four-year institution and 5.2 percent more likely to be enrolled in college courses two years after graduating from high school. Similar findings were found for the more limited number of linked CTE programs in New York City.[23]

Given the proven success of these programs, college systems are slowly moving toward implementation. For example, in 2009 the large City University of New York (CUNY) system initiated Carpe Diem ("seize the day"), a five-year pilot program that linked ninth graders at three vocational high schools with four associate degree programs (in hospitality management, construction management and civil engineering, entertainment technology, and career and technical teacher education) at the City Tech branch of CUNY.

These students had already chosen to enroll at a vocational high school so that Carpe Diem expanded the possibilities, particularly for the sizable population of students who had not considered attending college. During the high school freshman and sophomore years, the students who choose to enroll will attend college awareness workshops and take preparatory classes that provide soft skills and other job-related skills. For example, they will take a speech course to develop the communication skills necessary for interaction with customers, fellow workers, and supervisors. Summer learning is a requirement.

During their junior and senior high school years, students select up to four college-credit-bearing courses that can be applied to one of the associate degree programs. To improve student math skills, project-based learning is an important part of the curriculum. Students also meet with industry partners and are able to gain internships to learn more about the particular occupations offered.

Finally, beyond high school occupational programs, a greater effort must be made to improve teen access to paid employment. As chapter 2 summarized, both year-round and summer teenage employment has decreased dramatically over the last decade. For example, the summer employment rate among native-born teenagers declined from 52.8 percent in 2000 to 33.5 percent in 2009.

The reason for such a dramatic decline in summer employment rates is perplexing. Some researchers point to low-wage immigrants who can increasingly substitute for teen labor. In 2007, the share of teenagers either working or actively seeking work was 45 percent in the ten states where

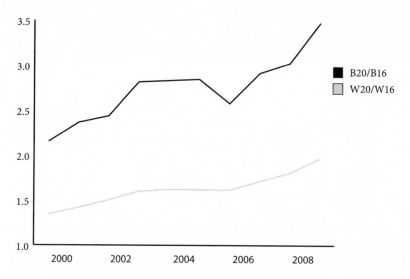

Figure 4.1. Ratio of adult to teen employment rates, by race, 2000-2009

immigrants were the largest share of workers but 58 percent in the ten states where immigrants were the smallest share of workers. These researchers estimated that, on average a 10 percentage point increase in the immigrant share of a state's workforce reduced the labor force participation rate of U.S.-born teenagers by 7.9 percentage points. Other researchers contend that at least one-third of the teen employment decline can be explained by the substantial increase in teenagers who attend summer school, both in high school and in college. Whatever the reason, this dramatic employment decline means that fewer teenagers become accustomed to the world of work that can provide them with the knowledge and discipline necessary to succeed in life.

Not surprisingly, the employment problems are more severe for black than white teenagers. For both black and white workers, employment rates are substantially higher for adult workers (twenty years and older) than for teen workers (sixteen to nineteen years old). However, the gap is dramatically larger among black workers. In 2000, adult black workers had an employment rate 2.15 times the rate for black teenagers; among white workers, the ratio was only 1.35 (figure 4.1). This disparity indicates that black teenagers face a relatively more difficult time than black adults. Over the next decade, the situation for both black and white teenagers worsened, but the racial gap remained.

Why do black teenagers have such difficulty finding employment? Certainly, racial stereotypes adversely affect black teenagers. Whatever qualms employers have with hiring adult black workers, they are much more severe when considering black teenagers. Second, teenage more than adult employment is dependent upon informal networks. Black youth have far fewer personal contacts that can link them to jobs than do white youth. In addition, national firms that use more formal hiring practices are still reluctant to locate outlets in black neighborhoods, which further lessens the ability of black youth to gain employment.

Improved Role of Testing

A more general problem black workers face is their poor academic performance: low grades in their courses and on general skills tests.[24] These findings cause many to fear that the use of testing during the hiring process would adversely affect black applicants. It is important to remember, however, that in the absence of testing, firms use informal judgments that may also adversely affect black workers. So long as the information provided by job tests about minority applicants is not systematically more negative than firms' beliefs derived from informal screens, job testing would not have a disparate impact on minority hiring.

To judge whether or not black employment is adversely affected by job testing, David Autor and David Scarborough surveyed a national retail chain whose 1,363 stores switched from informal to test-based worker screening. These firms experienced a 10 percent rise in job tenure, suggesting that there were efficiency gains. Consistent with prior research, minorities performed worse on the test, yet testing had no measurable impact on minority hiring, and productivity gains were uniformly large among minorities and nonminorities.[25]

There is also some national evidence that shifting from personal interviews to testing increases the share of black workers hired. In their multicity study, Moss and Tilly found the "person hired is two-thirds more likely to be white if a personal interview was used as a screen." By contrast, when testing was used, there was a tendency to reduce the odds of hiring whites. Thus, there is strong qualitative and quantitative evidence that, as a result of the negative stereotypes that influence many employers, the use of accurate criminal records and direct testing will not adversely affect and may aid black employment.

The role of testing was central to the recent Supreme Court ruling on the promotion procedure used by the New Haven Fire Department. In 2004, the city of New Haven decided not to use the results of a promotional test for firefighters because it was concerned that the test may have discriminated against minority applicants. White firefighters who scored well on the test sued the city, and the rest is now history: the U.S. Supreme Court ultimately ruled that a city cannot set aside the results of an employment test unless there is a "strong basis in evidence" that a test is discriminatory. Without judging the Supreme Court decision, let us look more closely at the New Haven testing procedure.

For its promotion procedures, New Haven used exams with a written portion that accounted for 60 percent of the grade and an oral portion that accounted for 40 percent. Forty-one firefighters took the captain exam, with none of the eight black test takers ranking higher than sixteenth. Seventy-seven firefighters took the lieutenant exam, with none of the nineteen black test takers ranking higher than fourteenth.[26]

The 60-40 weighting was quite arbitrary. As it happened, on both exams, black firefighters did relatively better on the oral portion. Among black test takers, one ranked sixth on the oral portion of the captain exam, and four ranked among the top eleven on the oral portion of the lieutenant exam. Thus, a shift in weighting would have enabled at least a few black firefighters to rank high enough to gain promotions.

Cognizant of this fact, elected officials in New Haven sought to revise its procedures to recruit new fire fighters. Previously, the procedure was as follows: All applicants took a written exam, and only those who passed moved on to take the oral portion of the exam. As with the promotion procedure, the remaining applicants were ranked by their weighted average on these two exams. In 2007, the written exam continued to be the first screen for applicants. However, now it was proposed that rankings would be determined solely by the oral exam scores of the remaining applicants.[27]

While an increased emphasis on the oral portion would have improved New Haven's recruitment of black (and Latino) firefighters and increased the promotion of black candidates, there was another problem with the city's testing procedures. As the creator of the test admitted, neither the written nor the oral portion of the promotion exam measured a test taker's ability to supervise or lead other firefighters in the line of duty. That is, the exam did not test applicants on the soft skills required to be effective supervisors or managers.

This was the complaint of a number of New Haven's black firefighters. "Just because you scored three more points than I did, that doesn't make you a better officer," said Wayne Ricks, a black veteran of twenty-seven years who did not score high enough on the lieutenant exam to qualify for the promotion list. "You need to be good with people, especially when you go into the communities and there might be a language barrier or a culture barrier. Not everyone is comfortable going into 'the hood.'"[28]

The Firebirds Society—an organization that represents black New Haven firefighters—favors an alternative called "assessment centers," which are designed by testing professionals to evaluate the particular skills needed for a certain job. Rather than distributing written questions and following up with an oral exam, this method intersperses a combination of interviews, group discussions, written exercises, oral presentations, role play, and emergency scenarios in order to closely simulate the job environment. Assessment centers are now used by fire departments from Ohio to the District of Columbia.[29]

These findings have some implications for affirmative action policies. Using cross-sectional employer data, Harry Holzer and David Neumark analyzed a variety of measures of employee credentials and performance for different demographic groups of employees. The measure of credentials included educational attainment while performance measures included wage/promotion outcomes as well as a subjective ranking by supervisors.

The study examined whether or not observed gaps in credentials and performance between whites and minorities are larger among establishments that practice affirmative action in hiring than among those that do not. Comparing minorities with whites, there was clear evidence of weaker educational credentials among the former group but relatively little evidence of weaker performance.[30]

How could affirmative action result in minorities with weaker credentials but not weaker performance, if educational credentials generally are meaningful predictors of performance? Evidence indicates that firms engaging in affirmative action (1) recruit more extensively; (2) screen more intensively, and pay less attention to characteristics such as limited work experience that usually stigmatize candidates; (3) provide more training after hiring; and (4) evaluate worker performance more carefully. In addition, these firms use other predictors of performance and a variety of methods to enhance performance among those who are hired. Thus, there may be selectivity bias that allows these firms to uncover applicants whose educational and formal credentials *understate* their productivity potential, and the use of support activities after candidates are hired allows these employees to close any performance gap that would have occurred.

More intensive hiring procedures enable firms to identify those applicants with weaker academic credentials who can become capable workers.

These successful efforts suggest that many employment procedures place too much weight on academic credentials and the use of fact-based and memorization testing. A shift to exams that measure the necessary practical skills can increase both equity and efficiency. This not only will reduce the racial scoring gap but also will overcome the negative stereotypes that seem to be sustained during personal interview procedures.

Policy Implications

During the George W. Bush administration, civil rights enforcement waned. Charles Savage reported that the Government Accountability Office found "several cases—including the curtailed voter intimidation inquiry—in which supervisors rejected the recommendations of career lawyers to go forward." For example, lawsuits brought by the division to enforce laws prohibiting race or sex discrimination in employment fell from about eleven per year under President Bill Clinton to about six per year under President George W. Bush.[31]

These findings dovetail with recent reports that black college graduates—the group that has been most sensitive to Equal Employment Opportunity (EEO) enforcement—are increasingly purging their black identify from their résumés. For example, Michael Luo reported:

> After graduating from business school last year and not having much success garnering interviews, [Johnny R. Williams] decided to retool his résumé, scrubbing it of any details that might tip off his skin color. His membership, for instance, in the African-American business students association? Deleted. . . . Similarly, Barry Jabbar Sykes, 37, who has a degree in mathematics from Morehouse College, a historically black college in Atlanta, now uses Barry J. Sykes in his continuing search for an information technology position, even though he has gone by Jabbar his whole life.[32]

If black college graduates are having difficulty competing for job openings, imagine the problems faced by black applicants in the informal labor markets that often dominate employment among less educated workers. Smaller firms do have legitimate economic reasons to use these methods of attracting job applicants, especially because they are less costly and less time-consuming than advertising and interviewing all applicants. We believe, however, that these practices often sustain biased employment practices. For this reason, the Civil Rights Division should not only reestablish EEO practices in professional employment but also strive to improve the monitoring of smaller firms that employ non–college graduates. Enhanced enforcement of EEO laws could include greater use of tester studies to establish discriminatory behavior and more systematic review of EEO data from employers that are not government contractors.[33]

This chapter has also highlighted how employment decisions are quite sensitive to the hiring process. We found that an overreliance on personal interviews can weaken the employment prospects of disadvantaged workers and that tests that simulate workplace decision making are more effective than standardized testing. In addition, criminal records or academic credentials should be judged in the context of the individual's overall résumé, not as decisive initial screens. These findings suggest that an important activity for the Civil Rights Division would be to disseminate information to human resource personnel so that they can more effectively formulate hiring procedures.

While reducing discriminatory hiring practices is important, this chapter has highlighted additional factors that can close the racial employment and earnings gaps. Efforts should be made to increase the soft skills necessary for employment. Government funding of nonprofit organizations should be expanded and made more secure. In my interview, Rob Carmona cited problems with reliance on nonprofit funding. At the request of the Ford Foundation, Carmona oversaw the development of reentry programs in Camden, New Jersey. Though these programs were successful, a new foundation leadership decided to go in a different direction, abruptly suspending their funding, not even providing a wind-down grant.

Even government funding can be unstable. Carmona mentioned a particular reentry grant from the Department of Labor whose goal was the placement of 700 ex-offenders. Despite placing 720 individuals who had a recidivism rate of only 17 percent, the grant was not renewed. Carmona suggested that this problem could be solved if STRIVE and similar organizations would become line items in federal budgets similar to the Job Corps.

Evidence further indicates that occupational training may be just as valuable for many high school students as efforts to increase their enrollment at four-year colleges. This was certainly the view of Ivonne Barreras, director of CUNY collaborative programs when I interviewed her in 2009. Reflecting on her own background and that of many of the disadvantaged students in the New York City school system, Barreras noted, "These students come from backgrounds where no one in their extended family had ever gone to college. In many families, they are the only one literate in English and are often under pressure to earn money as soon as possible to help support the family. For these students, collaborative learning opens up access to occupational programs which does not preclude them from going on to a CUNY four-year degree after completing the associate program."

Even without formal occupational training, it is important to improve the employment situation of young men and women. The collapse of teen employment has undoubtedly increased the detachment and disillusionment of many youth, especially black teenagers from low-income neighborhoods. The gap between the growing youth demand for consumer goods and their ability to purchase them can only worsen the situation. While the Obama administration has made some efforts to respond to this situation by increasing federal funding of summer jobs, this is far too little. It should try to link government contracts to targeted employment requirements, including teen employment and internships. A college-for-all focus should be balanced with a teen employment agenda.

5

Combating Gender
Earnings Disparities

Increasingly, public concern for gender employment inequities has been muted. The disproportionate job loss among men and black workers directed energies elsewhere. Initial expectations were that the Obama administration's stimulus funds would focus exclusively on "rebuilding our crumbling roads and bridges, modernizing schools that are failing our children, and building wind farms and solar panels; fuel-efficient cars; and the alternative-energy technologies that can free us from our dependence on foreign oil and keep our economy competitive in the years ahead."[1] While there is certainly a need for bridges, roads, schools and investment in green technology, economist Randy Albelda feared:

> There is a crucial missing link in this package—both on the employment side and the investment side. That link is women. This might as well be called the macho stimulus package. Jobs in construction and many of those that come with green investment often pay decent wages with benefits. But they are overwhelmingly held by men. Outside of trickle-around effects, this stimulus package will not create jobs for women in any close proportion to the numbers that will be unemployed. . . . Like the need to rebuild our physical infrastructure there is as big a need in developing and expanding our social infrastructure.

Albelda believed that government should make "investments in direct care, education, and healthcare [which] would also go a long way in alleviating poverty. Many low-income women are employed in these sectors. Federal money to these industries that also required a commitment to minimum employment standards would make more of these 'good' jobs, lifting the bottom of the labor market."[2]

The actual stimulus package did contain a significant amount of the kind of funding Albelda sought: more than $30 billion on child care and early education; almost $100 billion on health care, $20 billion of additional funding for food stamps, and over $60 billion for education and job training.[3] Despite these needed allocations, the problems face by men and black workers remain an overriding priority, moving efforts to reduce the persistent gender earnings gap to the background.

While this gap decreased substantially in the last decade, male workers still earn 20 percent more than female workers. The gap persists despite women having, on average, more years of schooling than men. Because at least a portion of the gap reflects the exit of women temporarily due to family responsibilities, the impact of child care policies will be explored. Because the gap also reflects occupational differences between men and women, this chapter will explore the possibilities of increasing female representation in nontraditional female occupations and raising wages in traditional ones.

Gender Discrimination in Noncollege Labor Markets

Among women, there is a clear earnings gap between races. In 1999, black women earned, on average, 86.5 percent of what white women earned. Most studies find, however, after adjusting for differences in productivity-related variables, this gap is eliminated.[4] To the extent a modest disparity remains, it is due primarily to differences in the occupational distribution of black and white women.[5] Similarly, there does not appear to be a significant wage disparity between comparable white and Latino women.[6] As a result, we can focus here on gender disparities irrespective of race or ethnicity.

Over the last three decades, there has been a general decline in gender wage disparities. Whether measured by usual weekly wage or earnings of full-time workers, the gender gap has declined to about 20 percent from the 30 percent level that existed in the early 1990s. The disparate work histories between men and women, however, make it difficult to judge how much of this wage gap reflects gender discrimination. In particular, women tend to be concentrated in lower-earnings occupations than men. Is this a result of labor discrimination or simply due to women selecting occupations in the lower-paying "helping" professions that they find personally rewarding or that enable them to better balance family responsibilities and work? If it is a matter of choice, we should estimate the gender wage gap among men and women working in the same occupations. When studies are restricted to only full-time workers, after adjusting for education, work experience, industry, and occupation, the predicted gender wage gap is reduced to 7 to 9 percent.[7]

These estimates are sensitive to the measure of work experience used. For men, age is a useful proxy for work experience, but not so for women. Many women earn degrees at an older age and/or take time off from full-time employment because of family responsibilities. At least through the end of the last century, women continued to interrupt their paid employment as a result of child care responsibilities. In 1998, only 52.5 percent of women worked full-time. While this is a considerable increase from 41.0 percent in 1979, it is still well below the 81.1 percent share of men.[8]

Looking at the period 1983–98, 48 percent of women aged twenty-six to fifty-nine, compared with 84 percent of comparably aged men, had paid employment in all fifteen years; 33 percent of women but only 5 percent of men reported no earnings in at least four years. Women also worked fewer hours per year than men. For example, comparing only those who worked in all fifteen years, women averaged 500 fewer hours annually. As a result, over this period, the typical woman earned only 38 percent as much as the typical man rather than the 72 percent that would be expected if women had worked the same number of years and the same number of hours as men.[9]

This work experience gap influences assessments of gender earnings disparities. In particular, if women aged thirty-five to forty-three had the same years of work experience as men of the same age, the predicted gender wage gap would decline from 23.0 to 5.8 percent for those workers with no more than a high school degree.[10] Thus, helping working-class women balance family and work may have a greater impact on gender wage differences than combating discriminatory hiring and promotion behavior.

Enhancing Female Earnings

Public policies should strengthen the ability of women to balance their workplace and family responsibilities. Women in low-income households are younger: 54.9 percent of low-income mothers compared with 36.2 percent of other mothers are younger than thirty-five. Low-income mothers are also less educated, have more children, and are much less likely to be married than other working mothers (table 5.1). As a result, they have much lower-paying jobs with fewer fringe benefits and are more likely to work evening or night shifts. Indeed, almost two-thirds of mothers in low-income households work in sales, service, or production jobs compared with only about one-quarter of other working mothers.[11]

TABLE 5.1

Personal and Family Characteristics of Working Mothers,
Aged 18 to 64 (percentages)

	Low-Income*	Not Low-Income
High school education or less	62.0	32.2
Three or more children	26.9	13.2
Married	43.6	80.6

*All mothers with family income below 200% of the poverty threshold.

With lower wages, more unstable work schedules, and weaker support networks, many of these mothers are vulnerable to lost work days and unemployment. Those mothers with higher earnings were more likely to remain at the same job, as were those who had secure child care arrangements and company-sponsored health insurance. Indeed, among low-income mothers with children under six years old, those with no stable child care arrangements were twice as likely to experience job turnover as those with secure child care arrangements.

Policies that increase the monetary value of work induce an increase in the share of women in the workforce. For example, when the 1986 tax reform lowered the tax rate faced by married women, they substantially increased their labor supply. The same was true when the federal government increased the Earned Income Tax Credit over the next decade. Consistent with this evidence, a recent Finnish study found that when some municipalities increased the cash benefits given to mothers who stayed at home, their labor supply fell.[12]

While it would appear that reducing child care costs by providing increased access to government-funded facilities would increase female labor supplies, this is not always the case. Many married mothers have stable informal child care arrangements, most often with other family members. As a result, most married working mothers who qualify for new government child care supports simply shift away from these informal arrangements, with their work schedule unchanged.[13]

By contrast, single mothers with young children substantially increase their employment when they gain access to government-funded child care. One study found that among these mothers, those who received child care assistance were 40 percent more likely to remain employed two years later than those who did not.[14] These mothers have much less stable informal arrangements than married mothers. For many, changes in personal circumstances make many unstable over time. Grandparents become unable to continue child care for health or other reasons, and the lives of other family providers change, making them unavailable for either brief or extended periods. Interviews revealed that one-third to one-half of low-income mothers experienced unplanned changes in child care arrangements during a two-year period.[15]

Just as important, for many workers, job advancement requires educational training outside of scheduled working hours. Often finding informal arrangements for these additional hours is much more difficult, forcing many mothers to forestall these skill-enhancing efforts. Thus, government-funded child care can have an impact on family economic well-being beyond enabling mothers to sustain paid employment.

Government-subsidized child care has never been as widely available as needed. The vast majority of families who qualify under federal guidelines received aid. Most troubling, state programs that have lower income requirements only serve 30 percent of those eligible. To address these pressures, President Obama's stimulus package added $2 billion for subsidized child care programs for 2009 and 2010. A number of states, including Indiana and Illinois, used this added funding to begin offering child care support to parents looking for work. Unfortunately, many more states cut access by either placing more families on waiting lists or reducing the income levels for eligibility; others have reduced the subsidies that individual families receive. "The social safety net was always in patches, and now it's more frayed," said Helen Blank, director at the National Women's Law Center. "For a single mom, it's a lottery in many states whether she gets child care or not."[16]

These cutbacks have affected many women like Jaimie Smith, a twenty-three-year-old single mother who paid $1.50 a day for her three-year-old daughter to attend a government child care center in Tucson. This enabled Smith to work at a nearby Target at which she earned eight dollars per hour. Smith was aiming to resume college and then find a higher-paying job. When Arizona enacted more stringent renewal procedures, however, she was shifted to the waiting list, forcing her to use unstable informal child care. As a result, she began missing days at work. After a few months, Target put her on a leave of absence, telling her to come back after securing stable child care.

One problem is that these subsidies are often quite cumbersome and require enormous logistical efforts to keep arrangements intact. Families also report that changes in eligibility status can cost them their subsidies and force them to take children out of care situations that were working well.

Often parents are not aware—until the subsidy suddenly disappears—that fluctuations in their work schedules or incomes will trigger ineligibility. In addition, bureaucratic procedures and staff attitudes in agencies that manage subsidies often discourage parents who qualify from using this help.[17]

Stringent income eligibility rules have a disruptive impact on many working mothers, such as Alexandria Wallace, who was working three days a week at a call center for Verizon while attending beauty school to earn a license as a cosmetologist. A small raise, however, bumped her above the income limit, and she had to withdraw her daughter from the government-funded program.

Without stable child care Wallace was forced to quit her Verizon job and took a lower-paying one that enabled her to maintain eligibility. When she reapplied for child care, however, Ms. Wallace was put on a waiting list, forcing her to rely on makeshift arrangements. She was able to complete the cosmetology program, but her subsequent beauty salon employment became erratic because of the instability of the child care arrangements she had patched together. Reluctantly, she applied for cash assistance because it was the only way she could gain stable child care and enroll in a state jobs program that would enable her to secure new employment.[18]

For women forced to rely on private providers, government tax subsidies can reduce child care costs. Currently, the federal government has two distinct child-related tax benefits. Families with qualifying child care expenses can either file for the federal child and dependent care tax credit or instead pay these expenses through a dependent care account (DCA). The federal child care tax credit is nonrefundable and thus benefits families only to the extent that it reduces their taxable income. It currently is much more widely used than a DCA. Because low-income families often have little or no taxable income, these credits have only modest value to them. To combat this inadequacy, thirteen states have instituted *refundable* child care tax credits; if the family has no taxable income, it will receive the credit as a tax refund. Chapter 8 will look more closely at some of the problems working families face in maximizing their ability to gain tax benefits, particularly among the single near-poor.

Rather than expand child care subsidies that are targeted to low-income families, it might be more effective to simply universalize government coverage to all families with young children. Between 2000 and 2008, state-funded pre-K enrollment rose more than 50 percent. Nationwide, as of 2008, more than 2.1 million three- and four-year-olds were enrolled in publicly funded early education, with state-supported pre-K accounting for about half of all children served. However, in spite of this growth, less than 30 percent of the nation's three and four year olds are served in publicly funded early education.

One promising strategy that we support is for government pre-k programs to form partnerships with community-based programs, including child care centers, Head Start, faith-based programs, and family child care homes. These partnerships would enable local government programs to serve a larger population by helping them address some challenges, such as the lack of resources and expertise or the inability to meet the comprehensive needs of children with working parents. Already these efforts have proved success-ful in a number of states and should be replicated elsewhere.[19]

Changing Occupational Choices

As already mentioned, a significant share of gender wage disparities reflect gender occupational differences. Women are disproportionately in lower-waged occupations than men. Among workers with less than a four-year col-lege degree, women in male-dominated occupations have hourly earnings about 20 percent above those of women in female-dominated occupations. Thus, changing the occupational distribution of women may substantially increase their earnings.

One significant impediment to female entrance into these male-domi-nated occupations is the jobs' hourly requirements. Among full-time work-ers, women in male-dominated occupations work about 300 hours more annually than women in female-dominated occupations. Providing more accessible and more responsive child care arrangements for working moth-ers will enable more of them to enter the higher-paying occupations that require longer hours.[20]

Beginning in the 1980s, nonprofits and government agencies began devel-oping programs to train and encourage women to enter male-dominated occupations. At the time, nearly 40 percent of men worked in occupations in which there were virtually no women. In most of these occupations, there are more women now, but their share remains exceedingly low. For example, in 2008 the female share of construction workers was only 2.7 percent (table 5.2). Even among painters, it was only 6.3 percent. The female share of installation and repair workers was only 3.8 percent. Among transportation and moving occupations, the female share had increased substantially but was concentrated primarily among bus drivers. In 2008, women constituted only 4.9 percent of truck drivers. Similarly, despite substantial increases, the female share in many other male-dominated blue-collar occupations remained below 10 percent.[21]

TABLE 5.2

Employed Persons by Detailed Occupation and Sex, 2008

Occupation	Total Employed (000)	Percent Female
Total, 16 years and older	145,362	46.7
Management, professional and related occupations	52,761	50.8
Service occupations	24,451	57.2
Sales and office occupations	35,544	63.2
Transportation and moving Occupations	8,827	14.9
Bus drivers	651	49.0
Taxi drivers and chauffeurs	373	13.3
Industrial truck and tractor operators	568	8.9
Driver/sales workers and truck drivers	3,388	4.9
Farming, fishing, and forestry	988	21.1
Construction and extraction	8,667	2.7
Carpenters	1,572	1.5
Painters	647	6.3
Production occupations	8,979	29.7
Assemblers and fabricators	1,320	34.8
Machinists	409	6.9
Computer control programmers and operators	68	8.7
Welding, soldering, and brazing	598	4.7
Installation, maintenance, and repair	5,152	3.8
Automotive service and technicians	852	1.6
Radio and telecommunication equipment installers and repairers	200	11.4

Source: Bureau of Labor Statistics, Table 11: http://www.bls.gov/cps/wlf-table11-2009.pdf.

These findings are consistent with broader evidence that increasing female shares in traditional male-dominated occupations has been slow. Herve Quineau estimated changes in sex segregation indices, which measure the share of female workers who would have to shift in order for the female representation to be equal across occupations. Between 1972 and

Combating Gender Earnings Disparities |

2002, it decreased from 43.96 percent to 34.10 percent. However, sex segregation declined at a decreasing rate: 4.10 percentage points during the period 1972–83, 3.44 percentage points during the period 1983–93, and 2.32 percentage points during the period 1993–2002.

More relevant here, declines in the sex segregation index were increasingly the result of decreases in the share of total employment in male-dominated occupations rather than increased female representation in those occupations. During the 1972–83 period, almost two-thirds of the index decline was due to increased female representation in male-dominated occupations. By contrast, during the 1993–2002 period, less than one-quarter of the index decline was the result of increasing female representation.[22]

Instead of focusing on traditional male-dominated occupations, we might look to other occupations in which women have a stronger foothold. In particular, technology-based occupations may provide substantial upward mobility. Between 1996 and 2000, among all workers who shifted from non-technology-based to technology-based occupations, 42 percent moved up to a higher income quintile whereas only 18 percent moved to a lower income quintile.[23]

One such occupation is information technology (IT). When this field emerged in the 1980s, jobs required a four-year computer science degree. By 1985, women obtained 36 percent of those degrees. Since then, however, the share of women earning computer science degrees has fallen below 30 percent.[24] Jane Margolis and Allan Fisher contend that this decline reflects a hostile environment and internalized inadequacies that women experience. During their college careers, many women studying computer science face an unsettling technical culture and a variety of discouraging experiences. Many begin to doubt their basic intelligence and their fitness to pursue computing. One female student quoted by Margolis and Fisher perceived her misfit with the prevailing culture this way:

When I have free time, I don't spend it reading machine learning books or robotics books like these other guys here. It's like, 'Oh, my gosh, this isn't for me.' It's their hobby. They all start reading machine learning books or robotics books or build a little robot or something and I'm not like that at all. In my free time, I prefer to read a good fiction book or learn how to do photography or something different, whereas that's their hobby, it's their work, it's their one goal. I'm just not like that at all; I don't dream in code like they do.[25]

It is not clear whether or not this perception reflects the environment in many university computer programs. Most important, over the last two decades, the IT field has broadened so that the bachelor degree is no longer its main entry point. In Illinois, more than 40 percent of IT workers have either certificates or associate degrees. While women constituted only 26 percent of those with a bachelor's degree or more, they constituted 44 percent of those with either a certificate or an associate degree. It appears that certificate programs are particularly receptive to women: while 39 percent of enrolled students are women, they constitute 49 percent of those who successfully complete these programs. As a result, entry into the IT field has become quite receptive to women.

A national study of IT certificate programs was conducted by Karen Chapple. Some left-liberal theorists have argued that the spread of information technology allows the global economy to use networks that effectively select only certain places and people to participate in the new economy. The existence of networks thus, they claim, creates a duality, of the "switched-on" and "switched-off," deliberately and selectively including some groups and excluding others.[26] By contrast, Chapple found that these certificate and associate programs make it possible for workers from disadvantaged backgrounds to get a foot in the door and advance in IT, becoming valued contributors to the new economy. She contends:

> Rather than exacerbating social exclusion, the spread of information technology has made upward mobility possible through the changing role of intermediaries, the new emphasis on soft over technical skills, and the growing maturity of workplace culture and career pathways. New training programs have emerged to prepare an IT workforce that looks different from the college-educated, white, male-dominated computer culture of the past.[27]

Chapple highlighted two of the training programs she studied: Per Scholas in the Bronx, New York, and Training, Inc., in Newark, New Jersey. Both programs are free of charge and funded almost entirely by foundations and corporations. They offer fifteen-week PC technician training programs, targeting extremely disadvantaged groups. The curriculum includes some networking, hardware, and software components. Both graduate 100 to 150 students per year, with placement rates that remain consistently around 80 percent.[28]

These programs are among those that emphasized soft skills, with as much as one-third of the curriculum devoted to communication and workplace protocol, with the explicit goal of job placement. Most of the other providers also include soft skills training, from customer service to familiarity with corporate culture. Many were particularly focused on instilling the importance of the proper behavior. One program had students sign a code of conduct upon entering the program, including a pledge to pay a five-dollar fee for each instance of tardiness. Many providers, particularly the nonprofits, have dress codes and a three-strikes-and-out attendance policy.

The background of instructors was crucial to teaching soft skills. More than half of the instructors, particularly among private providers, had an IT background and were most likely to continue to work in the IT industry. Nonprofits are more likely to provide specialized assistance, including personal presentation skills, videotaping, and motivation counseling.[29]

The organization of IT training at the one community college Chapple studied was strikingly different. The background of the instructors was more academic than at the private or nonprofit providers. In addition, the college culture would frown on dress or conduct codes, particularly if they resulted in the automatic dismissal of students. As a result, the college had no soft-skill training as part of its curriculum. The program graduates 1,200 students per year. Although the college offers job fairs, there were very few resources for placement, so it was largely informal. In general, its graduates recommended its courses as being of high quality but otherwise felt little connection to the institution.[30]

Chapple followed the graduates for four years. For those with no more than a high school degree, these entry-level programs made a dramatic difference, more than doubling their earnings. While they were making somewhat less than those who entered with more education, these wage increases made a dramatic difference in their lives.

Chapple also measured more broadly the degree of success of these graduates. She allocated each to one of three categories. The *very successful* group comprised those graduates who were experiencing significant growth in both wages and workplace responsibilities. The *limited success* group comprised those who, while maintaining IT employment, were not experiencing substantial growth in either wages or work responsibilities. Finally, the *not successful* group comprised those who were unemployed or did not work in the IT field.

By the time of the exit interviews, three or four years after graduation, just over one-quarter of the sample experienced no success in IT. However, almost 40 percent experienced high success. Interestingly, the distribution among the three categories did not differ significantly between those who had no more than a high school degree and those who entered the IT program with more education. Importantly, these gains came despite a stagnating economy in the early 2000s. These findings indicate that IT certificate programs can be an effective vehicle for upward mobility for working women.

Efforts to increase female inclusion in IT should be strengthened, but policy makers should not focus solely on employment growth. Given that women will continue to constitute a disproportionate share of those at the lower rung of IT workers, they should also focus on reducing gender wage disparities. Policy makers would do well to learn from the experience of women in the telecommunication industry.

Within the communication industry, Wired Telecommunications has historically employed the largest number of workers. Women and workers of color found good, stable, well-paid jobs with the telephone companies. Indeed, at 11.4 percent, the telecommunication industry has the highest female share of any group of installation workers (see table 5.2). A strong union presence set the standard for good wages throughout the industry. Over the years, public policy promoted the equitable employment of women and minorities, to ensure the diversity in communications that is essential to our democracy. The civil rights movement of the 1960s and the riots and protests of the 1970s created pressure on the Federal Communications Commission (FCC) to apply EEO measures to the communication industry. New EEO measures included reporting to the FCC the employment shares held by women and racial and ethnic minorities and the positions in which they were employed, and reporting to groups such as the National Urban League about employment opportunities.

Through their historically central role, especially in office jobs such as customer service representatives and operators, and when unionized, women have access to high-quality jobs in this industry. As a result, just under one-half of all workers in the telecommunication sector are female; the figure is 54 percent in the fast-growing Wireless Telecommunications. These women have earnings that substantially exceed the U.S. average for women working full-time in nonsupervisory jobs in all other industries. While earning more than women in other industries, they still earn less than men working in the telecommunication sector. In Wired and Wireless Telecommunications, women earn 71 cents and 72 cents, respectively, for every dollar earned by a man.

Most troubling, EEO policies have been weakened with the recent rhe-torical and legal assault on affirmative action. A campaign that conflated the term "affirmative action" with preferential treatment undercut important employment practices, while judicial activism typified in *Lutheran Church–Missouri Synod v. FCC* contributed to the FCC's regulatory backpedaling. As a result, there is good reason to be concerned about how women and work-ers of color currently fare in the communications sector.[31]

The government also influences occupational choices through its Work-force Investment Act (WIA). This program, which was initiated at the time of welfare reform to aid single mothers' skill development, replaced the Job Training Partnership Act (JTPA). WIA organized a three-tiered system of core, intensive, and training services. While managers have substantial dis-cretion in determining the tier for each applicant, intensive services and training services are generally reserved for unemployed or underemployed individuals. To access training, qualifying participants are supplied with an individualized training account (ITA) that serves as a voucher to "purchase" training from an eligible provider.

While well-intentioned, the current procedure makes it difficult if not impossible to provide training to single mothers who are gainfully employed—training that may be critical to their ability to attain middle-class wages. In particular, given the dramatic increase in the employment rate of single mothers, the numbers receiving job training fell dramatically. Whereas in 1998, 43.7 percent of adult training exiters were single mothers, this number fell to 24.6 percent in 2003.[32]

WIA also seemed to be focused on traditional employment. More than one-half of program managers did not know if women were placed in non-traditional occupations (occupations that are less than 25 percent female). Not surprisingly, then, only 2.9 percent of women adult exiters were employed in nontraditional jobs after WIA. This is particularly discourag-ing because nontraditional occupations offer women opportunities for high wages, health benefits, and pensions not typically available in traditionally female fields.

WIA must also improve its efforts to accommodate the special needs of single mothers. To be effective, they must understand that single mothers are not alone—its policies must take into account that they are the primary caregivers to their children. Indeed, in a recent survey, 80 percent of train-ing providers reported that child care demands prevented women from succeeding in training programs, and 63 percent of the providers reported that a lack of access to transportation to a training site prevented women's success in their programs. Single mothers face multiple barriers to success in employment and training, and workforce staff must be cognizant of their needs, in addition to knowledgeable about all the potential services for which these women may qualify. To accomplish this, states need funding to provide the technical assistance to local staff to effectively serve these women.[33]

Enhancing Pay in Female-Dominated Occupations

Enabling women to better balance work and family and changing preparation and attitudes could help move more women away from traditional female occupations. Even in the best of circumstances, however, women will continue to dominate occupations that have more flexible work hours and are in the helping professions. First among these are various occupations in the health industry. An estimated 16.91 percent of all female employment is in health industry.[34] Among all women with associate degrees, 31.03 percent are employed in health care. The importance of this industry for the female workforce should only grow over time as health care consumption will continue to experience disproportionate growth. Thus, raising wages for these workers would go a long way toward improving gender equity.

There are two main groups of female health care workers. Many less educated women labor as aides and custodial workers, earning low wages and often enduring bad working conditions. They are employed in hospitals, nursing homes, and privately as home health care attendants. The most important ways that these workers can attain improved wages and working conditions is through unionization and government mandates. These mandates could be at the federal or local level. For example, when Chicago living-wage legislation covered home care attendants, their pay rose by almost two dollars per hour.[35]

Mandated sick leave policy could also enhance the well-being of home care attendants, most of whom do not have any paid sick leave.[36] In most cases, health care employment agencies allow workers to take *unpaid* leave to attend to their own or their families' health needs. However, these workers risk losing their job placement, since the client can decide to keep the replacement. If paid sick leave was mandated, these aides would have a greater ability to care for their own families' health needs without risking their placements. A number of localities, most notably San Francisco, have implemented mandates, but a national proposal, the 2007 Healthy Families Act, has languished in Congress.[37]

The second group consists of those women who have gained health care education credentials. Women with associate degrees in the health industry earn $9,600 more annually than those with other associate degrees ($39,622 versus $30,006). This evidence suggests that many young women should be encouraged to enter the health field and, more important, that supports should be provided to allow them to rise up the career ladder.

Sandra Watson, the director of continuing education at LaGuardia Community College, highlighted the importance of providing these supports. Thanks to extensive funding grants, LaGuardia students are provided with the necessary support services, like counseling, child care, and smaller classes, that are crucial to their success. Just as important, the school's programs provide career ladders in the health field. Students with the weakest skills begin in "Bridge to the Health Sciences." After completing this entry program that has employment links, they might choose to continue to the licensed practical nursing program, and after completing that program, they might choose to extend their education further through a registered nursing program.

Teen Childbearing and Employment

Certainly, there should be a focus on skill enhancements that would enable more working women to have higher earnings. This chapter, however, has noted the difficulties faced by single mothers—difficulties that create barriers to their skill-enhancing and career choices. While more accessible and more affordable child care is helpful, delaying childbearing may be an important component of the ability of at-risk women to advance. We believe that one important component of any program to reduce teen pregnancy is *direct* employment of at-risk teenage women.

In 2006, for the first time in fifteen years, teen birthrates rose. Though the increase was slight and has not continued, observers feared that the rise verified a growing malaise among disadvantaged young women. Left liberals saw it as evidence that public school sex education should be energized and shifted away from the abstinence-only priorities of the Bush administration. The focus on school programs to stem teen birthrates is most clearly seen in a Kids Count publication from 2009.[38] In more than seventeen pages of detailed policy recommendations, there is not one sentence on the role direct employment can play in reducing pregnancies among at-risk young women. Instead, recommendations emphasize safe-sex education and esteem-enhancing school programs, an approach that contrasts with the approach taken toward at-risk young men where employment efforts are seen as crucial to enhancing their long-term futures.

As it happens, there is some evidence that employment issues strongly influence childbearing decisions of young, at-risk *black* women. For young black women in poor neighborhoods, it is often a struggle to overcome a sense of powerlessness. Kristin Luker felt the choice of pregnancy was dominated by these attitudes. Arline Geronimus and others suggested that with a bleak economic outlook, it becomes rational to have children young when these poor women are healthier and have a stronger child-support network.[39] This framework infers that strengthening economic conditions will have a positive effect, inducing more young, at-risk black women to forgo motherhood during their teen years. Indeed, Cynthia Colen and colleagues found that during the 1990s, declining unemployment rates could explain a substantial share of the decline in black teen birthrates. They surmised, "During times of economic prosperity, when teens or their elders may perceive improved financial returns to education or immediate job opportunities, a great percentage of African American teens in high-poverty communities may be both encouraged and personally motivated to delay childbearing."[40]

The employment prospects of young black adults certainly can influence the childbearing attitudes of teen black women, but peer pressures may play an even more important role. The attitude of one's peers toward motherhood and the pressures from one's boyfriend to engage in unprotected sex are important determining factors. The Kids Count authors propose school counseling to build up self-esteem that would enable young women to resist the pressures from boyfriends and peers. We believe, however, that direct employment offers the best chance of resisting these pressures.

First, employment stems harmful pressures by giving young women an alternate set of peers. Katherine Newman found that the social relations formed with fellow workers insulated many young people from engaging in the risky behavior common to their neighborhoods. As noted earlier, David Shipler found that for many welfare leavers, it was the advice they received from coworkers that led to better life decisions.[41] Second, the pressures that many young black women face from their boyfriends are influenced by financial considerations. Employment can give young women a source of money so that they do not need to rely on boyfriends for spending money, as receiving spending money is a risk factor for never using condoms.[42] Thus, helping young women gain paid employment will give them a different social network and some financial independence that can effectively counter the pressures they face in their schools, neighborhoods, and intimate relationships.

Conclusion

This chapter points out that child care support does not simply enable women to maintain employment. It also makes it feasible for many working mothers to enroll in job training and educational programs that enable them to enhance their careers. For many, it is the only way they can sustain the additional hours associated with working in many traditional male-dominated occupations. Paid sick leave would also help them sustain employment.

As working mothers' pay increases, they gain less from government-subsidized child care. For these mothers, improved child-related federal and state tax benefits can substantially reduce the costs of child care. Most important would be expansion of pre-K programs in public schools. Fortunately, support for government pre-K programs does not appear to be a politically partisan issue. A number of southern states, including Oklahoma and Georgia, have pre-K participations rates among the highest in the nation. Federal support for the expansion of these programs may be an effective way to prod more localities to initiate them.

Programs that aid female access in traditional male-dominated occupations should continue. Indeed, WIA training programs should help increase female access rather than continuing to funnel women into traditional female occupations. Training programs should also be made available to working mothers who want to enhance their skills rather than being reserved solely for the underemployed and unemployed. Of course, for these programs to be viable for working mothers, support services, especially child care, must be provided.

Evidence also indicates that government programs should provide further access to occupations that already have significant female representation. There is strong evidence that the cultural and educational barriers that women have faced are much less severe than they were decades ago. This is certainly the case with IT certificate programs. Some evidence suggests that four-year programs have become more supportive as well. In particular, data from Illinois indicate that the female share of graduates is virtually the same as the female share of enrollees, which strongly suggests that there is no systematic discouragement of female computer science students once they enroll. Some women undoubtedly faced an alienating or hostile environment that caused them to drop out. These women, however, may be offset by other women who were able to complete the program only with university encouragement and support.

We should also not ignore the biased environment women face outside of female-dominated occupations. Evidence from the telecommunication industries suggests that even when there is a favorable environment, female workers still lag behind their male counterparts in wages and promotions. Upgraded EEO enforcement can reduce these inequities.

Finally, a comprehensive look at issues related to family formation is beyond the scope of this book. A later chapter will look at one aspect: strengthening healthy relationships between parents. Teen childbearing is another aspect but is dealt with only briefly there. In this chapter, evidence was presented that linked teen birthrates to both future employment prospects and, possibly more important, direct teen employment. Just as there is a concern for the direct employment of young at-risk men, there should be a similar appreciation of the importance of such employment in the lives of at-risk young women.

6

Refocusing Community College Programs

Today almost half of all college-bound students start out in community colleges, which are the overwhelming destination for high school graduates whose parents lack a college degree. Historically, their primary mission was the transfer function: preparing students to move on to four-year colleges. In the last twenty years, however, there has been a movement toward also preparing students for immediate entry into the workforce with certification programs and two-year associate degrees. This chapter will argue that community colleges should reorganize spending and hiring priorities to strengthen and expand their occupational programs. In addition, they should strengthen their work with employers to encourage more internship and apprenticeship programs that allow students to earn while they learn and gain valuable occupational experience in their fields. These programs are in the best interest of the majority of community college students, who are often ill served by the emphasis given to the transfer function.

Our position is not popular with many educational theorists. From the beginning, many of these individuals attacked any shift to occupational programs. Labeling such a shift "cooling out," they claim that it creates a new form of tracking where occupational programs dissuade students away from the more financially rewarding four-year degrees into dead-end, low-paying occupations. These critics of occupational programs are particularly troubled by the increasing entry of black and Latino students into the community college system. Given the long history of racist school tracking in the K-12 system, they fear that tracking is now being reproduced at the college level.

To some degree, lines hardened after the 1996 welfare act. Critics were upset that the government provided very few long-term educational programs to prepare welfare recipients for work. First among this group are Katherine Shaw and Jerry Jacobs. After editing an issue of the *Annals of the*

American Academy of Political and Social Sciences that slammed the shifting emphasis of community colleges to occupational programs, they collaborated with others to publish *Putting Poor People to Work (PPPW)*, a finalist for the prestigious C. Wright Mills Award.[1] Condemning President Clinton's "Make Work Pay" philosophy, the authors asserted that welfare recipients were "increasingly directed toward the most ineffective forms of training rather than toward higher-quality college-level education. . . . Under welfare reform, a significantly higher percentage of recipients participating in any type of education or training pursue only short-term, noncredit training."[2] As in their *Annals* publication, the authors claim that the work-to-work programs had undermined the traditional mission of community colleges as primarily institutions that prepare students to enter four-year programs. They lament, "Historically community colleges held their academic mission as primary, but now there is mounting pressure on them to adopt a workforce-preparation mission . . . [and] divert ambitious lower-class students away from four-year schools, channeling them instead into lower-status vocational programs."[3]

Certainly given the long history of inappropriate tracking, one should not take lightly the risks that encouraging occupational programs may have. Moreover, the United States, more than most developed countries, is a "second chance" society where we believe that employment trajectories should not be determined solely by the choices individuals made in their teenage years. These concerns, however, should not blind us to evidence that for a substantial share of weakly prepared students, occupational programs offer the best alternative.

As we shall see, a large share of students coming to the community college system have abysmal academic skills, which results in very low graduation rates. This evidence does not, however, cause most critics to change their assessment. They focus on the earnings gap between those who complete four-year degrees and those who do not. Those who succeed, they assert, enter the middle class, whereas those who do not are sentenced to a lifetime of economic deprivation. Given the choices, these critics believe that there is no alternative to their focus on the transfer function. After all, who can support an alternative if it consigns a large share of college students to a lifetime of destitution even if they succeed?

The emphasis on four-year degrees is based upon the large current gap between the *median* earnings of those who attain four-year degrees and those without one. For example, the median usual weekly wages of workers, twenty-five years or older, with four-year degrees (and no higher) was $1,029;

for those with only some college or an associate degree, it was $726; for those with an associate degree, it was $782.[4]

This comparison is only one part of the story: there is a large dispersion of earnings at each level of educational attainment. In 2009, the lower quartile of workers with four-year degrees had a usual weekly wage of $724 or lower. As a result, more than one-half of all workers with some college or an associate degree earn more than the lowest quartile of those with a four-year degree.[5] This large overlap in earnings suggests that the left-liberal interpretation is faulty: four-year degrees do not guarantee superior earnings, nor do occupational degrees consign workers to a lifetime of dead-end, low-wage jobs.

Similar results were found in a Gates Foundation study that looked at the peak quarterly earnings over a three-year period of Florida workers in their midtwenties. The lowest quartile of those with a four-year degree had annualized peak quarterly earnings of $29,000 or less. By contrast, the median annualized peak quarterly income of comparably aged Florida workers whose highest educational attainment was completion of a certificate program was $37,044.[6] Tabulations I have done from the 2000 census indicate the same degree of earnings overlap among workers aged thirty-five to forty-four.

The unintended consequences of stressing the transfer function are substantial. Students are dissuaded from entering occupational programs they could have completed and instead encouraged to maintain their goals for four-year degrees that they are unable to attain. Even those who succeed in transferring to four-year colleges face an uphill battle. Ritze found that even the small share of students who completed a two-year program at the local community college had persistent difficulties when they transferred to four-year colleges. In their first year after transferring, these students attained an average GPA of only 2.52, well below the four-year college norm.[7]

While a member of the admissions committee, I tabulated the characteristics of students who entered as first-time Brooklyn College freshmen in 1987. At the end of five years plus one summer, 459 had graduated and another 105 were "almost" graduates, having completed at least 90 but less than the required 120 credits. The almost graduates were much more weakly performing students. Whereas 18.7 percent of those who graduated in five years had a GPA of less than 2.5, 55.2 percent of the almost graduates did. Whereas 22.2 percent of five-year graduates had at least a 3.5 GPA, only 5.7 percent of almost graduates did.[8]

The almost graduates were disproportionately those who had a low high school average and/or required remediation. Whereas 19.1 percent of five-year graduates had a high school average of less than an 80, 44.2 percent of almost graduates did. Whereas 31.4 percent of five-year graduates required some remediation, 61.9 percent of almost graduates did. This indicates that even among those weakly prepared entering students who are successful in completing a four-year degree, their performance lags. On average, they take longer to graduate and have weaker GPAs. Thus, even those low-performing high school students who graduate will likely have earnings below the median of those with four-year degrees.

Weakly prepared students who were able to graduate from less demanding four-year colleges also face employment difficulties. I interviewed one such woman, Belinda, who had been a drug addict and an absent mother for more than a decade until she pulled her life together in the mid-1990s. Working two jobs, she put herself through college, eventually obtaining a four-year degree from a private college that specialized in business programs tailored to weakly prepared students. When I spoke with Belinda in 2004, almost one year after she graduated, she was bitter. She had yet to obtain even one job interview in her field, and the college placement office was useless.

Belinda is not alone. Increasingly, weakly prepared black and Latino students are enrolling in and graduating from schools that disproportionately enroll minority students. For black students, most identifiable are the Historically Black Colleges (HBCs), but there are many more colleges that serve this role. In 2006, 19.29 percent of all black female four-year graduates came from the HBCs. In addition, another 19.25 percent of black female graduates came from colleges where black women constitute at least 25 percent of female graduates. As a result, 38.54 percent of black female graduates came from a small group of colleges that produce only 7.56 percent of all female graduates.

This pattern is even stronger among Latinas. Whereas 42.44 percent of all Latina four-year graduates are from schools where Latinas constitute at least 25 percent of their graduates, these colleges produced only 7.25 percent of all female graduates. Similar results exist for the production of black and Latino male graduates. These Latino- and black-serving colleges are uniformly among the least competitive private and public schools nationally. For black women, excluding the HBCs, the three largest degree grantors were DeVry University, Strayer University, and the University of Phoenix, all for-profit proprietary schools.[9] There is no guarantee that Belinda or other graduates from these colleges would have been more successful if they had completed a more focused occupational program. But Belinda's experience and evidence provided later in this chapter suggest that four-year graduates with weak academic skills from weak programs tend to earn significantly less than the median earnings of all four-year graduates.

Student Background and Performance

Unfortunately, completion of an associate degree at a community college, let alone transfer to a four-year institution, may be beyond the reach of a substantial share of young adults. For this population, occupational certificates provide the best chance for moving forward. This certainly appeared to be the case for a large share of welfare recipients, who were overwhelmingly women who had not had a successful high school experience. Kristin Luker noted that for many young poor women, doing poorly in school *preceded* pregnancy: "As many as one-fourth to one-third of teenage mothers drop out before they get pregnant," and many others "may already be drifting away from school long before pregnancy gives them an official excuse to do so."[10] LaDonna Pavetti and Gary Burtless found that welfare recipients have much weaker basic skills than the general population, as measured by the Air Force Qualifying Test (AFQT); at least two-thirds of welfare recipients in the early 1990s scored in the lowest quartile on this test, one-third scoring in the lowest decile.[11]

These deficiencies suggest that a large proportion of welfare recipients, including those with high school degrees or GEDs, would perform poorly in a college setting where academic coursework is stressed. This was the finding when in the 1990s California expanded services to welfare participants at its community colleges. Despite the extensive support services provided, almost one-third of welfare participants leaving California community colleges had completed no college credits; another 30 percent earned fewer than twelve credits.[12]

This specter of failure may be one of the reasons systematic evaluations by the Manpower Development Research Corporation (MDRC) consistently found that work-first programs proved to be substantially more successful than other welfare-to-work programs that emphasized some education and training. At eleven sites nationally between 1991 and 1994, welfare recipients were randomly selected for a welfare-to-work program or a control group that remained in the general welfare population. Welfare-to-work programs were divided into those that emphasized Work First activities and those that emphasized a short-term human capital development (HCD) approach. Each participant was followed for five years, with the four Work First programs increasing earnings by $1,500 to $2,500, and the number of quarters employed from 0.7 to 1.1. By contrast, the two HCD programs with low enforcement failed to raise employment while the other five HCD programs increased earnings by $800 to $2,000 and the number of quarters employed by 0.3 to 0.8.[13]

Studies did find that among adult women, welfare reform lowered school attendance—dropping from 3.6 percent to 2.7 percent for women without a high school degree. Evidence indicates that for these employed women, "there may be very large costs or minimal benefits to completing high school." This was particularly true for those welfare mothers whose "only motivation for staying in or continuing high school" was the welfare requirement. These researchers concluded, "Thus, most or all of the adverse effect of welfare reform on schooling appears to be due to the increased employment among the target group."[14]

As chapter 2 noted, employment provided these workers with more than needed income. It also provided many with purpose and feelings of self-worth. For example, a nursing administrator in Massachusetts told me that recipients, after completing a ten-week home health care attendant program, viewed it as a major accomplishment, bringing their children and parents to the graduation ceremony. What most surprised my son when he did labor organizing at Baptist Hospital in Beaumont, Texas, was how much workers were upset because, as a result of cutbacks, they had neither the staff nor the equipment to do a satisfactory job cleaning the floors and rooms. The pride these women felt is not an isolated phenomenon. Many women realize that, through stable paid employment, they become a positive role model to their children. In Milwaukee, Cutina, a welfare leaver I interviewed, told me, "All of my children think more of me, no longer see me lying around. Can tell them all you want but they go by what they see you're doing for yourself. They respect me more because I respect myself more. I'm way better than I was before. Just can't see myself going back."

Another woman I interviewed showed me how work can provide meaning and stability in troubled lives. Sally left an abusive relationship and, with her daughter, was forced to move in with her father after being homeless for a time. The situation remained chaotic because of the antagonism between Sally and her father's new wife. At the time, Sally was employed at a center for emotionally disturbed children. When she told me how she liked caring for these children, I asked, "Isn't it sometimes upsetting taking care of these children?" She smiled and answered, "I liked being at work to get away from the problems at home."

Academically Underperforming Students

A second group that would benefit from certificate programs consists of the many students who fail to graduate from high school. While nationally the vast majority of white students graduate from high school, this is not true for blacks and Latinos. For example, in Chicago, the 2003 high school graduation rate was 38 percent for black men and 54 percent for black women. The Chicago rate for black men is in the middle of the pack among school districts nationally that enroll the largest number of black students. It is higher than the 20 percent rate for Detroit and the 32 percent for New York City. Nationally, the black male high school graduation rate was 47 percent compared with 57 percent for Latino men and 75 percent for white men.[15]

Even among high school graduates, many have skill deficiencies that limit their ability to complete college. This has become an increasing problem, given the growing number of first-generation students entering college—students whose parents had attained no more than a high school degree constituted 73 percent of those enrolled in certificate programs and 53 percent of those enrolled at community colleges.[16] Past evidence collected by the National Center for Educational Statistics indicated that there was a core of first-generation students who had solid academic credentials. Almost one-quarter of 1992 first-generation high school graduates had taken a trigonometry course. Among this group, 57 percent attained four-year degrees within eight years. Similarly, among the 18 percent who had high test scores, 54 percent attained four-year degrees.[17]

The vast majority of the remaining first-generation students, however, had weak college preparation. Among those who began in community colleges, 60 percent were required to take remediation courses; this figure was 45 percent for those who first enrolled in four-year colleges. These students also had other impediments that hindered their academic performance: more family and work responsibilities and less social capital that would help them navigate college life.[18]

The weak outcomes of first-generation college students are particularly evident among black Americans and Latinos who first enrolled at community colleges in the late 1990s. After six years, while 40 percent of white students had earned some degree or certificate, only 27 percent of blacks and 31 percent of Latinos did. For black students, the largest share of those credentials were certificates; only 10 percent of black students had attained either an associate or bachelor's degree, compared with 20 percent of Latino and 30 percent of white students. This racial gap could not be explained by black students taking longer and thus still being enrolled in school. The shares of 1996 enrollees who had either completed a four-year program or were still enrolled in one were 7, 14, and 21 percent, respectively, for black, Latino, and white students.[19]

TABLE 6.1

Percentage of 2002 and 2003 Chicago High School Graduates Who Scored at Least an 18 on the ACT or had a GPA of at Least 2.5 in Core Courses

	Black	Latino	White	Asian
Male	27	38	63	68
Female	47	52	74	86

The poor progress of most black students in community college partly reflects weak academic skills combined with the triumph of a "college for all" attitude. Evidence for this is found in the experience of the Chicago public school system in the last decade. Beginning in 1997, Chicago made a concerted effort to improve the college preparation of its students by dramatically expanding its offerings of honors and Advanced Placement courses throughout the system. Between 1998 and 2003 there was a 96 percent increase in the number of graduating students who had taken at least one Advanced Placement course. This effort increased the educational aspirations of students attending Chicago's public high schools. Among high school seniors, 78 percent hoped to obtain bachelor's degrees, and an additional 14 percent expected to obtain associate degrees.

Unfortunately, the vast majority of Chicago high school graduates were weakly prepared for college. Virtually all colleges that have any selectivity reject all applicants with ACT scores lower than 18 (where the average score is 21) *and* had a high school GPA of less than 2.5 in core courses. Among all 2002 and 2003 Chicago public school graduates, only 41 percent had a GPA above 2.5, and only 20 percent of black men did. Indeed, only 27 percent of black male high school graduates met at least one of these two thresholds (table 6.1). This situation is consistent with findings of an earlier national study, which estimated that less than one-half of African American and Latino high school graduates had grades and test scores that would minimally qualify them to attend four-year colleges.[20]

Among black Chicago 2002 and 2003 high school graduates, a bit over 60 percent enrolled in college within a year of graduation, as did slightly less than 50 percent of Latino graduates. Given their poor academic records, it is not surprising that only a small share enrolled in selective colleges, while 40 percent of African Americans and 45 percent of Latinos enrolled in community colleges. Given the limited share of students starting out in community colleges who eventually attain bachelor's degrees, some have suggested that it would be better if students could begin in four-year colleges. The six-year college graduation rates for white and Asian Chicago public high school graduates who initially enrolled in four-year colleges in 1998, both men and women, were 45 percent. By contrast, the college graduation rates for black and Latino men who first enrolled in four-year colleges were only 22 and 28 percent, respectively. For black and Latino women, graduation rates were 28 and 34 percent, respectively.

These graduation rates were linked strongly to high school GPAs. For example, the graduation rate was 16 percent for those with GPAs between 2.1 and 2.5; 27 percent for those with GPAs between 2.6 and 3.0; 43 percent for those with GPAs between 3.1 and 3.5; and 63 percent for those with GPAs of 3.6 or higher. Thus, pushing weakly prepared college-bound students directly into four-year colleges does not seem to be a viable solution.[21]

The Remediation Hurdle

The results for the Chicago school system are common nationally. While cities have been able to increase graduation rates, the skills these students possess have not improved. New York state education officials released a report indicating that "only 23 percent of students in New York City graduated ready for college or careers in 2009, not counting special-education students. That is well under half the current graduation rate of 64 percent, a number often promoted by Mayor Michael R. Bloomberg as evidence that his education policies are working."[22] Sadly, New York City's rate was well above those in other cities in New York. In Buffalo, Rochester, Syracuse, and Yonkers, the share of high school students attaining the necessary skills was below 17 percent.

Typical of the national picture, three-quarters of the students who entered community college in New York City in 2009 needed to take remediation courses to prepare them to take credit-bearing courses. Once assigned to remediation courses, students have difficulty succeeding. A typical example is the outcome of an Ohio study that looked at the educational progress of students five years after they had enrolled full-time in one of the state's community college. Among those who did not have to take a math remediation course, 29 percent had completed a two-year associate degree, and 16 percent were either still enrolled in or had completed a four-year college degree program. By contrast, among those full-timers who had to take a remediation math course, less than 18 percent had completed their associate degree, and only 9 percent were either still enrolled in or had completed a four-year college degree program. Comparable results were found for students who were required to take a remedial English course.[23]

Success rates are particularly low for those students who need remediation in a number of areas. In Miami-Dade Community College, less than 25 percent of students who were deficient in three areas successfully completed remediation; only 4 percent had completed an associate degree within five years. By contrast, almost two-thirds of all students deficient in only one area successfully completed remediation; 20 percent had completed their associate degree within five years.[24] In another study funded by the Community College Association, Robert McCabe found that only 5 percent of seriously deficient entering students completed at least twenty college credits.[25]

Given such low success rates, it is not surprising that colleges seek ways for students to avoid taking remediation courses. After a threatened suit by the Latino community, California colleges chose to eliminate any basic skill requirement as a prerequisite for credit-bearing courses. Elsewhere, administrations provide waivers so that probably more than 20 percent of students referred to remediation were able to circumvent the requirement.

Buttressing these circumvention efforts are national studies that measure educational outcomes of students with similar academic deficiencies. These studies generally track students who were on the borderline for taking remediation courses, not the students with more severe skill deficiencies. When those who enroll in the recommended remediation are compared with those who do not, most studies find that there is little difference in graduation rates or college credits earned.[26]

I am not surprised that these borderline students could do just as well whether or not they took the recommended remediation. Before Brooklyn College stopped admitting students who failed basic skills exams, the school offered prefreshman summer remediation programs that were quite successful in helping borderline students pass when they retook the basic skills tests at the end of the summer. The evidence indicated, however, that remediation rarely has transformative effects. Except for a very small share of students, remediation helped students *marginally* improve their weak skills, but for many, this was enough to qualify them to take credit-bearing college courses.

Given the very modest skill improvements, remediation will not have a substantial bearing on the ability of students to move forward in their college careers. Counseling, course selection, personal circumstances, and personal effort will swamp any effect that the marginal improvement in basic skills might have. Indeed, the longtime director of the Department of Educational Services at Brooklyn College did not look so favorably on this summer program. If these students had to take remediation courses during their freshman year, they would also be required to have the accompanying counseling services that the director thought were extremely valuable for first-generation college students. By passing their skills exams during the summer, these students missed out on these services. Given their still below-average academic skills, they remained vulnerable to failure but without the support that could help them navigate through their difficulties.

If remediation has only a modest impact on skills of borderline students, then it is unlikely to enable more weakly prepared students to succeed. In 1999, Bronx Community College in New York City instituted a special program to help the more poorly prepared students navigate through their remediation courses. Expending substantially more resources on support services and small classes, this Freshman Initiative Program (FIP) was able to substantially increase pass rates on all three remediation exams by about 20 percentage points.

The FIP program enabled more students to continue at the community college. Unfortunately, it did not have a significant effect on overall retention rates and other measures of progress. After the institution of FIP, the passing rate on credit-bearing courses increased by only 2 percent, the rate of course withdrawals decreased by only 3 percent, and the number of students on probation dropped by only 1 percent. Even after instituting the program, the six-year graduation rate increased only slightly, remaining well below 30 percent.[27] Thus, improved remediation of the weakest students had little long-term effect on their ability to navigate the community college system.

Unintended Consequences of Emphasizing the Transfer Function

Summarizing the evidence presented:

1. A substantial majority of students enrolling in the community colleges have insufficient skills to successfully complete credit-bearing college courses.
2. Remediation has only a marginal impact on skill development so that those with significant skill deficiencies are not helped sufficiently to succeed in their academic programs.
3. Many students who transfer to four-year programs do not complete those programs.
4. Most of those who complete the four-year degree do so with below-average GPAs and probably from weaker four-year schools.

From this evidence, one might conclude that for a very large share of those who enroll in the community college system, attainment of four-year degrees is unrealistic. These students should be quickly counseled into shifting into certificate or associate degree programs that prepare them directly for the job market. This conclusion, however, is rejected by most educators, who instead emphasize the growing importance of the college credential: "What counts in the labor market is the quantity of education an individual has completed, not the quality of learning."[28] In support, these educators point to the economic literature, where it is suggested that educational degrees have a "signaling mechanism" that enable employers to judge which applicants have the proper behavioral traits and which do not. From this perspective, lifetime earnings have little relation to college performance; even the weakest four-year graduates from the weakest colleges can expect to attain, on average, close to the median earnings of all college graduates.

By contrast, we believe that this widely held view is incorrect. In particular, empirical support for this signaling mechanism is problematic. In a widely cited survey of the literature, John Riley concluded, "In labor economics, the connection between [signaling] theory and testing has been rather loose."[29] Moreover, much of the testing was done in earlier times when college graduates were relatively scarce. As the number of college graduates has grown, an increasing share are hired for jobs that do not necessarily require four-year degrees. Employer surveys during the 1990s found that "the college graduates in lower level jobs are those whose actual skills do not reflect their credentials."[30] This sorting suggests that employers incorporated quality differences when making hiring decisions. There is also some evidence that class rank has a significant influence on lifetime earnings.[31] Thus, we believe college performance influences the earnings of four-year college graduates.

Unfortunately, the broad acceptance of the belief that the college credential is paramount has had a profound impact on the attitude and behavior of community college faculty. Rather than "cooling out" students, Rosenbaum, Deil-Amen, and Person believe that today, there is much more "warming up": community colleges faculty seek to strengthen student desires to seek four-year degrees rather than discourage these goals. Thus, low success rates cannot be primarily the result of faculty discouragement.

Most community college faculty and counselors make every effort to maintain student confidence and goals. They minimize the students' weak skills by blaming the high schools and relabel remediation courses as developmental. As a result, most remediation students do not realize the long odds they face in finishing an associate degree, let alone preparing themselves for transfer to four-year colleges. As Rosenbaum, Deil-Amen, and Person lament, "Although national data indicate that the dropout rate for students with three or more remediation course areas is much higher than for those with only one, we find that students with high remedial enrollment do not in fact perceive their chances of completing their degree as lower than other students."[32]

Many faculty and counselors consider their prime mission to convince students who have goals of completing two-year occupational programs to adjust their educational ambitions upward. A typical attitude was that of a professor teaching a college algebra course that was required for students in applied degrees, not designed for transfer. To his class, he stated, "I assume you want to try to transfer these credits to another college."[33]

In addition, full-time faculty members with strong transfer orientations are active as advisers to student government, clubs, and other student activities. All these efforts create an environment that counsels students, despite their considerable skill deficiencies, to forgo occupational programs in the hopes that they can attain the four-year degree. These efforts persist despite consistent evidence that for many students, reducing their college goals from four-year to associate degrees significantly reduces their dropout rate.[34]

These faculty attitudes are strengthened by their personal goals. Given the historic transfer function, the vast majority of the community college faculty have academic doctorates, seek academic publications, and strive to gain parity with faculty at four-year colleges. Not surprisingly, at community colleges, faculty who come out of industry and teach in the occupational programs are treated as inferior and have little say in strategic college decisions. They are seen by the traditional academic faculty as a worrisome nuisance that reluctantly must be accepted but certainly not embraced.[35]

Their personal goals and perception of the decisive benefits four-year degrees provide cause most community college faculty to strongly resist efforts to reduce the transfer option. Instead, lowering remediation standards becomes quite acceptable for many educators frustrated with high failure rates. For example, in response to the low mathematics pass rate, McCabe suggested, "Either adjustments in expectations or major improvements in high school preparation are needed—perhaps both."[36]

There is certainly a risk that some students who could have been successful in four-year programs end up in less lucrative occupational careers, and black and Latino students may be particularly vulnerable. But for many students, enrolling in occupational programs *increases* options rather than constraining them. Occupational students have enhanced employment possibilities that they would not have if they had enrolled in the general education programs that are recommended for students hoping to transfer to four-year colleges. And given the substantial earnings overlap, many of these occupational students can earn at least as much as if they had been able to squeak by and just graduate from a less prestigious four-year program.

Just as in the case of high school dropouts, employment successes cause some students to curtail their education. In 1995, LaGuardia Community College celebrated the tenth anniversary of its program to aid mothers making the transition from welfare to work. It published a booklet highlighting the postcollege experience of twenty-eight students who had responded to a mailing. From this group of successful students, only five were either still in a four-year program or had graduated from one.

Almost all were working full-time in a field related to their associate degree program and were grateful for the opportunities LaGuardia provided to them. This was clearly a group that had the educational skills and personal determination necessary to complete four-year degrees. However, given their family situations and the successful careers their LaGuardia training made possible, the vast majority chose not to pursue further education.

These LaGuardia graduates certainly thought that their occupational education helped them succeed and did not feel they were tracked into dead-end, low-paying careers. Indeed, many first-generation college students with weak academic skills choose to enroll in occupational programs offered by the private-sector proprietary schools. Between 1995 and 2002, enrollment in proprietary schools grew by 157 percent while the enrollment at two-year colleges grew by only 18 percent. In New York State, enrollment in colleges and universities grew by 15 percent while in proprietary schools, it grew by 46 percent.[37]

More than 39 percent of those enrolled in proprietary school certificate programs were black or Latino, and 58 percent of financially independent students at these schools had annual incomes of less than $20,000. By contrast, only 28 percent of community college students were black or Latino, and fewer than 38 percent of financially independent students enrolled there had annual incomes of less than $20,000.[38]

These enrollment trends were matched by trends in career educational credentials awarded. Between 1997 and 2006, the share of certificates awarded by proprietary institutions rose from 39.0 to 43.5 percent, while their share of associate degrees awarded rose from 15.7 percent to 25.6 percent.[39] Unfortunately, the outcomes for proprietary career schools are uneven; educational entrepreneurs do not always serve the best interests of their students. At a 2005 congressional hearing on enforcement of antifraud laws in for-profit education, Congresswoman Maxine Waters highlighted some of these abuses:

> I had GED courses conducted in my office so that my constituents could pass the math portion of the GED to get into the construction training programs. . . . Many of these students . . . had defaulted on previous student loans used to attend a trade school, and thus did not qualify for any current financial aid including Pell Grants which they needed to support themselves while attending Community College to obtain training. At one graduation ceremony at the Employment Preparation Center, I asked how many of the graduates had been ripped off by a trade school, and all hands but one went up.[40]

When Drake Business School in New York City closed, LaGuardia Community College attempted to help its students. In an interview, Gail Mellow, president at LaGuardia, told me, "We found it impossible. Even though some of these students were at the end of their sophomore year, their level of preparation was so low that they were not passing our basic skills tests." Union Community College, the largest New Jersey provider of occupational programs, provides a notable example of the important role community college can play. When I interviewed its director of the college's welfare-to-work programs in 2005, he noted that placements have become more difficult, to some degree, because "in the last few years there has been a noticeable decline in the skill and motivational levels of recipients." The college, however, has become more creative by, for example, outfitting a "job van" to more efficiently link students with interviews with prospective employers. The college has also expanded its job fairs, enabling it to maintain its 40 percent placement rate.

One of Union Community College's most effective innovations has been to "develop a flexible and customized system that addresses the lifelong learning and skill training needs of existing and potential workers in concert with the skills demanded by employers." As the Work for Development director at the Rutgers Labor Center, Mary Gatta, notes, "The workforce development system must encompass a holistic approach that not only provides services but also creates and institutionalizes a structure that is flexible and amenable enough so that all workers can avail themselves of these services."[41]

Gatta evaluated an online learning program provided to low-earning single mothers in five New Jersey counties. A similar program was administered at Union Community College, where mothers were provided with computers and enrolled in courses that combined home computer-simulated training with once-weekly in-class instruction. This program has been enormously successful, with job placement rates of more than 60 percent.

Many other community colleges have responded effectively. In Florida, there are lines at both ends of some Pinellas Tech programs: students wait for class slots, and companies wait to hire them. Two-thirds of the school's students complete requirements for professional certification or state licensing, and 82 percent end up employed in their fields of study. Columbus State Community College in Ohio provides customized training for more than 4,000 employees at almost 60 different companies. The Hagerstown Community College Advanced Technology Center in Maryland has delivered training to more than 650 companies and 29,000 employees since 1990. Spartanburg Technical College in South Carolina offers a corporate program in which more than 80 percent of graduates have accepted employment with their sponsoring company after graduation.[42]

Changing Environment

While some community colleges, especially those in rural or smaller urban areas, have responded positively to the occupational demands of both students and industry, most community colleges in larger urban areas have not. As Grubb and Lazerson noted:

> Locating occupational education within a comprehensive institution has to some extent doomed it to second-class status. The highest-status track remains the transfer program. . . . Community colleges are funded with academic education in mind, and the high cost of labs, workshops, materials, and small classes make it difficult to support a wide variety of occupational programs.[43]

Indeed, in recent years urban community colleges see as their main competitors neighboring four-year institutions. As a result, they favor expanding their emphasis on academic education. During the last ten years, "community colleges have either maintained or strengthened their emphasis on academic and general education. Other trends, such as high-profile growth of honors programs and the growing movement for community colleges to offer baccalaureate degrees, suggest that community colleges, for better or for worse, are increasingly seeking to follow a traditional academic collegiate model rather than focused occupational or technical alternatives."[44]

This indifference to the needs of first-generation college students who are interested in pursuing occupational degrees manifests itself in an unwillingness to correct some obvious deficiencies. Because occupational programs are often not perceived to be a core function at community colleges, they are vulnerable to cutbacks. As one administrator lamented, occupational programs "fight for funding, yet they have track records business leaders and legislators should admire."[45]

Due to shared governance between educators and administrators, community colleges often do not respond quickly to changing business needs, especially when doing so would be perceived as infringing on faculty prerogatives. Colleges may balk at having courses at work sites or at times most suitable for a company's employees. Many faculty members are less enthusiastic about these relations because they often must modify traditional or unique academic courses to meet industry needs.

Administrators and faculty members also may view contract training or specialized skill preparation as a distraction from the more fundamental missions of the community colleges, such as access or transfer. This is one contributing factor in the inability of occupational programs to have permanent job placement positions paid through general university funding. Instead, program directors have to write grants and find outside funding sources for this crucial link between training and employment.

As already documented, the for-profit two-year and four-year colleges have filled the void by offering more focused occupational curricula. Many of these schools take advantage of students, saddling them with high debt and limited credentials. In 2010, Tamar Lewin exposed a particularly abusive policy at Kaplan University, one of the schools that disproportionately enrolls black female students. Carlos Urquilla-Diaz, a former Kaplan administrator, "recalled a PowerPoint presentation showing African-American women who were raising two children by themselves as the company's primary target. Such women, Mr. Urquilla-Diaz said, were considered most likely to drop out before completing the program, leaving Kaplan with the aid money and no need to provide more services."[46]

Under pressure from government agencies, many for-profit schools have been trying to improve their performance in order to gain national accreditation. As a result, these for-profit schools have strengthened their advantages and, if properly chosen, offer clear benefits for students seeking occupational degrees. Whereas for-profit two-year colleges enroll only 4 percent of all students enrolled in two-year colleges, their students obtain just over 10 percent of all associate degrees and almost one-quarter of all certificates awarded.

Indeed, the success rate at for-profit colleges is much higher if we include for-profit four-year colleges, since these schools generate substantially more two-year than four-year degrees. Not only are there higher completion rates, but "a more rapid completion rate for both associate degrees and certificates for the for-profits."[47] Community college faculty think of themselves as traditional college faculty and so closely guard their prerogatives: shared governance and course development. By contrast, faculty at for-profit colleges make sure that course offerings mesh with students' obtaining degrees. For-profit instruction is more likely to use labs and to tie academic courses to practical applications and to the occupational curriculum. Researchers have also found that "student services such as admissions, counseling, and career placement were more integrated and better developed at the for-profit than at comparison community colleges. The for-profit placed more emphasis on job placement and tracking students after they had graduated or left."[48] In particular, whereas community colleges rely most often on their institutional reputation, for-profits emphasize building relationships with employers to facilitate graduate placement.[49]

Remediation is one area where community colleges can learn from the better for-profit schools. Due to their emphasis on the transfer function, most urban community colleges develop remediation that is deemed necessary for students desiring to go on to academic programs. By contrast, for-profits tailor remediation to the occupational programs in which the student is enrolled. These efforts not only increase pass rates but also reduce the number of non-credit-bearing courses weakly prepared students must take.

Rosenbaum, Deil-Amen, and Person highlight this issue when they tell the story of Sheila. A single mother of two who had done poorly in high school, Sheila, despite working forty hours per week, attended community college full-time and was able to maintain a B average. She was becoming discouraged, though, with how long it was taking her to earn her associate degree and was under pressure from her mother, who was helping with child care. Enrolled in an academic associate degree program, Sheila did not realize that many of the remedial courses she was required to take did not confer college credit. Nor was she aware that she could have avoided these courses if she had instead enrolled in an applied associate degree program. Sadly, the authors found that Sheila's experience was typical of the experience of many students. Whereas "45 percent of community college students responded that they had later discovered that at least one course that they had taken would not count toward their degree, this was true of only 16 percent of private occupational college students."[50]

Unfortunately, community college faculty members resist these adjustments. This more focused approach is discouraged because it tracks students even if the alternative is very low passing rates. It is also discouraged because more focused remediation may require teaching material that is not traditionally the domain of mathematics instructors, such as quantitative reasoning: the ability to look at simple graphical representations (e.g., histograms, pie charts) in order to infer information.

Even though educational testing includes quantitative reasoning as part of general literacy, most colleges do not have explicit courses to systematically teach this skill to their students. For example, the City University of New York has a rising junior exam: a test taken by all students in the four-year colleges after they have attained forty-five credits to measure their basic skills. If they do not pass this exam, they are barred from registering once they attain seventy-five credits. One-third of the exam consists of answering questions related to two graphs. The scores on this section have been so appallingly low that scoring has been continually adjusted so that even the most meager attempts are given some credit.

One of the reasons for such poor performance has been the reluctance of the CUNY colleges to develop courses in quantitative reasoning, since these skills are not part of mathematics department curriculum. Instead, the basic mathematics course used for general education consists of statistical probability and low-level algebra. While these topics offer the possibility of students continuing on to calculus, they do little for developing student abilities to understand basic graphs and charts. As a result, the few CUNY colleges that attempted to offer quantitative reasoning had to abandon their efforts because they were unable to find sufficient faculty members from traditional disciplines to teach it. Thus, faculty prerogatives and notions of academic standards stand in the way of developing the mathematic literacy most valuable for students, especially those with an occupational orientation.

Recommendations

This chapter has documented the poor outcomes for weakly prepared students who enter the community college system. We suggest that an expansion of occupational programs may be an important way to increase educational attainment of these students and to improve their long-term economic well-being. Many left liberals are repelled by policies to strengthen occupational and credentialing programs, fearing that they will trap students in dead–end, low-paying jobs. When these students are disproportionately black and

Latino, occupational policies conjure up racist images from the past. Just as with affirmative action, however, students may be unsuccessful if they are placed in academic programs beyond their skills. High dropout rates, not four-year degrees, could be the outcome of well-intentioned policies.

Educational outcomes can be significantly improved only if these colleges have more realistic goals for these students and disabuse themselves of self-serving notions concerning their role in the educational system that continue to dominate their policies. Faculty should stop highlighting individual success stories that allow them to rationalize keeping the transfer function alive for *all* incoming students and focus instead on the low probabilities of four-year degree attainment for many. Most important, they should discard the notion that even students who just eke out a four-year degree, especially from a weaker school, will automatically have superior earnings potentials than those with occupational certificates or associate degrees. The very large overlap in earnings should undermine claims that occupational degrees consign workers to dead-end, low-wage employment tracks.

Once there is a more realistic assessment of the needs, goals, and potentials for weakly prepared students, as well as the financial value of many occupational certificates and associate degrees, community colleges can better serve these students by adopting the *best practices* found in the for-profit sector. This would require more secure funding for support services and giving a greater role to occupational instructors and program directors than they currently have.

A refocusing of community colleges is particularly valuable for black students. During the 1980s, the collapse of central-city manufacturing and the crack cocaine epidemic undermined family and employment stability in many urban black communities. Children growing up in such a disrupted and depleted environment were at risk for educational failure, as are many of their own children. While an "academic college for all" vision may soothe consciences of some educators and advocates, it does not help a large share of victims of circumstances who can benefit most from support for direct employment and occupational programs.

7

Strengthening Partnerships

As we have documented, family income is strongly correlated with the structure of the modern family. Over the last fifty years, the United States and other countries have experienced sharp increases in childbearing taking place outside marriage and in child rearing taking place outside a two-parent household. In the United States, the proportion of births to unmarried couples has jumped eightfold, from 5 percent in 1960 to more than one-third in the early 1990s, reaching a new high of nearly 40 percent in 2006.[1] Of the 4.27 million children born in 2006, 1.64 million were born to unwed parents. In 1960, about 1 out of 8 children did not live in a two-parent family; by 2004, the figure jumped to about 1 in 3 children living away from at least one parent.[2]

These trends have seriously complicated overall efforts to reduce poverty and inequality, as well as initiatives aimed at closing income gaps between blacks and whites. Children in single-parent families are four to six times more likely to fall below the poverty line in a typical year than are children in married-couple families.[3] Chronic child poverty is even more concentrated among single-parent families.[4] The gaps are as wide among black families as among all families. In 2007, about 44 percent of black, single-mother families were poor, a rate more than five times the 8 percent rate experienced by black married couple families with children. The intergenerational impacts of single parenthood on poverty are especially troubling. Children of single parents do worse in school and face an increased risk of poverty when they become adults.[5] Single parenthood is also linked to a higher incidence of other social problems, such as higher rates of school dropout, alcohol and drug use, adolescent pregnancy and childbearing, and juvenile delinquency.[6]

For a long time, many policy makers have discussed the negative impacts of the changing American family, especially among black Americans. In 1965, a report by Daniel Patrick Moynihan (then a Labor Department official) stirred up a major controversy. The report expressed deep concern over the state of the Negro family, citing a rise in unwed births, high rates of divorce, and high proportions of children growing up in female-headed families.[7] It linked family instability to a "tangle of pathology" in which male joblessness led to the breakup of marriages, which, in turn, was reinforced by the welfare system. It is striking that at the time the births to unwed parents made up about 25 percent of all black births. Since then, the nonmarital birthrate has reached over 25 percent for non-Hispanic whites and has jumped to nearly 70 percent among blacks. Nearly half of all Hispanic births are to unmarried parents.

During the 1970s and early 1980s, some academics criticized the Moynihan report for "blaming the victim."[8] Even today, not everyone agrees that rising single parenthood and marital instability contributed significantly to the weak progress against child poverty. Consider these comments from a 2004 *New York Times* editorial: "It is undeniably true that women tend to become poorer after divorce and that children from single-family homes are more likely to grow up in poverty. But the fiscal lift that occurs when middle-class couples marry and combine resources does not come about in neighborhoods where jobs have long since disappeared and men in particular tend to be unskilled and poorly educated."[9] Kim Gandy, president of the National Organization for Women, was even more blunt: "To say that the path to economic stability for poor women is marriage is an outrage."[10]

According to this view, prospective spouses of low-income women are themselves too poor or too limited in their earning capacity to contribute significantly to the family's resources. Their marriage would presumably leave the children in poverty in any case.[11] So, does marriage really reduce poverty and improve economic well-being? Why or why not? Do gains from marriage extend to less educated men and women? Maybe marriage helps the middle class but not the unskilled and poorly educated that the *New York Times* editorial writer referenced.

The issue resonates with public-policy makers. The preamble to the 1996 welfare reform cited stemming the growth of nonmarital births and encouraging more two-parent families as central policy objectives. Concerns about the welfare system's financial incentives for divorce and single parenthood have influenced policy makers for decades. Laws to strengthen the enforcement of absent fathers' child support obligations are aimed in part at discouraging nonmarital births, separation, and divorce. The Bush administration established the Healthy Marriage Initiative to focus on improving the skills of couples so that they could form healthy relationships and take better care of their children. This chapter first assesses the evidence about how marriage and family structure affect poverty and economic well-being, then turns to policies that may directly influence living arrangements, marriage, and the quality of couple relationships.

Marriage and Economic Well-Being

The evidence strongly points toward marriage as raising the living standards of all types of people. One study examined what would have happened to child poverty and inequality if the 1989 marriage rates were the same as in 1971. To project the additional 1989 marriages, the study matched unmarried mothers with unmarried men with similar levels of education, race-ethnic origin, and age. To determine the incomes of these simulated married-parent households, the study added the incomes of the men and women in these unions but subtracted welfare and related benefits from mothers' incomes. The study found that these additional marriages would have prevented the growth in child poverty and cut in half the growth in income inequality. A more recent study estimated that if family patterns had not changed between 1960 and 1998, the overall child-poverty rate would have declined by 25 percent, and almost 50 percent for black children.[12]

Other studies also show economic gains from marriage using a variety of methods. In one, current marriage was associated with a two-thirds reduction in poverty, with larger-than-average impacts among women at a high risk of poverty.[13] Another looked at a large sample of young women who became pregnant outside marriage and gave birth. The first step was to estimate the likelihood that these women would marry within six to nine months after the birth, using a number of variables known to predict marriage, such as race, income, and family background. Women were divided into groups based on their likelihood of marriage, and then the outcomes of those who married were compared with those who did not.

The results were striking. Mothers who married ended up much better off than mothers with the same disadvantages who did not marry. So did their children. Among those in the bottom quartile of "propensity to marry," those who married before the baby was six months old were only half as likely to be raising their children in poverty five years later as those who did not.[14]

One way to downplay the importance of marriage is to cite cohabitation as an alternative. After all, cohabiting couples have two potential earners and can take advantage of scale economies, just like married couples. Although the differences between married and cohabiting couples in some European countries may be modest, studies in the United States show clear economic disadvantages for cohabiting relative to married couples, even among those with the same race, education, parental background, number of children, and ability measures. Further, cohabiting couples are far less stable than are married couples, a fact that complicates child rearing.[15]

Researchers highlight two sources of instability: *partnership instability* and *multipartner fertility*. The mother's search for a long-term partner creates stress for mothers and children and leads to jealousy and mistrust by the other biological parent. Defined as men or women having children with different partners, multipartner fertility causes fathers to spread their time and money across several children and can generate problems between past and current partners. As multipartner fertility accompanies unwed childbearing and as unwed parenthood increases much more among less educated than among more educated mothers, changing family patterns are apparently lowering economic mobility in the United States.

In the words of Princeton sociologist Sara McLanahan, past president of the Population Association of America, the long-term shifts in U.S. marital patterns are generating "diverging destinies" for children.[16] The divergence is increasing as children from married, two-parent families thrive and children from less advantaged, single-parent families face serious obstacles to economic mobility. Differences in childbearing and child rearing by education are especially striking. Although college-educated women delay marriage, most ultimately marry and do so before having children. As a result, only about 7 percent of births to women with a college degree were to unmarried couples.[17] The picture is dramatically different among less educated women; more than half of their births take place outside marriage.[18]

The detail on family structure only heightens our concerns. Compared with never-married mothers, single parents who were once married but are now divorced or separated are more likely to have built-up assets and more likely to obtain financial help through child support payments and voluntary support from their children's fathers. Their children are more likely to have spent several years with and have a closer connection with their biological fathers. Unfortunately, children are increasingly living with never-married single parents. Between 1968 and 2006, the share of children who were living with a never-married mother increased from less than 1 percent to more than 10 percent. These children now make up more than 36 percent of children in single-parent households, up from 5 percent in 1968.

What about the men who are the unwed fathers of these children? At the time of the child's birth, about half the unwed fathers are cohabiting with the mother and the baby; another 30 percent are in close romantic relationships with the mother and visiting the child quite often. Unfortunately, their presence and involvement erode rapidly over time, especially if the parents remain unmarried. Five years after the child's birth, 37 percent were living with the child, but 37 percent had had no contact with the child in the previous two years.[19] Making matters more complicated is the high rate at which unwed parents have children with other partners. For almost one in three children born to unwed parents, either the mother or the father already had a child with another partner. By the time the child reaches age five, the rate of multipartner fertility rises to 75 percent.[20]

Why Might Incomes and Living Standards Improve with Marriage?

Many theories and empirical studies address the question of why incomes and living standards might improve with marriage.[21] One common economic theory is that marriage allows for specialization, thereby raising the productivity of one partner in the market and one at home. Another strategy is for couples to maximize their living standards by having both partners work and buy housework services. Sharing housing and other goods in a marriage offers scope for economies of scale. Marriage also offers a kind of insurance against unexpected events; if one partner experiences unemployment, the second can enter the workforce or work longer hours. Although specialization, economics of scale, and risk diversification are available to cohabiting couples as well, these benefits are more likely to arise in marriage because it is a far more stable living arrangement. Not only does marriage involve a long-term and formal commitment, but exiting marriage imposes significant costs.

Norms matter as well. Marriage is associated with a level of maturity, responsibility, fidelity, and loyalty not found as often in other couple relationships. These norms encourage spouses to work, spend, and save more responsibly, say by paying a mortgage on a home instead of spending a lot on leisure travel and eating out.[22] In addition, the trust engendered by marriage norms inspires a long-term perspective that allows spouses to feel confident enough to invest together in education and training, a home, and financial assets.[23] By contrast, cohabiting couples are less likely than married couples to pool their resources or to specialize, perhaps because their relationships generally end sooner.

Marriage looks more desirable but more precarious to people at the low end of incomes. Drawing on in-depth interviews, Edin and Kefalas find that low-income mothers aspire to marriage, but only after they are sure that they and their potential spouses can earn enough to support the family. Holding a job may not be enough. The male partner must be earning enough for the family to reach the middle class. To these mothers, marriage is less a mechanism for reaching the middle class than a crowning achievement for already having done so.[24] This is unfortunate. Instead of moving forward with a husband motivated to work hard for his family, many mothers end up in cohabiting or other romantic relationships that are much less stable and often lead to low incomes and material hardship.

Married men experience higher levels of employment and earnings and lower rates of unemployment. The evidence for this "marriage premium" among men goes back many years and covers several countries. Taking into account education, work experience, race, and the size of the metropolitan area, in 2005, married men had a 39 percent earnings advantage over never-married men and a 21 percent advantage over divorced and cohabiting men.[25]

As strong as this evidence appears, the reality is less clear because men who marry might have higher capacity in the job market, even compared with unmarried men with the same education and background. Many studies have tried to account for this possibility by comparing the earnings of men when they marry to the same men when they were unmarried. Not only did marriage increase wage levels, but it also increased hours worked. Especially striking is the fact that remarriage also led to increases in earnings. Putting the wage and hours effects together, becoming or remaining married raises earnings by about 21 to 24 percent relative to staying single (i.e., never married). For black men, the earnings advantage from a continuing marriage over never being married is similar (17.9 percent).[26]

A substantial earnings premium shows up in a recent study of men who fathered children outside marriage. Researchers found marriage (almost always to the mother of their child) leads to increases in wages and working hours well beyond what would have taken place if the men remained unmarried.[27] The marriage-induced gains for this group of men—most of whom are black or Hispanic—was as high as for all men.

Another reason marriage enhances economic well-being is the added support married couples receive from family, friends, and civic organizations in their communities. Married couples are more than twice as likely to get financial aid from the father's kin, compared with families headed by single mothers or cohabiting couples.[28] Married families in crisis also get more assistance from civic institutions such as churches and food pantries than do single mothers or families headed by a cohabiting couple.[29] This "access to help" from family, friends, and others in the community partly accounts for the fact that married couples experience fewer episodes of missed meals, evictions, and utility shutoffs than cohabiting couples or single parents. These patterns extend to less educated married mothers, who get significantly more help from family and friends than do low-income and less educated mothers who are not married.

The added help to married couples might result from social norms linking extended families (especially the father's kin) to couples and grandchildren. Moreover, the norms of maturity and responsibility associated with marriage provide extended families and civic institutions with greater confidence that any material support will be used in a responsible fashion (say, to buy a house rather than pay for a trip to the Bahamas). The norms of commitment, loyalty, and fidelity associated with marriage provide kin with greater confidence that any financial aid given to a married couple will redound to the benefit of their biological kin and not be diluted by a breakup. Finally, the fact that marriage is still privileged as the normative institution for the bearing and rearing of children—especially in religious circles—probably helps to explain why religious and civic institutions provide more assistance to married families than to families headed by cohabiting couples or single parents.

Health and Other Benefits of Marriage for Adults

Although social policies concerning the family emphasize impacts on children, adult well-being should matter as well. It turns out that adult gains from marriage extend far beyond the economic sphere to what matters most—health and happiness. Let us start with mortality. Married adults have significantly lower mortality rates than unmarried adults, though the marital advantage is greater for men than for women.[30] Marriage likely reduces mortality because upon marriage, adults in general, and men in particular, tend to reduce dangerous and harmful behaviors (drinking, brawling, etc.) and develop more healthful habits (e.g., eating more nutritious food on a regular basis). Because single men are more likely to have worse "habits" than do single women, it is not surprising that marriage exerts a greater impact on the mortality rates of men than of women. One recent careful study that captured the timing and sequence of marital transitions found that relative to married individuals, divorced men have a 60 percent higher risk of mortality and single women a 50 percent higher risk.[31]

In addition to living longer, married adults are on average happier and healthier than unmarried adults. The correlation is especially strong in families with children. Happiness patterns and trends in Britain and the United States reveal large positive impacts associated with marriage, net of any gains in income.[32] Other careful research on the German population found similarly large happiness gains from marriage.[33] Moreover, to the extent that marriage raises incomes, these studies understate the full impact of marriage on happiness.

Married adults report being in better health than divorced, widowed, and separated adults,[34] but devising ways to estimate whether marriage contributes to these health differences can be difficult. Estimates might overstate health impacts of marriage if personal attributes (say, good genes) that are not measured increase both the chance of marriage and the chance of good health. It turns out that some studies find the reverse, that less healthy men are often more likely to marry.[35] This would suggest that estimates of marriage link to health are sometimes understated. Overall, studies suggest that marriage conveys substantial health benefits and that more harmonious marriages lead to especially large positive health outcomes.[36]

Government Policies and Marriage

Given marriage's beneficial effects on alleviating child poverty and improving child development and adult welfare, the public interest in encouraging healthy marriage might seem obvious. But, in fact, several government policies create financial disincentives for low-income couples to marry. Further, when the Bush administration proposed the Healthy Marriage Initiative, aimed largely at providing classes on marriage and relationship skills to low-income couples, it was widely dismissed as at best ignoring contemporary realities and at worst an effort to put women back into subservient positions. Some worried that the government would be entering the marriage business, matching people and pushing marriage on unsuspecting single mothers. While these views distorted the reality of the initiative, the controversy highlights how much debates about marriage relate more to culture wars than to serious issues affecting children and families. The passionate debates about gay marriage attract far more publicity than the decline in marriage among parents and the increasing disadvantages children face when growing up without at least one biological parent. Many advocates of legalizing gay marriage are skeptical about broader efforts to strengthen heterosexual marriages. Advocates of *mandatory* classes in sex education for young students in public schools often oppose public support for *voluntary* marriage education classes for adults.

Where, then, does the government stand on marriage, and where should it stand? Do existing policies and programs encourage or discourage marriage? Should the government try to remain neutral with respect to marriage, even in cases involving bearing and rearing children? Let us start by examining past and current policies that directly or indirectly influence marriage, especially among low-income families.

Are Existing Benefit Policies Pro-Marriage or Antimarriage?

The 1996 welfare reforms and the subsequent dramatic reductions in case-loads have diverted attention from past concerns that the welfare system encouraged illegitimacy, divorce, and single parenthood. The welfare system's antimarriage incentives had been highly publicized and targeted by researchers and politicians at least since the early 1960s. Married-couple families were virtually excluded from receiving benefits under Aid to Families with Dependent Children (AFDC), the primary cash assistance program for the non-elderly poor. For many critics of welfare this suggested that the loss of cash benefits strongly discouraged single mothers from marrying. This assessment ignored the child-related benefits available only to families with wage income: the refundable EITC and, more recently, the child credit. As a result of these two credits, few mothers on cash assistance have marriage penalties if they marry a working man with modest earnings. Similarly, for couples in which mothers earn little (say, under $6,000) and fathers earn a modest amount (say, $10,000 to $14,000), the EITC and child credit can encourage marriage, offsetting the negative disincentives from other programs.

By contrast, it is *working* single mothers with modest earnings who suffer substantial marriage penalties. If these women remain single, they have sufficient earnings to receive close to the maximum benefits available from a number of government programs: EITC, child credit, and food stamps. Many of them also receive child care and housing subsidies. Their incomes are also sufficient to place them in the phase-out range of most of these programs: more *family* income reduces benefits received. For example, for each additional $100 of family income, they would lose $24 of food stamps, at least $17 of EITCs, and $30 of housing subsidies—a 71 percent phase-out rate of benefits.

Let us consider a mother raising two children in Maryland who earns $1,040 per month and is receiving a housing subsidy, food stamps, a child care subsidy, and the EITC. The benefit programs would have boosted her family income from her $1,040 in earnings to more than $2,500—not counting health insurance benefits for her children. Now, suppose her potential husband also earns $1,040 per month. Their marriage would reduce the monthly subsidies she received by $776. These declines in government benefits not only discourage this Maryland mother from marrying but sometime could discourage her from working additional hours to earn extra income.

Benefit programs may also discourage marriage by allowing single mothers to maintain their independence from a male partner. The notion of an "independence effect" on women's decision to marry or stay married arose in the context of results from the Seattle-Denver Income Maintenance Experiment (SIME/DIME). The intervention tested in SIME/DIME reduced the disincentives to marry by allowing assistance to married parents on the same basis as for other poor households, but the intervention also provided single mothers with modestly higher and less stigmatizing support than what they could receive under AFDC. Surprisingly, though SIME/DIME benefits improved the incentive for single parents to marry, access to the SIME/DIME income support did not increase the likelihood of marriage and may have actually lowered it, possibly because women's eligibility for more favorable benefit plans helped them remain independent.[37] The independence effect could also cause women's increased employment and earnings to reduce marriage.[38]

The disincentives and independence effects are hard to overcome without generating other problems. Raising incomes of single mothers is critical for reducing poverty, but if the increases lead to marriage disincentives or independence effects that split up parents, the impacts may be self-defeating. One option for lowering disincentives to marry would be to have separate, more generous benefit schedules for married and single parents. However, this step would add significantly to program costs, assuming benefits would not be cut for single moms.

Over the last decades, several program changes have complicated how safety net programs and tax benefits influence incentives to marry. Increasingly vigorous child support enforcement raised the costs to men who become noncustodial fathers, whether because of fathering a child outside marriage or divorcing or separating from the child's mother. At the same time, increased child support can make mothers more independent. The 1996 welfare reforms increased the likelihood that mothers heading families will work in the formal market. The major expansion of the EITC substantially increases the rewards for work; over low ranges of income, each added dollar brings a higher tax credit, thereby lowering progressivity and in some circumstances raising the gains to marriage. At the same time, other income-related benefits such as child care vouchers lowered mothers' gains from marriage.

Another major family policy—strict enforcement of child support awards—may exert a mix of incentives. When couples have a nonmarital birth or when parents separate or divorce, state agencies are charged with enforcing the financial obligations of both parents for their children.[39] The enforcement steps may involve establishing and recording legal paternity, establishing child support orders, and collecting the money owed in these orders. To make sure noncustodial parents make support payments, their earnings are generally subject to mandatory withholding. Imposing significant child support obligations on men (or women) who leave their children could deter them from separating or divorcing. In addition, the prospect of eighteen years of child support payments should act as a disincentive to father children outside marriage. On the other hand, the ability of the custodial parent—nearly always the mother—to collect child support payments might increase her independence and make her more likely to separate or divorce. Other unintended consequences of child support policy are the weakening of earnings incentives of low-income noncustodial fathers and reducing the likelihood of remarriage.[40]

Other policies with potential direct or indirect effects on nonmarital births, marriage, separation, and divorce include sex education programs in schools (including abstinence-only programs), other types of teen pregnancy prevention, and assistance to young people in attaining better jobs and careers. The sex education programs have been contentious, with occasional objections from parents and even legal appeals, especially when the curricula are used for junior high or lower grades.[41] The evidence on impacts is mixed, perhaps because of the widely varying curricula, objectives, and levels of participation. Although some sex education and teen pregnancy programs appear to delay sexual activity and reduce unprotected sex, the follow-ups are generally too short to determine their impact on the nonmarital birthrate or single parenthood.[42]

One recent study followed twelve- and thirteen-year-old black teenagers after they took variety of sex education courses. Included was an innovative abstinence-only course that stressed postponing sexual intercourse until a later age in order to avoid sexually transmitted diseases and to have more mature relationships. The study found that about one-third of the young teens who received an eight-hour abstinence lesson had sexual intercourse within two years of the class. By comparison, more than half of the students who were taught about safe sex and condom use reported having intercourse by the two-year mark, and more than 40 percent of students who received either an eight- or a twelve-hour lesson incorporating both abstinence education and safe sex reported having sex at two years.[43]

Providing education through schools oriented around career clusters shows promise in increasing the earnings of less educated males and the likelihood of marriage and two-parenthood among low-income, mostly minority young people. The Career Academy students attend small schools that provide a supportive environment, that combine academic and technical curricula oriented around a specific industry or industry cluster, and that involve partnerships with local employers who often provide work-based learning opportunities. Although the Career Academies did not explicitly aim to improve family structure, they managed to increase marriage rates for young men by nearly 30 percent and raise the share of fathers in two-parent families by 40 percent. To evaluate Career Academies, researchers used an experimental design to randomly assign prospective high school students to the standard high school program or to career academies.[44] The results suggest that improving initial careers, especially among young men, increases the share of married men and the share of children growing up with their fathers.

Causes and Potential Solutions to Single Parenthood Issues

Competing explanations of the causes of single parenthood and declining marriage rates among low-income and minority men and women certainly influence debates over policy. One view, usually but not always associated with political liberals, is that one-parenthood is mainly related to the declining job market prospects of less educated men. Because the decline in the number of men who are "marriageable" in the sense of having adequate earnings capacity is the main culprit, policy makers should focus on increasing their earnings. Let us call this the "jobs hypothesis." A second view, usually but not always associated with political conservatives, is that weakening social mores concerning marriage, fidelity, and the importance of parenting along with inadequate education and relationship skills are largely responsible. From this perspective, teaching relationship skills and emphasizing the value of marriage in child rearing are potentially effective interventions. Let us call this the "skills-attitudes hypothesis." As we will see, because both causes appear to play a role in marriage and the avoidance of single parenthood, perhaps both sets of policies can improve family outcomes.

To understand whether men's earnings affect marriage and marital stability, studies must take account of characteristics (such as good looks and an engaging personality) that researchers do not observe but that may lead to both higher earnings and more marriage. In these instances, we can mistakenly attribute higher earnings as the cause of marriage when instead the positive correlation between marriage and earnings is the result of the unobserved characteristics.

Most good studies that deal with this problem still find that higher earnings tend to increase marriage and reduce divorce.[45] However, not all evidence points in this direction. For example, one study found that job losses due to a plant closing did not increase divorce rates.[46] Another analysis showed that better job options for men did increase marriage, but the size of the impacts was modest and accounted for little of the decline in marriage over the 1970s and 1980s.[47] Other research indicates that raising the earnings of black men and women to the comparable earnings levels of whites would actually reduce marriage rates of black women, partly because both men and women could be more selective in choosing a spouse or partner.[48]

What about the roles of social norms, attitudes, and relationship skills as factors influencing marital outcomes? These factors are much harder to define than earnings impacts, let alone quantify. Fortunately, today we know much more than we did only a decade ago because of the development of the Fragile Families and Child Wellbeing Study, which interviewed parents of nearly 5,000 children born in urban hospitals. The first interviews took place around the time of the birth; follow-up interviews have taken place one, three, five, and seven years later. More than 3,700 of these births were to unmarried parents.[49] Although the research findings from these data are too numerous to report here, several are relevant to factors influencing marriage, especially among low-income parents.

First, the vast majority of unmarried parents (about 80 percent) are either living together or in a close romantic relationship at the time of their child's birth. They are committed to raising their children together, and most believe that marriage is better for children. What is most striking is that most believe they will marry the other parent. In fact, 88 percent of the men believe the chances are better than fifty-fifty that they will marry. Second, the evidence suggests that good relationship skills and pro-marriage attitudes are important for marriage, as is success in the job market, especially for the father. One study compared both sets of factors and concluded that differences in the combination of attitudes toward marriage, gender trust, supportiveness, and conflict in the relationship played the bigger role in determining which couples actually married.[50]

Even the impact of job holding interacts with attitudes about marriage. In-depth and continuing surveys with a small subgroup of parents drawn from the overall sample revealed that low-income women believed in waiting until the couple achieved a good measure of economic security before marrying instead of taking marital vows and building economic security together over time. It turns out that many low-income and minority young people learn about marriage from very few cases in their families and communities and often from media portrayals of marriage.[51] Often, these sources distort the realities of marriage as well as the requirements for and the advantages of healthy marriages. The distinction between cohabitation and marriage patterns is another area in which misinformation is widespread. Many are unaware that cohabitation typically involves much higher breakup rates and that longer-term cohabiting unions are more prone to domestic violence than are marriages.[52]

Policies and the Future

Reducing single parenthood and nonmarital childbearing are central to the fight against poverty and inequality, but what policies might work in this sensitive family arena? Usually, a good first step is to end policies that make the problem worse. Unfortunately, even this step can be difficult because of conflicts among goals.

Let us start with the disincentive problems built into our income support system. We can reduce marriage penalties in only two ways. One is to lower benefits for single parents, a change that could drive more children into poverty. The second is to raise benefits for two-parent families. This step can increase the costs of benefit programs substantially if not well targeted. Specific policies to reduce disincentives will be discussed in the next chapter.

Another trade-off arises when we look at gender-based help for improving job outcomes. Increases in men's earnings appear to contribute more to marriages and marital stability than do increases in women's earnings. Yet, because of historical discrimination against women in the labor market, a range of affirmative action and other programs have focused on helping women. Despite the disproportional adverse effect the current economic downturn has had on men, many political analysts were focused on making sure that women got an equal share of the stimulus funding.

Men are falling far behind women in completing college, and as the previous chapter on gender inequities discussed, efforts are being made to increase female representation in the more lucrative occupational programs. Taking these steps may be appropriate for equal opportunity reasons but does little to help men or the prospects for two-parent families. It is understandable that policy makers are intent on helping single mothers who are raising children in difficult circumstances. At the same time, policy makers should be equally if not more attuned to improving job prospects for men.

The problems less educated men face may be exacerbated by current immigration of legal and undocumented less educated men, who are increasingly in competition with less educated native-born men. More broadly, current immigration puts strains on government support programs that weaken their ability to serve those in need. A subsequent chapter will detail the adverse consequences of current immigration strategies and suggest changes in national policies.

Fortunately, several promising approaches are not subject to difficult trade-offs or changes in national policies. Helping young people get off to an early start in careers is one possibility. Career Academies not only substantially raised the earnings of young men, especially those with a high or medium risk of dropping out of high school, but the experience generated gains in marriage as well. Another idea is to provide job services to both members of a couple.[53] When this concept was tested in Chicago as part of a job readiness and job search assistance program for seventeen- to twenty-four-year-old couples, there were additional gains for women and men. In addition, among parents who both completed the program, nearly 90 percent remained together one year later. A good follow-up to this approach would be to expand apprenticeship training, which offers young people the opportunity to learn careers without losing income, to learn through hands-on training instead of pure classroom instruction, and to be exposed to adult mentors who might guide them in family as well as career matters. We now have solid evidence that apprenticeship generates big earnings gains. Although whether improvements in family stability would follow is an open question, the Career Academies' impacts indicate that such gains are plausible.

When rolled out by the Bush administration, healthy relationship programs were controversial. Many feared that they would be thinly disguised attempts by Christian conservatives to reinforce and reestablish traditional patriarchal relationships. These concerns spurred the liberal journalist Katherine Boo to interview women who participated in an Oklahoma program run by Pastor George Young at the Holy Temple Baptist Church. A voluntary program, it did recruit woman from low-income neighborhoods like the Sooner Haven housing project, but none of its participants were currently on cash assistance.

Pastor Young did not romanticize marriage. As Boo pointed out, "The data [presented] was bleak by design; the social scientists on whom Oklahoma relied believe that a crucial part of making and keeping a marriage is disabusing oneself of sentimental notions. Marriage is not sexual or emotional bliss between soul mates, they contend; it is a job requiring as much patience, self-sacrifice, and discipline as any other."[54]

Instead, Young focused on conflict management. Boo reported, "Pairing off for role-playing, the students learned to refrain from saying to a man who disappointed them, 'You're an oily, two-timing toad,' and to say instead,

'When you did *x*, in situation *y*, I felt *z*.'" Boo emphasized that "they practiced swallowing their rage, articulating their grievances specifically and respectfully, recognizing when a fight might turn violent, and listening with open minds to imaginary mates."[55]

Boo noted that the women involved enjoyed the honest, intimate conversions they engaged in during their marriage classes. They did not believe, however, that their efforts alone would translate into successful relationships. "My thing is: how do you get a man to talk about marriage when you're pretty sure he's still sleeping with his baby's mother?" a nurse's aide asked, expressing a problem so familiar at Sooner Haven that it is known by the term "baby-mama drama." Indeed, Boo felt that these marriage promotion efforts were doomed because of the history these women have had with men. She reported:

> All but one of the women in the room had grown up without a father in the home. At least two had been sexually abused in the first ten years of their lives. Those who had children had been left by their children's fathers. Three had been beaten by men they had loved, and two had been involved with violent criminals. In short, it required an imaginative leap to believe that a committed relationship with a man would rescue a woman from poverty.[56]

Once the evidence accumulated, it became clear that these policies had no serious negative trade-offs. They have demonstrated effectiveness in experimental studies for producing gains in communication processes, conflict management skills, and overall relationship quality.[57] Premarital programs appear to reduce the likelihood of divorce.[58] While these studies generally had small samples and short follow-ups, and rarely included low-income populations, the results from the broader literature on healthy marriage interventions have been sufficiently compelling to influence policy in the United States and other countries.[59]

One recent experimental project involving low-income families aimed at increasing fathers' involvement and improving couple relationships. The Supporting Father Involvement program provided information, sixteen-week classes, and case management to 289 low-income families in four rural California counties.[60] The families were randomly assigned to a fathers group (where the classes and counseling tilted toward parenting), a couples group (where the classes and counseling tilted toward couple relationships), and a control group. Both the fathers and couples interventions increased father involvement and decreased parenting stress, anxiety, and conflict over the child. There were gains in family earnings as well. Moreover, the couples approach led to higher improvements for children and earnings. The results show that fathers are more likely to become involved with their children when they have a good relationship with the child's mother.

Further tests of the relationship skills and marriage education strategy are under way, sponsored by the U.S. Department of Health and Human Services. The projects extend to mentoring programs involving married couples, training clergy and others to deliver marriage education, and courses in high school about healthy dating practices and information about the advantages of marriage. The intensity and duration of the interventions vary, and some are expanding their scope to connect with employment-oriented services and financial literacy. Two large random-assignment demonstration projects provide classes on relationship skills, counseling, and related assistance to experimental groups while following control groups that applied for but were excluded from receiving demonstration-funded services. The goal is to determine how such interventions work for low-income unmarried couples with children and for low-income married parents. A third demonstration is testing the impact of having a critical mass of marriage-related services and community mobilization on marriage outcomes in low-income areas of three cities.

Although the findings from all the demonstrations will not be available until 2012, early indications from the Building Strong Families (BSF) demonstration are disappointing. In only one in eight sites—Oklahoma—did the intervention consistently improve the quality of couple relationships and increase the proportion of couples still romantically involved, when measured fifteen months after participants applied to BSF.[61] However, the demonstration generated modest, statistically significant improvements in relationship quality among black couples and reduced the incidence of depressive symptoms among men and women. These impacts come from programs that involved treatment group couples in only twelve hours of group sessions on relationship skills. Moreover, the initiatives are still in their early stages. As additional research and demonstration evidence accumulates, we will learn whether relationship skills training can play a constructive role in helping couples and children.

8

Revising Government Tax Policies

The proposals in this book are dominated by attempts to fit workers more easily into existing labor markets by enhancing their skills, improving the accuracy of employer assessments of those skills, and providing government benefits that supplement wages. For left liberals, this approach is too narrow, too limited, and too likely to reproduce class, race, and gender disparities. Rather than primarily changing workers, they reason, policies should require employers to change their structures and behavior independent of market forces.

In labor markets, many advocates for the poor are unwilling to rely on market-driven policies. Instead, they give priority to interventionist policies: unionization, minimum-wage and living-wage legislation, and the legislating of mandatory sick leave, vacation, and maternity leave policies. These are the policies that should be pursued rather than those that continue to allow firms to benefit unfairly at the expense of their workers.

There is no question that many of these favored policies are valuable and should be pursued. Indeed, we applaud the significant number of states that have legislated minimum-wage scales that are above the federal requirement of $7.25 per hour. And we certainly agree that many of the other policies advocated by left liberals can be helpful to working families. We believe, however, that left liberals should place more emphasis on benefit-enhancing federal and state tax policies.

The Earned Income Tax Credit is the main supplemental wage policy. At the federal level, it provides more than $5,000 annually in benefits and in a number of states an additional $1,000 or more. With the refundable child tax credit (CTC), single mothers working full-time year-round at a minimum-wage job now gain as much as $8,000 annually from these two federal policies. Together with food stamps, housing subsidies, and often other government supplements, these working women gain enough to move into the near-poor.

While the EITC and other means-tested government supplements have been crucial in lifting working mothers out of official poverty, they have an inherent shortcoming: after some income level, additions to income result in reduced government benefits. For many families, this limits benefits from additional wages. In addition, the EITC and most government supplements are based on family income. As a result, for working single mothers, marriage can often result in a substantial loss of government benefits—a penalty that may be an important impediment to marriage.

Finally, the cost of child care influences the ability to balance work and family. Child care costs are particularly important to single working mothers. While many of the poorest mothers have access to government-funded child care, the majority must rely on government tax credits. Unfortunately, the federal child care tax credit is nonrefundable and thus has only modest benefits for many of these families. While some states have generous refundable child care credits, they are poorly coordinated with federal policies. Thus, revisions of the child care provisions of the tax code should be considered.

Improving the Earned Income Tax Credit

The federal EITC was crucial to the success of welfare-to-work policies and remains an important income-enhancing program for all poor and near-poor working families. The EITC is a refundable credit: if the credit exceeds tax liabilities, the taxpayer receives the difference in cash from the Internal Revenue Service. While the credit is available to a limited number of childless workers, its benefits are overwhelmingly to families with children. In the phase-in range, the EITC is a wage subsidy; additional earnings increase the EITC received. Once the taxpayer's earnings push benefits up to the legal maximum credit, it remains constant over a range of income called the "plateau." Finally, after a certain income level, credits decrease as income rises until eligibility ends.

The specific parameters that determine the EITC received depend upon the custodial parent's marital status and number of qualifying children. However, the structure of the credit remains the same: a phase-in range, a plateau, and a phase-out range. The program costs more than $30 billion annually, making it the largest entitlement program in the federal budget aside from health programs and social security.

For a single mother with two qualifying children, the phase-in rate is 40 percent. In other words, for each additional $100 of wages in the phase-in range, the taxpayer is entitled to an additional $40 credit. For 2009, the phase-in range extended to $12,550, at which income level families obtain the maximum credit of $5,028. Between incomes of $12,550 and $16,450, the credit remained constant. Above $16,450, it is phased out at a 21 percent rate so that these families are no longer eligible for credits at incomes above $40,250. The EITC is indexed for inflation so that the maximum credit and the cutoff points for each range increase annually.[1]

The EITC is more effective in moving families over the poverty line than any other governmental program. Participation rates are high compared with those for other income support programs; more than 85 percent of those who are eligible for the credit apply for it. A major motive for preferring a tax credit such as the EITC to traditional public assistance is the boost to work incentives. From 1984 to 1996, employment rates for single mothers increased substantially, and researchers attribute a significant share of this increase to repeated expansions of the EITC. Indeed, in the pre-1994 environment, the EITC acted as an effective "carrot" to prod some recipients to choose work rather than welfare.[2]

Given its demonstrated antipoverty benefits, twenty states and the District of Columbia have refundable EITC programs. The seven most generous localities provide an EITC equal to at least 20 percent of the federal EITC. As a result, working single mothers with two children in these areas receive an additional $1,006 or more.[3]

These credits have enabled low-income families to purchase automobiles and make other large expenditures that allow them to move forward. However, for families in the phase-out range, credits decline as earnings rise. Together with the phasing out of benefits from other means-tested programs, including food stamps and child care subsidies, the net gains from additional earnings might be quite meager for many families.

The implicit tax rate measures the net gains to families from additional income. It equals the proportion of any earnings increase that goes to the government as *either* additional taxes or a reduction in benefits from government programs. At the beginning of the phase-out range, for each additional $100 of earnings, credits fall by $21 for a single mother with two children. Though she has neither federal nor state income tax liabilities, the mother must pay additional social security and Medicare taxes of $7.65. In addition, she is probably receiving benefits from other means-tested programs. For each additional $100 of income, food stamp benefits decline by $24, and rent payments in public housing projects or Section 8 housing increase by $30. As a result, working mothers who collect food stamps and have housing subsidies would only net $17.35 from the additional $100 of earnings so that they would be facing an implicit tax rate of 82.65 percent.

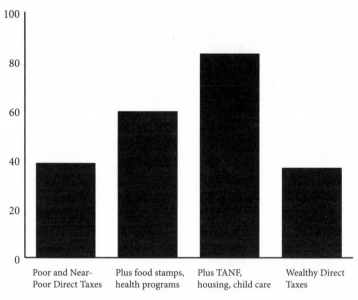

Figure 8.1. Implicit tax rates, by benefits obtained and by income, 2004

The implicit tax rate is even higher—and the net gains to working mothers still lower—if they also are eligible for medical or child care subsidies; eventually the family's additional income will be subject to federal and perhaps state income tax. Indeed, for some working mothers who are receiving all these subsidies and credits, additional earnings might actually cause net income to decline! In 2002, fully one-third of all single mothers with two children who received the EITC and at least two Wisconsin in-kind transfers had an implicit tax rate equal to 50 percent or more.[4]

At the national level, figure 8.1 assesses the implicit tax rate for single mothers with two children and incomes between $10,000 and $40,000. In 2004, these single poor and near-poor mothers had, on average, an implicit tax rate of 35.9 percent if we include only their direct state and federal taxes such as social security and the EITC. This rate is slightly higher than the 33.2 percent rate for households with incomes between $90,000 and $200,000. Just as the Wisconsin study found, the implicit rate increases appreciably for poor and near-poor families if they qualify for additional means-tested benefits programs. For families enrolled in the food stamp, Medicaid, and S-CHIP program, the implicit tax rate increases to 58.8 percent; if they qualify for cash welfare, housing assistance, and child care subsidies, it increases to 88.6 percent.[5]

A high implicit tax rate makes it difficult for many families to distance themselves from poverty because extra work adds so little to net income. Indeed, from a social standpoint, it may be best for these households to *reduce* market labor time, especially if their children are young. Studies have shown, however, that few EITC recipients understand the relationship of earnings to their implicit tax rate. Almost all families receive the EITC as a lump sum at the end of the tax year and are generally unaware how the credits are calculated. As a result, the EITC probably has only a modest effect on labor supply decisions for households in the phase-out range.[6] Our main concern, however, should not be whether or not the EITC distorts employment decisions. Instead, we should be concerned with the inappropriateness of having low-income families facing higher implicit tax rates than upper-middle-class families and how this can trap them in near poverty.

The Politics of the EITC

While it would be nice to assess promotion of and adjustments to the EITC on its merits, often political considerations have dominated the discourse. This begins with the credit's origins: the negative income tax proposed by the godfather of conservative economics, Milton Friedman. Friedman's underlying idea was simple: if households lack income to purchase economic necessities, simply give them cash transfers. Given its conservative origins, left liberals have always been ambivalent toward this policy, more so as it was championed in the 1990s as an alternative to raising the minimum wage.

More generally, unions have always had misgivings about fighting for government wage supplements, fearing that they might undermine pressures on employers to raise the direct wages they pay. Moreover, unions believe that it is better to gain wage increases directly through labor negotiations or federal mandates, including minimum-wage and living-wage legislation, rather than relying on legislated federal tax benefits.

One unavoidable problem, however, is the impact that means-tested programs have on workers when they receive wage increases. As the studies described here indicated, many low-wage workers face a high implicit tax rate so that much of the wage increases that unions gain for these workers is offset by reduced government benefits. For example, in Chicago, union efforts were crucial to enacting living-wage legislation. This legislation resulted in an immediate two-dollar-per-hour increase in the wages paid to home health care attendants. However, because these workers lost benefits from means-tested programs, like the EITC, the net increase was only one dollar an hour.[7]

The low priority unions placed on federal legislation that provided tax benefits to their workers was evident in 2000. At the time, the Economic Policy Institute (EPI) proposed a revision of the EITC, later dubbed the Simplified Family Credit. As will be discussed later, this reform, by having a substantially lower phase-out rate than the EITC, would have modestly reduced the implicit tax rate for many families.

In a development that startled EPI leaders, this proposal won bipartisan support and at a news conference was endorsed by Democratic and Republican members of the House of Representatives. The Republican support reflected the belief that since welfare legislation had shifted many women into the workforce, these efforts should be supported by federal tax dollars. The legislative initiative floundered, however, because the EPI chose other priorities closer to union interests and did not put in the time and manpower to build further support necessary to move this legislative proposal through Congress.

A second political consideration that limited left-of-center support was the expected beneficiaries of this legislation. Because the proposed legislation was focused on aiding families whose incomes placed them in the EITC's phase-out range, the primary beneficiaries would have been near-poor families.

As it happened, these families are quite deserving of additional child-related tax benefits. David Ellwood and Jeffrey Liebman demonstrated that this group gained fewer child-related tax benefits than either lower-income or higher-income households. These families had too much income to benefit as much from the EITC as poor families and too little income to benefit as much as higher-income families from dependent allowances and the federal child care tax credit. Dubbing the current system the "middle-class parent penalty," they recommend changes in the tax code that would provide more equitable treatment through revisions like the Simplified Family Credit.[8]

These considerations, however, were not that important to advocates for the poor. Organizations like the Children's Defense Fund were focused on increasing benefits to the most needy—those who lived in poverty. While they were not against the proposed revisions, they were unwilling to make them a priority when considering legislative initiatives.

A final consideration reflected a desire by some to maintain a distinct EITC program rather than transforming it into a more comprehensive child-related credit. Individuals associated with the influential Brookings Institution and Center on Budget Policies and Priorities desired to reduce the implicit tax rate faced by working families *without* eliminating the EITC as a distinct government program. These organizations were instrumental in extending the plateau region of the EITC so that the phase-out would be pushed to higher incomes, reducing its overlap with the phasing out of food stamps.

More important, they helped guide a new child-related tax benefit through the legislative process—the refundable child tax credit of \$1,000 per child. The initial intention was to have a phase-in rate of 15 percent that would begin at an inflation-adjusted \$10,000. For a family with one child, the CTC would continue phasing in until the full credit would be attained at \$16,667; for a family with two children, the full CTC would be phased in through \$23,333. As a result, in a significant portion of the EITC phase-out range, the phasing in of the CTC would lower the implicit tax rate. Specifically, while additional income of \$100 would reduce the EITC by \$21, families would be receiving an additional CTC of \$15.

This effort to use the CTC to reduce the implicit tax rate of some near-poor families proved unsuccessful. First, in the final stages of the legislative process, the bill was adjusted so that for much of its phase-in region, the CTC phase-in rate equaled 25 percent.[9] As a result, the full benefits were phased in faster than planned so that the CTC did not provide as much as an offset to the phasing out of the EITC as anticipated.

Moreover, by beginning its phase-in at an inflation-adjusted \$10,000—\$11,750 in 2007—the CTC did not target the poorest families. To redirect benefits to poorer families, antipoverty organizations succeeded in lowering the threshold income at which the child credit begins to phase in: to \$8,500 in 2008 and \$3,000 in 2009. This accomplished their goal of providing more benefits to a modest number of the most-needy families but eliminated the ability of the CTC to offset the high implicit tax rate faced by near-poor families. With the 2009 income threshold, the child credit is now completely phased in *before* the phasing out of the EITC begins for families with one or two qualifying children.

As a result, one of President Obama's economic advisers, Jeff Liebman, noted:

> Despite the EITC and child credit, the poverty trap is still very much a reality in the U.S. A woman called me out of the blue last week and told me her self-sufficiency counselor had suggested she get in touch with me. She had moved from a \$25,000 a year job to a \$35,000 a year job, and suddenly she couldn't make ends meet any more. I told her I didn't know what I could do for her, but agreed to meet with her. She showed me all

her pay stubs etc. She really did come out behind by several hundred dollars a month. She lost free health insurance and instead had to pay $230 a month for her employer-provided health insurance. Her rent associated with her section 8 voucher went up by 30% of the income gain (which is the rule). She lost the ($280 a month) subsidized child care voucher she had for after-school care for her child. She lost around $1600 a year of the EITC. She paid payroll tax on the additional income. Finally, the new job was in Boston, and she lived in a suburb. So now she has $300 a month of additional gas and parking charges. She asked me if she should go back to earning $25,000. I told her that she should first try to find a $35k job closer to home. Also, she apparently can't fully reverse her decision to take the higher paying job because she can't get the child care voucher back (the waiting list is several years long she thinks). She is really stuck. She tried taking an additional weekend job, but the combination of losing 30 percent in increased rent and paying for someone to take care of her child meant it didn't help much either.[10]

The Simplified Family Credit

Periodically over the last decade, a number of policy analysts have called for a revision of the patchwork system of child-related tax benefits provided by the federal government. In particular, proposals began to circulate in 2000 that recommended combining the dependent allowance, the EITC, and the CTC—the three child-related federal benefits that are universal. Figure 8.2 indicates the sum of the federal benefits from these three programs for 2009 for single mothers with two qualifying children.

The solid black line in the figure reflects the current set of benefits with the 21 percent phase-out rate for the EITC. As income initially rises, combined benefits grow as the family is in the phase-in range of the EITC and the child credit. At income of $16,450, the family receives combined benefits of $7,473: the maximum EITC of $5,028, the full CTC of $2,000, and $445 from the dependent allowance. As incomes increase, the EITC is phased out at 21 percent, substantially reducing combined benefits. In this EITC phase-out range, the rate at which combined benefits decline is also adjusted slightly for changes in the value of the dependent allowance.

At income of $40,250, the entire EITC is phased out so that families now only receive benefits of $3,095: $2,000 from the CTC and $1,095 from the dependent allowance. This continues until income reaches $57,500, when the 25 percent tax

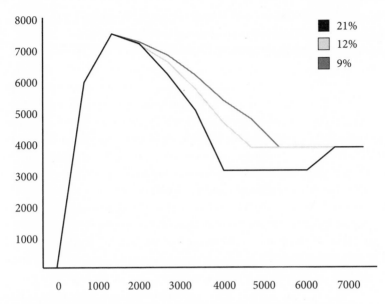

Figure 8.2. Combined federal tax benefits from dependent allowance, EITC, CTC, by phase-out rate, 2009

bracket would have begun absent the dependent allowance. Now the benefits from the dependent allowance increase until at income of $64,800 combined benefits equal $3,825: CTC of $2,000 and dependent allowance of $1,825.

As discussed previously, initial efforts to combine these three tax programs proved unsuccessful. With George W. Bush's election in 2001, the Republic tax priorities shifted, and efforts to reform the child-related provisions of the federal tax code waned. Recently, however, there has been renewed interest. In particular, policy advocates associated with the right-of-center American Enterprise Institute have proposed combining not only these three programs but also the child and dependent care (CADC) tax credit and educational credits as well.[11] They suggest that credits would be phased in at a 60 percent rate until they reach a maximum of $8,000 at income of $13,333. The plateau would end at $20,000, at which point credits would be phased out at a 22 percent rate. Their objective is to reduce the benefits received by taxpayers with upper-middle-class incomes. As a result, they are prepared to phase out benefits completely at incomes of $56,363.

Except for their desire to target benefits more directly to lower-income families, the proposal does little to change the high implicit tax rate that near-poor families experience. By contrast, the Simplified Family Credit proposal, recognizes two things: (1) benefits should be maintained for middle-income and upper-middle-income families, reflecting the universal nature of the current CTC and dependent allowances; and (2) it is important to lower the implicit tax rate near-poor families now face.

The simplest proposal would maintain the maximum benefits of $7,473 with a lower phase-out rate until combined benefits are reduced to those received by middle-income families: $3,825. Figure 8.2 illustrates these proposals depending upon whether the phase-out rate is 9 percent or 12 percent.[12] These changes modestly lower the current combined phase-out rate from the 21 percent phase-out rate that the vast majority of near-poor families with two or more qualifying children experience.[13]

It is the case that families with incomes above the current EITC eligibility cutoff at $40,250 would have an increase in the implicit tax rate they face because they would be in the phase-out range of the Simplified Family Credit. In particular, they would face the phase-out from the credit—either 9 or 12 percent—as well as the 15 percent tax rate on additional income.[14] However, because their income is more than 200 percent of the poverty line, these lower-middle-income families would not experience the phasing out of other benefits; thus, together with the payroll tax, this would be the extent of their implicit tax rate. Finally, they would have a substantial increase in their disposable income: well over $1,000 for most of these families.

Government Child Care Tax Credits

Today, there is a large group of single mothers with annual wages between $20,000 and $40,000. These near-poor mothers have increasing difficulty obtaining government-subsidized child care slots. In 2008, seven states limited eligibility to families with incomes below $25,000, as did thirty states with incomes below $32,000. Even if eligible, many of these families must make substantial co-payments. For example, in nineteen states, a family at 150 percent of the poverty level—$26,400 in 2008—had monthly co-payments of at least $200.[15]

Another way for the government to improve these women's ability to balance work and family would be to provide substantial tax benefits to defray child care costs. Unfortunately, the federal CADC tax credit has not been very helpful. It is a nonrefundable credit and so has only modest benefits for these working families. Specifically, for a single mother with one qualifying child, the maximum tax benefits are no more than $900; for those with two children, they are no more than $1,500.

These tax benefits do too little to defray costs, which can easily run to $5,000 a year or more if one uses a qualifying vendor.[16] As a result, a majority of near-poor working mothers must rely on informal arrangements when government child care or full-day pre-K slots are unavailable. Indeed, in 2002 only 12 percent of CADC dollars were obtained by tax filers with incomes below $25,000, whereas 68 percent went to families with incomes over $40,000.[17]

One straightforward way of correcting this problem would be to make the federal CADC fully refundable, as the Family Tax Relief Act of 2009 proposed. This legislation would have had a dramatic impact on poor families who have no taxable income, raising benefits to $1,050 for a family with income of $15,000 and $3,000 of child care expenses. In addition, the bill proposes to increase the reimbursement rate from 35 percent to 50 percent for the poorest families and the maximum qualifying expenses from $3,000 to $5,000 per child, providing even more generous benefits to working mothers.[18]

As an alternative to the federal CADC, families can choose to pay their child care expenses through a dependent care (DC) account. Child care expenses paid through these accounts are not included in adjusted gross income. As a result, the taxpayer has reduced federal income taxes, and reduced Medicare and payroll taxes.

These families further benefit from the impact of a DC account on EITC benefits. Near-poor families are in the phase-out range of the EITC program. Because a DC account lowers their adjusted gross income, it enables these families to keep more credits from the federal EITC program.

Single near-poor mothers with at least $5,000 of child care expenses obtain substantially more tax benefits from DC accounts than from the CADC tax credit. For virtually every single near-poor mother with one or two qualifying children, a DC account offers at least $800 more *federal* tax benefits than she could receive from the current CADC tax credit. For about one-half of these families, the federal gains are more than $1,000. In addition, these mothers would obtain further benefits from reductions in their state income taxes and additional credits in states that have a local EITC program.

Unfortunately, virtually no near-poor single mothers currently use DC accounts. One reason given is the belief that few of these women work for firms that provide flexible spending accounts that enable workers to pay for child care and health expenses out of pretax income. The evidence, however, shows that well over 30 percent of private-sector workers are employed by firms that offer these accounts, as does virtually every governmental agency.

Moreover, firms have a strong economic incentive to help their workers. Lowering the amount of payroll and Medicare taxes workers must pay also lowers the employers' share. In addition, DC accounts could reduce worker turnover. As a result, worker initiatives and government efforts can be quite successful in expanding the share of firms offering these accounts.

A second reason given for why near-poor mothers do not open a DC account is the need to plan in advance. Workers must decide before the year begins how much of their next year's salary, up to $5,000, they wish to allocate to a DC account. Once this decision is made by December, an equal amount of funds are placed into the account from each paycheck throughout the following year. If families end up having lower child care expenses over the year than is taken out of their paychecks, they lose the remaining account funds.

Risks, however, are quite small. Child care expenses can be reasonably predicted. More important, the government allows families to terminate their paycheck deductions if they change jobs or they or their child suffers an illness. Finally, many families expect to spend more than the $5,000 limit on these accounts. For these families, even if child care expenditures decline, they are very likely to still use all the $5,000 placed in the DC account. Improved counseling could be helpful so that more families could better weigh the risks and rewards that these accounts offer.

There is one final problem with these accounts, namely, how they interact with state child credit programs. In 2005, twenty-eight jurisdictions provided benefits to taxpayers with child care expenses. Let us look more closely at the thirteen that have fully or partially refundable credits: Arkansas, California, Colorado, Hawaii, Iowa, Louisiana, Maine, Minnesota, Nebraska, New Mexico, New York, Oregon, and Vermont.[19] All of these states, except Arkansas and Massachusetts, reduce benefit rates as income rises so that low-income households are targeted. All of these states, except for New Mexico, Minnesota, and Oregon, exclude from benefits expenses paid through DC plans.

The inability to qualify for a state refundable credit undermines substantially the overall tax benefits from using DC accounts.[20] For example, let us look at its impact on a New York mother of two children with an income of $30,000 and $5,000 in child care expenses. She gains $1,042 of additional tax benefits at the federal level if she switches to a DC account instead of using the federal CADC tax credit. In addition, she will gain $570 in state benefits from the lowering of her income tax and the ability to retain a larger state EITC. However, by paying her child care expenses through a DC account, the mother is ineligible for $1,400 of refundable child care credits. While she would still have a net gain of $212 from the shift to a DC account, these negligible gains are not worth the record keeping and planning required.[21]

In New Mexico, as long as modified gross income is low enough ($21,424 in 2007), one can claim a refundable credit regardless of the choice of child care benefit taken at the federal level.[22] The Minnesota refundable credit allows funds paid through a DC account to qualify as long as child care expenses paid through a DC account are added back into state income for tax purposes.[23] Oregon has a *refundable* Working Families Tax Credit (WFTC) that does *not* exclude child care expenses paid through DC plans. In order to target the WFTC to low-income families, benefits decline with income. For three-person families with incomes that were no higher than $34,500 in 2007, they can claim a credit equal to 40 percent of their child care expenses, up to a maximum of $1,200 per child. This percentage declines with additional income until families reach an income level at which they lose eligibility: $42,951 for a three-person family.[24]

In extolling the virtues of this program, the Oregon Legislative Office noted that as a result of making the credit refundable, the total expenditures rose by more than 300 percent between 1997 and 2003, becoming the single most important state program to aid low- and moderate-income families. In 2003, it provided an average of $814 to 25,763 families, with most of the benefits going to families with incomes between $20,000 and $30,000.[25]

With an Oregon-type provision, our New York working mother would now obtain the full state CADC benefits ($1,400) so that the additional benefits from shifting from the federal CADC tax credit to a DC account would be $1,612; if she had one qualifying child, the gains would be $1,579. Now the combined federal and state tax savings from choosing a DC plan would be at least 70 percent of the family's outlay, making quality child care viable for most near-poor New York mothers.[26]

New York tax officials were not sympathetic to adopting an Oregon-type procedure. They claim that this would be unfair, since families choosing DC plans would gain *both* state income tax savings and state child care credits. Fairness is quite subjective. After all, means-tested programs are based not on fairness but on a desire to help the less fortunate. Thus, the Oregon-type procedure could be viewed as an additional means-tested program that helps those in need.

These New York tax officials were more equivocal with respect to the Minnesota alternative: including DC expenditures in taxable income in order for these families to qualify for the state CADC tax credit. In response to my inquiry, one official wrote:

In the abstract, it might make some sense for the state to allow taxpayers to make a choice at the state level independent from their choice at the federal level, that is, allow taxpayers to add back their DC contribution if they wish for New York purposes to claim the child care credit without any limitation resulting from the DC contribution. In some instances, this strategy would increase the New York benefit. Overall, however, we are not in favor of such a change because . . . this approach would make an already complex determination faced by unsophisticated taxpayers even more complex.[27]

As to making the program more complicated for unsophisticated taxpayers, we find this position unconvincing. First, this new provision would require only adding a phrase (italicized in the following) to the qualifying expense statement on New York Tax Form IT-216: "Also, expenses reimbursed by a state social service agency or *from a dependent care account* are not qualified expenses unless you include the reimbursement in your income."

As to unsophisticated taxpayers, as a result of the welfare-to-work transition, increasingly low- and moderate-income single householders have been using tax preparation services. Besides the for-profit tax firms (H&R Block, Liberty, etc.), a number of nonprofit organizations aid these householders in tax preparation and tax advice. These tax preparers should be able to clarify the issues and implications, given that under the revised procedure, the gains from shifting to DC accounts is about $1,300 for families with incomes of $30,000; this does not include the further benefits for those who are subject to New York City taxes, child care subsidies, and EITC.[28] Even if some version of the Simplified Family Credit was enacted, benefits from a DC account would remain substantial.

It would probably be the case that the take-up rate among near-poor mothers would initially be quite modest. However, the efforts of nonprofits and tax preparers can have a strong impact on decisions. Finally, many other states have similar current policies, including California. It is likely that once one large state makes changes, other states will seriously consider following suit.

Marriage Penalties

Prior to World War I, the federal tax system touched only the wealthiest Americans. When it became more universalized after the war, the dominant family type was a married couple with a stay-at-home mother. The tax code enabled these couples to obtain a marriage bonus: total taxes were reduced when working men married. The only married couples that would pay more than if they remained single were those where both spouses had relatively equal incomes—a very small minority at the time.

As more women entered the labor market and as they began attaining an increasing number of well-paying jobs, the share of equal-earning couples increased. This change caused a slow rise in the share of couples who suffered a marriage penalty: paying more taxes when married than if they had the same earnings but were two single individuals. In the late 1970s, a compensatory policy was enacted to mitigate this problem. It allowed a modest portion of the second wage earner's pay to be deducted from the household's taxable income. However, the 1986 tax reform eliminated this option so these equal-earning couples continued to suffer a marriage penalty.

By 2000, equal-earning couples made up a significant share of married couples so that Congress set out to rectify the problem, rejecting the previous compensatory policy that had targeted the aggrieved families. Conservatives, complaining that this second wage earner provision was biased against stay-at-home mothers, demanded that the solution must not distinguish between working and nonworking spouses. Legislation enacted in 2004 made sure that the direct federal income tax married couples paid would be no higher than what they would have paid if they were unmarried. However, because the benefits were not targeted to families who were suffering marriage penalties, the vast majority of the benefits went to couples who already were obtaining marriage bonuses. Moreover, 81 percent of the benefits went to couples earning at least $75,000, and most of this to couples earning more than $100,000.[29]

This concern for eliminating marriage penalties did not significantly address the situation faced by many single mothers. Many of these mothers, almost two-thirds of whom had incomes below $40,000, would experience income losses if they choose to marry. Let us detail the sources of these marriage penalties in order to formulate effective corrective policies.

Most mothers with wage income under $10,000 are not receiving the maximum EITC or the full benefits from the child tax credit. For many of these mothers, marrying a working man might actually increase credits received and, hence, provide a marriage bonus. By contrast, for the vast majority of working mothers with earnings above $10,000, marrying a working man would entail marriage penalties.

The largest marriage penalties are experienced by single women with two children and earnings between $14,000 and $18,000. All these mothers are receiving close to the maximum EITC, child credits, and food stamps available. Many also receive substantial housing and child care assistance or reside in states with a local EITC or other supplemental programs. For these wage-poor mothers, the total value of transfers is at least $7,000, but for many it is well over $10,000. As mentioned in the last chapter, by marrying low-earning men, they will lose a substantial share of these benefits; by marrying men earning at least $20,000, they will lose virtually *all* income transfers. Thus, these mothers face a severe marriage penalty.

There are a number of reasons why responding to this problem has not been a priority among policy advocates. Left liberals and many others are fearful of government efforts to encourage marriage. This concern was heightened when a number of conservatives proposed financial incentives to encourage women from low-income backgrounds to marry. For example, Kansas senator Sam Brownback proposed up to $9,000 in marriage bonuses to poor District of Columbia mothers who choose marriage. Wade Horn, assistant secretary for the Administration for Children and Families at the U.S. Department of Health and Human Services, publicly supported a similar West Virginia proposal and a Heritage Foundation proposal that women at high risk of bearing children out of wedlock should be given up to $5,000 if they bear their first child within marriage.[30]

Particularly for those who perceive heterosexual marriages as inherently patriarchal, these efforts reinforced their hostility to President Bush's healthy marriages initiatives. These concerns, however, were misplaced. Far from promoting marriage, for many wage-poor mothers, the government actively discourages marriage by inadvertently imposing substantial financial penalties. Thus, while there may be a very strong pro-marriage political rhetoric, for many couples, government tax and transfer policies can be very antimarriage.

A second reason that there have been very limited efforts to overcome marriage penalties faced by wage-poor mothers is the belief that marriage promotion policies have been ineffective. This viewpoint is based not so much on empirical evaluations of the Bush initiatives as on an overriding belief that pro-marriage policies cannot work. Low marriage rates, increasing cohabitation rates, and a growing share of births to unwed mothers both here and in many European countries seems to indicate a pattern of behavior that public policy cannot stop.

Some advocates who believe that the government should promote marriage see parallels with changing attitudes concerning smoking and exercise.[31] They correctly point out that no one could have predicted thirty or forty years ago the generational changes in these behaviors. We are not so hopeful that government policies could affect marriage trends significantly.

However, we believe the government should be neutral so that marriage penalties must be eliminated.

Finally, even among some who believe marriage penalties should be eliminated, this problem is not seen as widespread enough to warrant making it a priority. While it is certainly true that marriage penalties are substantial for the particular subgroup—those working mothers with incomes between $14,000 and $18,000—data seem to indicate these women make up a small share of poor and near-poor mothers. In an influential study, Urban Institute economists Gregory Acs and Elaine Maag analyzed the tax effects of marriage on those couples whose combined income was below 200 percent of the poverty line. As expected, they found that penalties "are most likely to accrue to families with two earners, adjusted gross income above $30,000 and one or two children." However, when they simulated the impact of marriage on all of the low-income couples, they estimated that almost three-quarters would gain marriage bonuses while only 15 percent would suffer marriage penalties. Thus, these wage-poor mothers constituted only a small share of low-income couples.[32]

Acs and Maag readily admit that these wage-poor mothers have substantial marriage penalties that justify policy intervention even if they are a small share of poor mothers. Second, their study did not take into account the dramatic decline in the income level at which the child credit now begins to phase in. The study assumed that the phase-in would begin at about $12,000 (in 2008 dollars), so that many poor mothers gained substantial child credits *only* if they married a working man. With a $3,000 starting point, however, even many low-earning mothers now qualify for substantial child credits, reducing the benefits from marriage. In addition, the exclusion from the study of cohabiting couples with combined incomes above $40,000 leaves out many situations in which a substantial marriage penalty would arise.

Probably most important, Acs and Maag look only at tax implications, not the impact of marriage on the full range of subsidies available to poor and near-poor families. In particular, the tax system provided a bonus because of the phasing *in* of EITC and child credits when poor mothers marry. By contrast, all the other nontax benefit programs—medical, housing, child care, and food stamp subsidies—provide maximum benefits at zero income. As a result, no poor mothers would gain additional subsidies from these programs by marrying, while many would have some subsidies phased out. For this reason, only among the poorest couples—those with combined incomes of less than $20,000—would bonuses persist even after taking into account the impact of nontax subsidy programs. For most other couples, the loss of these nontax subsidies will usually far outweigh whatever bonus is available through the tax system.

Even if we agree that something should be done about the marriage penalties faced by low-income working mothers, the solution is not straightforward. These penalties reflect the working of not only the tax system but also the many means-tested programs that aid poor and near-poor families. Thus, there is no one policy that can respond to all the programs that impact on the marriage penalty.

Part of the solution could include reducing the phase-out rates all families experience when their income rises. Certainly, shifting to a Simplified Family Credit with a 9 or 12 percent phase-out rate would reduce the marriage penalty for many couples. States and the federal government could consider universalizing programs similar to the child credit that is extended to all families. They could move in this direction by lowering the phasing out of medical and child care subsidies so that coverage is extend further up the income scale.

Another possibility would be for programs to have separate subsidy schedules for those already covered and for new applicants, which is the current child care subsidy policy in at least eighteen states. In Connecticut, for example, for new applicants, eligibility for child care subsidies in 2008 was limited to families with incomes below $38,726. By contrast, for families already receiving child care subsidies, the exit eligibility income limit was $58,089.[33] This two-tier subsidy system is already embedded in the EITC program. The plateau section is extended for married couples, which partially offsets the phasing out of credits associated with marriage. This procedure could be extended to food stamp, medical, and housing subsidy policies to lessen subsidy reductions when single mothers marry.

The marriage penalty could be fully eliminated if we gave couples the option of continuing to file as single individuals even after they marry. A less dramatic change would be to convert the EITC into a wage supplement for individual workers, not individual families. In this case, when couples marry and file joint returns, they would still compute their EITC benefits as if they were individual filers. This procedure would at least eliminate completely the share of the marriage penalty that results from the phasing out of EITC credits.

The marriage penalty could also be reduced if couples had the option of using income averaging to determine the combined child credit and EITC received. Income averaging would mitigate their influences on the marriage decision. For more than twenty years, income averaging was a part of the federal tax code, allowing federal taxes to adjust gradually to a rapid change in taxable income. It was eliminated as part of the general tax reform in the

1980s. However, given the substantial marriage penalty for many couples, this policy should be considered at least for EITC calculations.

One possibility would be to allow newly married couples to determine their combined EITC and child credits as a running average. For example, let us assume that a just-married couple had in each of the previous four years received EITC and child credits equal to $7,000. Now in their first year of marriage, they qualify for only $2,000. Suppose that the tax form allowed them to compute their actual combined EITC and child credits by averaging the amount they qualified for over the last *five* years. In this case, the current year's combined credit would equal $6,000 ([$28,000 + $2,000]/5). Assuming the couple's income remains the same, this *credit* averaging would slowly bring down the annual credits received until at the end of five years it would reach $2,000.

In addition to reducing the marriage penalty working women face, averaging EITC and child credits over a five-year period would also reduce the implicit tax rate faced by single parents and already married couples. Recall that a substantial share of near-poor families are married couples with only one wage earner. Many of these families will have a substantial spike in incomes when the nonworking spouse reenters the paid workforce. Under current conditions, this change will result in a substantial drop in child-related benefits received. With averaging benefits, however, this decline would be moderated over the first five years. Similarly, for single parents who receive substantial earnings increases, averaging benefits would also moderate the drop in resulting drop in benefits. Of course, this provision should be optional so that those families experience declining income will get the full EITC increase they are eligible for under the current system.

Conclusion

This chapter has highlighted some of the inadequacies of the present tax system that have a significant economic impact on working families. Financial subsidies to these families could be improved by reforms in the federal tax system and better coordination with state tax policies. Reducing the implicit tax rate enables low-income working families to keep more of their wage gains. If we allowed child care expenditures paid through federal dependent care accounts to qualify for state CADC tax credits, near-poor families would be better able to afford care for their children. If we reduced marriage penalties, financial considerations would weigh less heavily on decisions to wed.

Our recommendation for restructuring the EITC relies on equity considerations. Lowering the implicit tax rate faced by low-income families, particularly single mothers, is a matter of fairness. Even if it has no impact on labor supply decisions, we should be concerned when this rate is higher than the tax rate faced by wealthier households. In addition, equity considerations justify this restructuring because it would end the middle-class parent penalty whereby many near-poor and lower-middle-class families gain less in child-related benefits than do either wealthier or poorer families.

Many policy makers justify using the tax system to change human behavior: cigarette taxes to cut down smoking and gasoline taxes to stimulate movement toward more efficient and smaller automobiles. Certainly, raising taxes is less intrusive than actually banning cigarettes or gas-guzzling cars. Indeed, we favor these taxes because there is sufficient evidence that cigarettes are harmful to smokers and gas emissions to the environment. By contrast, we are not convinced that marriage is more valuable to families than cohabitation and so we are unwilling to justify reducing marriage penalties in order to raise the marriage rate.

Instead, we rely on a long-standing economic objective: taxes should be structured so that they do not influence personal or market behaviors. This should certainly be the focus of taxation on nonwage income. It should not distort investment strategies, causing decisions to be based upon tax avoidance reasons rather than market performance considerations. If the government should remain neutral on marriage, we must eliminate marriage penalties as much as is possible. While benefit averaging is proposed primarily to moderate the marriage penalty, it also will reduce the implicit tax rate of single parents and married couples who are in the phase-out range of the EITC and experience rising income.

There is one final issue that these policy recommendations raise: Are taxpayers able to rationally respond to the proposed changes? Virtually all studies find that recipients have virtually no understanding of how the EITC works and only the vaguest notion of the overall implicit tax rate they face. This is not a serious problem, since the benefits they receive from a restructuring of the EITC do not require them to change their labor market decisions.

By contrast, the other two policy recommendations made in this chapter are effective only if single mothers change their behavior. They gain from better coordination of federal and state child care subsidies only if these mothers open up DC accounts. They gain from adjustments that lower the marriage penalties they face only if mothers choose to marry. This suggests that part of the efforts of advocacy groups and tax preparation firms must be to increase awareness so that families can make more informed choices.

9

Redirecting Immigration Policies

Over the last few decades, despite overall economic growth, there has been growing income inequality, persistently high poverty rates, and wage increases for less educated workers that have not kept pace with inflation. This book has enumerated a number of labor and tax policy initiatives to combat these problems. We also believe, however, that part of the problem stems from current immigration policies. It has been claimed that immigration has had harmful effects on the employment of less educated and teenage workers and that immigrants cause financial burdens because of the government services and benefits they receive. This chapter will assess these claims.

Much of the discussion of immigration has centered on what to do about the estimated 10 million undocumented individuals currently residing in the United States and how to reduce their numbers in the future. Important moral and ethical considerations dominate the competing perspectives on this issue, especially when those undocumented individuals have children living here. These factors also influence judgments regarding the appropriate level of *total* legal immigration. Without minimizing these issues, our focus will be on redesigning policies that should govern the *distribution* of legal immigrants.

The Impact of Immigration on Economic Measures

Let us begin by assessing the impact of immigration on income inequality. The simplest method is to compare incomes of those at the top of the income distribution with those at the bottom. Most observers point to the last twenty years of the twentieth century as the period in which inequality grew the most. In 1979, families at the 90th percentile (those with incomes just higher than 90 percent of all families) earned incomes 4.58 times as great as families at the 10th percentile (those with incomes just higher than 10 percent of all families). By 1997, the 90/10 ratio had risen to 5.58.[1] Most analysts suggest that this growth in inequality reflected falling earnings of those at the bottom

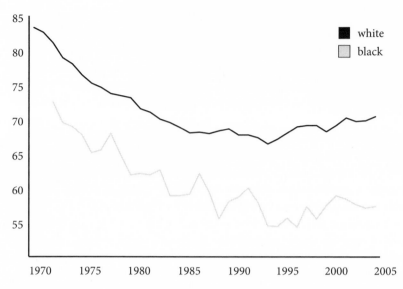

Figure 9.1. Labor force participation rates of men, 55–64 years old, 1970–2005

of the economic ladder due to declines in manufacturing employment, the share of workers represented by unions, and the declining value of the minimum wage adjusted for inflation. These factors certainly are part of the story.

We have documented the harmful effect that industrial restructuring had on young black men. It also had a harmful effect on older men. In their late forties and early fifties, these men lost employment as manufacturing relocated. Many had difficult transitions and were unlikely to maintain their previous earnings. This problem is captured by the changing labor force participation rates of men aged fifty-five to sixty-four. Through 1985, participation rates fell dramatically as company reorganizations forced many of these men from steady employment into chronic joblessness (figure 9.1). Afterward, the rates bottomed out and, thanks to the Clinton-era economic boom, began to rise modestly but came nowhere close to their 1975 levels.[2]

In 1979, the federal minimum wage was $2.90 per hour. In 1997, it equaled $5.15 an hour as the full effect of the 1996 minimum-wage increase had taken effect. However, after taking into account inflation, the purchasing power of the minimum wage had *declined* by 20 percent. Ten years later, federal minimum-wage legislation was passed so that by 2009 it reached $7.25 per hour. This increase was not quite enough to keep pace with the inflation rate, so that the purchasing power of the minimum wage continued to decline.

During the 1980s and 1990s, unionization rates declined, especially among private-sector workers. In 2000, 13.4 percent of all nonsupervisory workers were union members—a drop from 20.1 percent in 1983. Over virtually the same period, the share of private-sector workers who were union members was almost halved, to 7.8 percent.[3]

These changes certainly exacerbated income inequality. Immigration may also have contributed to these trends. One way to measure the impact of immigration on income inequality is to estimate what it would have been in 1997 if there had been no post-1979 immigration. Somewhat surprisingly, their elimination only reduces the 90/10 ratio slightly, from 5.58 to 5.49. This meager impact suggests that during this period, inequality among recent immigrants was almost as great as for the rest of the U.S. population.

Income inequality among immigrants during this period reflected large educational disparities. Among post-1979 immigrants, 36 percent were high school dropouts while 25 percent had at least four years of postsecondary education. For the native-born labor force, only 16 percent were high school dropouts while 24 percent had at least four years of postsecondary education. Thus, educational disparities were more substantial among recent immigrants than within the native-born labor force, which could explain why income inequality among recent immigrants has been substantial.

There was also growth in national poverty rates from 9.2 percent in 1979 to 10.3 percent in 1997. Much of this increase reflects the decline in married couples from 82.4 percent of all families in 1979 to 76.6 percent of all families in 1997. As a result, even though the poverty rate among married couples declined over this time, and the poverty rate of single-headed households increased only slightly, the overall poverty rate *increased* because single-headed households, which have a higher incidence of poverty, became a larger share of all families.[4]

Given the large share of recent immigrants with very low levels of education, poverty rates in 1997 would have been significantly lower if there had been no immigration. For example, between 1979 and 1997, the poverty rate among families with children rose from 16.6 percent to 17.9 percent. If we excluded recent immigrants, however, the poverty rate in 1997 would have been only 16.3 percent.[5]

Wages of Native-Born Workers

By excluding immigrants from our income comparison, we measured only the *direct* impact of immigration on overall income inequality and poverty rates. This approach ignores the impact immigrants may have on the earnings and incomes of native-born families. In 2004, immigrants constituted 31.8 percent of all U.S. workers with less than high school degrees and 66.8 percent of those workers in California. Suppose that this very large group of less educated recent immigrants caused wages of native-born workers at the bottom of the economic ladder to decline while it raised the wages of highly paid native-born workers. In this case, the *indirect* impact of immigration could explain a substantial share of the rise in income inequality and poverty rates. Let us therefore assess the impact of immigration on each of the groups.

Better-Paid Native-Born Workers

There are a number of ways that better-paid native-born workers might benefit from less educated immigrant labor. In the 1970s, Michael Piore suggested that the remaining vitality of garment districts in Los Angeles and New York City was determined primarily by their ability to utilize these immigrants. Subcontractors employed them to produce unfinished garments, which were then processed by parent companies.[6] Thomas Muller suggested that it was only the continued infusion of cheap foreign-born labor that enabled older urban areas to maintain any economic vitality: "For any stagnating urban economy, any productive economic activity is a plus. A Newark, NJ, is not likely to attract large research laboratories and certainly not a Japanese automaker. But with both commercial space and immigrant labor available at low cost, older cities can attract labor-intensive manufacturing and service industries."[7]

Muller pointed to the prosperity of the shoe industry in Los Angeles: "Without these immigrants . . . local shoe manufacturers would find it difficult to survive. Unskilled blacks could not fill the role of these immigrants, who had extensive shoemaking training in Mexico and were accustomed to working for rock-bottom piece rates."[8]

The sustained production that these immigrant workers provided enabled many professional workers—accountants, designers, distributors, and so forth—to maintain their employment. This additional production also generated jobs through the economic multiplier effect: employed workers increase their consumer demand for goods produced by firms that do not use immigrant labor. By contrast, if these immigrant workers were unavailable, production would be lost and so, too, many of these allied jobs.

Immigration also has had a substantial *service* effect. The additional government services and infrastructure provided to immigrants increases professional employment of social workers, educational personnel, and medical providers. For these government service providers, immigration has a positive impact on their economic welfare.

Finally, high-waged workers are often direct consumers of services provided by immigrants. George Vernez estimated that 60 percent of employed Salvadoran women in the Los Angeles area are private household workers.[9] As a result, immigration lowers the cost of household child care and cleaning services. Besides the direct financial benefits to households, the lower cost of these services often enables women to maintain career employment. Finally, home care attendants for the elderly are disproportionately immigrant women. Without this supply, many more of the elderly could not afford to stay in their homes and would be forced to choose alternatives that they consider inferior, such as nursing homes or residence with other family members. All of these individuals benefit from the presence of less educated immigrants.

These benefits are offset to only a modest degree by the competition higher-income families face from college-educated immigrants. A substantial share of these immigrants are unable to use their professional skills when they immigrate to the United States due to licensing restrictions, forcing them to shift instead to entrepreneurial activities. Many chose to provide professional services to members of their immigrant communities rather than compete with native-born workers in the broader economy.

Finally, many of these more educated immigrants have technical and scientific skills in occupational and professional areas where there are substantial shortages of workers. More than one-half of all students graduating from U.S. engineering schools are foreign born. Even the labor supply of recent immigrants is insufficient to overcome the shortage of math and science teachers, which has forced many schools to recruit teachers from abroad. In 2003, "the National Education Association estimated that up to 10,000 foreigners already were teaching U.S. students in primary and secondary schools, mainly to fill vacancies in math, science, foreign languages and special education."[10]

While many school systems rely on recruiting firms, Baldwin County, Alabama, sent its district officials around the world in 2007 and "brought back Michel Olalo of Manila and 11 other Filipinos to teach along the shores of the Gulf Coast and Mobile Bay and in the communities in between. That raised some eyebrows in Baldwin County, where nine out of 10 people are white, just one in 50 is foreign-born and, as the county's teacher recruiter Tom Sisk noted recently, 'Many of our children will never travel outside the United States.'"[11]

Industry and university research institutes also face substantial shortages of technical and scientific workers. The National Commission on Math and Science Teaching for the 21st Century, chaired by former U.S. senator John Glenn, noted:

> "Many American companies now have to import the computing talent they need to stay competitive. Two years ago the Congress had to pass special legislation to permit the entry of computer workers, in rapidly escalating numbers from abroad. The so-called "H-1B Visa Bills" progressively raised the ceiling to permit the entry of some 300,000 temporary, native-born, skilled computer workers between 1998 and 2002.[12]

The numerical limitation was temporarily raised to an annual quota of 195,000 during the dot-com boomlet. In addition, excluded from the ceiling were all H-1B immigrant who worked at universities and nonprofit research facilities. Laws also exempt up to 20,000 foreign nationals holding a master's or higher degree from U.S. universities from the cap on H-1B visas.

These annual quotas were lowered to 65,000 in recent years. They still indicate, however, that foreign-born workers continue to fill a persistent shortage in technical and scientific occupations that make them complementary to college-educated native-born workers. Thus, better-paid native-born workers have benefited substantially even after taking into account the impact of college-educated immigrants.

Less Educated Native-Born Workers

Given the large share of immigrants with low levels of education, we should anticipate that immigrants adversely affect the economic welfare of less educated native-born workers. In 1997, the National Academy of Science (NAS) published a report on the economic impact of immigration which found that "almost one-half of the declines in real wages for native-born high school dropouts from 1980 to 1994 could be attributed to the adverse impact of unskilled foreign workers."[13] David Jaeger estimated that immigration accounted for 15 to 25 percent of the increase in the high school–college wage gap during the 1980s.[14] Similarly, George Borjas estimated that immigration after 1979 was responsible for an 8.9 percent wage decline for native-born high school dropouts.[15]

Historical studies also documented examples of immigrant workers displacing native-born workers. For example, Vernon Briggs noted:

Black janitors had their union broken in the 1980s by nonunion Hispanic workers. Management in the hotel industry in Los Angeles . . . was able to lower its wage rates and benefits by switching from a Teamsters local union made up mostly of black workers to a Seafarers' local whose members were mostly recent immigrants. In a 1982 strike at a Los Angeles tortilla factory, native-born workers were replaced by illegal immigrants . . . and wages were cut by 40 percent for those workers who returned.[16]

Christine Zlolniski documented a similar dynamic in Silicon Valley, where the employment of janitors grew even faster than the employment of computer engineers. She found that "janitorial work devolved from a stable, well-paid entry-level occupation for minority and long-settled immigrants, to an unstable, low-wage, dead-end job for recent, mostly undocumented immigrants who arrived in the region in the 1980s."[17]

A more recent study focused on the labor supply response of native-born dropouts to an influx of immigrant workers.[18] Using data from 1995–99, it divided its sample into two groups: twenty-eight cities where immigrants constitute more than 25 percent of the dropout workforce, and forty cities where they constitute less than 25 percent. The study found that a rise in the number of immigrants impacted adversely on the labor force participation rate of native-born dropouts, especially in the more immigrant-dense cities. If the immigrant share increased by 10 percent, the labor force participation rate of native-born dropouts would decline by an average of 2.7 percent in the twenty-eight immigrant-dense cities but by an average of only 0.3 percent in the other forty cities.

Finally, a Canadian study also found that immigration had adverse wage effects on native-born workers. Using the long form from the 1981, 1991, and 2001 national data, this study estimated that a 10 percentage-point immigrant supply increase would lower the wages of native-born workers by about 3 percent. This adverse effect was overwhelmingly concentrated in the blue-collar manual occupations, especially during the 1990s. In particular, a 10 percentage-point immigrant labor supply increase was responsible for an 8.2 percent wage decrease in this occupational grouping.[19]

Alternative Explanations for Adverse Effects

Many researchers do not believe that these studies justify restricting the entry of less educated immigrants. They contend that the weakening position of less educated native-born workers was largely the result of structural factors, not immigration. One structural explanation centers on the movement of industrial jobs out of the central city to suburban industrial parks. As a result of continued racial housing segregation, white workers could move to the new locations but not black workers.[20] Thus, it appears that an important part of the growing black-white employment gap was "the closing of older plants in the central cities of the Midwest."[21]

Similarly, the *Wall Street Journal* analyzed data from 35,000 companies that are required to file reports with the federal Equal Employment Opportunity Commission (EEOC). These companies reported that from 1990 through 1991, their total employment increased by 126,000, while blacks lost 60,000 jobs in their companies. The companies claimed structural factors, not racism, explained these changes. For example, General Electric cited the closing of older plants in Maryland and Illinois in which blacks had been employed disproportionately. Sears cited the relocation of two distribution centers from inner cities to suburbs, to which blacks without cars could not commute.[22]

Marta Tienda has pointed out a weakness in this structural explanation. She found that in Chicago, the relocation of manufacturing firms did not hinder Mexican immigrant employment. These immigrants also faced the housing segregation that trapped them in the central city, and yet their unemployment rates were less than half those of black workers. Tienda concluded that discrimination among employers who prefer Hispanic workers, not structural factors, was an important reason for the weakening labor market position of black workers.[23]

Consistent with her findings, a more recent study found that racial and ethnic networking was a more powerful employment predictor than residential location near job density. It stated, "The key policy implication is that if networks are important, then location-based policies . . . are likely to prove ineffective. . . . And moving residents to other locations, which may sever network connections, may prove completely ineffective or even counterproductive."[24]

Others contend that manufacturing jobs that blacks disproportionately held were shifted to low-wages service jobs that only immigrants were willing to take. Daniel Hamermesh tested this hypothesis by looking at the relative amenities of the jobs held by immigrants compared with those held by native-born workers. He found no evidence that immigrants take jobs with adverse amenities; they may work for lower pay but do not take otherwise undesirable jobs.[25] Interestingly, it was black workers who seemed to have the most undesirable jobs as measured by night shift work and injury rates.

Thus, to the extent the shift to service industries has lowered black employment, it was not a result of their unwillingness to accept undesirable jobs.

There are also some situations in which black and immigrant workers may not be in competition with others. One study found that in metropolitan areas where there was a relative growth of "better" jobs, black workers rose up the occupational ladder while immigrants replaced them in the bottom-rung jobs.[26] A companion study found that when jobs were plentiful, immigrant and native-born black men both benefited from increased immigration. By contrast, immigrants displace black workers when, like today, there is significant unemployment.[27]

Finally, reasonable observers can differ on what the myriad of studies tell us. For example, Harry Holzer has reviewed much the material presented here and concludes, "Though the extent to which less-educated immigrants compete with and harm their native-born U.S. counterparts has been very heavily debated in the economics profession, the overall findings of this literature suggest quite modest negative impacts." For Holzer, these modest adverse effects are more than offset by the benefits these low-wage immigrants provide not only to high-waged workers but also to low-income consumers "in the form of cheaper and more available food, housing, and medical care."[28]

Competition for Niche Employment

Rather than looking at broad citywide measures, some researchers instead assessed specific employment niches to determine the impact of immigration on black employment. These researchers reasoned that, to the extent employers prefer immigrants, black displacement should be observed within occupations and industries. In addition, displacement should be more apparent in job settings that put a premium on the informal networks thought to be more prevalent in these immigrant communities.

Mary Waters assessed the employment dynamics of New York City cafeteria workers in a major financial corporation and found an almost complete turnover from African American to Caribbean American workers between 1980 and 1996. This displacement was at least partially due to the shift from using help-wanted advertisements to relying completely on recommendations from current employees. As a result, employment networking became dominated by Caribbean employees.[29]

Roger Waldinger claimed that these immigrant networks were important even in settings, like hospitals and hotels, where employers use formal hiring practices for most job openings but continue to use employment networks to fill their low-end jobs. Consistent with surveys of employer attitudes, Waldinger also suggested that employers might seek Latino workers because they fear the potential bargaining power of an all-black workforce.[30]

A New York City study identified sixteen occupations in which male employment was disproportionately native-born black in 1980. In these niches, the study found that over the next decade, total employment grew by 5.3 percent while immigrant employment grew by 50.6 percent.[31] In contrast to Waters's study, however, this study did not find that immigration adversely affected *total* black employment. The ability of native-born black men to sustain employment in their niches was due to two factors: (1) nine of the niches had significant public-sector employment where black men were insulated from informal network hirings; and (2) black men were able to maintain their employment shares in the two fastest-growing niches—security guards and heavy trucking.[32] This study did find, however, that immigration adversely affected the wages of native-born black men.

Michael Rosenfeld and Marta Tienda analyzed ten varied occupations in three cities to judge the impact of immigration on niche employment. They found that black workers who were squeezed out of low-employment occupations were those with the *lowest* wages. In all three cities, black maids and machine operators at the lowest pay levels were displaced. Given the lack of occupational mobility of the lowest-paid workers, Rosenfeld and Tienda concluded, "We have shown that black workers who remain behind in the low-skill jobs confront fewer job opportunities and sharply increased rates of unemployment."[33]

These studies provide some understanding of the situations in which immigration weakens the economic position of less educated black workers. Only when a metropolitan area has strong employment growth with an increasing share of better jobs does immigration benefit black workers. In other situations, strong immigrant networks adversely affect either the employment and/or the wages of black workers, particularly those that are the lowest paid and most vulnerable.

Tax Burden

The impact of immigrants on wages is not their only effect on the economic welfare of working families. Immigrants utilize welfare, food stamps, social security disability and retirement, health care, and educational programs. They also receive federal and state tax benefits, including the EITC and the child and dependent care tax credits. To the extent the taxes they pay do not cover the government expenditures and credits they receive, immigrants create a tax burden that must be paid by others.

While in a few places, like Nebraska, immigrants pay taxes to cover the government expenditures they receive, this is not the typical case.[34] For 1994, the National Research Council report calculated that immigration created a net burden on government at all levels of between $11 billion and $22 billion. The NAS study estimated that the average immigrant-headed household in California used almost $3,500 more in state and local services than it paid in taxes, amounting to an extra tax burden for each native-headed household of nearly $1,200. In New Jersey, the average immigrant family consumed nearly $1,500 more in services than it paid in taxes, creating a tax burden on native-born families of more than $200 per year while more recently in Florida, the tax burden annually was estimated to equal about $2,000 per immigrant household.[35]

These short-term costs, however, may disappear in the long run as immigrants become more settled, and there might be net tax benefits when their children grow up and enter the workforce. The NAS projected federal expenditures and tax revenues following the entry of a representative immigrant into the country in 1994. Initially, immigration creates annual burdens on taxpayers, reflecting the social services and tax credits immigrants receive. Beginning in 2016, however, the NAS study estimated that the taxes the immigrant family and its grown children pay would be greater than the government expenditures and tax credits they receive. By 2044, the cumulative net benefits would be $11,000, suggesting that immigration does not create a long-term tax burden.

These long-term projected net benefits are not necessarily a basis for maintaining current immigration policies. First, using a reasonable alternative federal tax policy, there would still be a net *loss* of $15,000. In addition, the NAS estimate of net benefits was only at the federal level, where immigrant families pay payroll taxes despite continued low income. At the state level, they would pay very low state income taxes, and many of their consumer expenditures would be exempt from state and local taxes. Thus, the substantial state expenditures they receive, including educational services, would not be offset by taxes paid.

Maybe even more important, it is not necessarily enough to look at the tax burden from *all* immigration. We might consider reducing the level of immigrant from subgroups that are estimated to have a long-term net tax burden. In particular, the NAS report estimated the lifetime cost of an immigrant based on different educational levels. The average immigrant high school dropout would cost American taxpayers a total of $89,000 over his lifetime, and an immigrant with only a high school degree would still cost taxpayers $31,000. Thus, we should look closely at these less educated immigrants in order to understand the tax burdens they generate.

In 2005, 62 percent of working-age Mexican immigrants had less than a high school degree, and only 5 percent had a college degree. Almost two-thirds of Mexican-immigrant households were poor or near-poor, and one-quarter were below the poverty line. With such low incomes, they use food stamps, housing assistance, Medicaid, and a number of other means-tested assistance programs, including WIC, disproportionately. For example, whereas Medicaid is used by 15 percent of native-born households, it is used by 37 percent of Mexican-immigrant households. Only 15 percent of native-born households are eligible for the EITC, compared with nearly one-half of Mexican-immigrant households.[36]

In 2009, 1.13 million individuals entering the United States gained legal resident status. The vast majority came under family unification provisions: 634,000 were parents, children, or spouses of U.S. citizens or resident aliens; 63,000 were brothers or sisters of U.S. citizens; and another 50,000 were additional relatives of U.S. citizens. The older immigrants generally work, so that 34.6 percent of immigrants who arrived after the age of fifty-five received social security income. Alan Gustman and Thomas Steinmeier documented the social security subsidy received by the typical immigrant worker. The subsidy is greatest for older immigrants who earned at least $10,000 annually and worked in the United States for between ten and twenty years. These immigrants would receive social security benefits of between 70 and 80 percent of those paid to native-born workers with comparable earnings who were employed for their full work-age life.[37]

While immigrants constitute 12 percent of the U.S. population, their children constitute almost 20 percent of the school-age population. These more than 10 million immigrant children account for all the increase in school enrollment over the last two decades. Given the poorly educated backgrounds many come from and their lack of English-language skills, these immigrant students place extra burdens on school systems; these burdens might adversely impact on other students, particularly if government funding does not keep pace with the growing needs.

Without a sufficient growth in expenditures, immigrants obtain educational-support funding that reduces the educational resources received by disadvantaged native-born students. Michael Fix and Wendy Zimmerman analyzed the impact of these poor immigrant populations on Title 1 funding, the largest single grant program for K-12 schools. Though the increased utilization of Title 1–funded services by immigrant populations did not reduce the number of black children served, it was generally associated with a substantial drop in expenditures per pupil.[38] Building on this evidence, Julian Betts estimated that immigration in the 1980s lowered the high school graduation rate of blacks and native-born Hispanics by 1 and 3 percentage points, respectively.[39]

Second-Generation Mexican Americans

The tax burdens of recent Mexican immigrants may not be offset by the higher earnings of their offspring. Increasingly, evidence seems to indicate that these subsequent generations do not have higher levels of economic well-being. A 2009 study highlighted these concerns. By and large, mothers from Latin American countries take care of their health during their pregnancies and give birth to robust children, but those children fall behind their peers in mental development by the time they reach grade school, and the gap tends to widen as they get older. The new study suggests the shortfall may start even before the children enter preschool, supporting calls in Washington to spend more on programs that coach parents to stimulate their children with books, drills, and games earlier in their lives. "Our results show a very significant gap even at age 3," said Bruce Fuller, one of the study's authors. "If we don't attack this disparity early on, these kids are headed quickly for a pretty dismal future in elementary school."[40]

Edward Telles and Vilma Ortiz documented the lack of educational and occupational progress across generations. Matching Mexican Americans who had been surveyed in the 1960s with their children and grandchildren, they found the following:

Mexican American schooling remained fairly flat in succeeding generations-since-immigration. Assuming equally resourced children, education actually worsened. Greater parental education, household income, social and cultural capital, and fewer children all contributed to more schooling. However, when these factors are held constant, the highest levels of schooling are for those who immigrated as children but were educated in the United States and the lowest for the grandchildren and great grandchildren of immigrants.[41]

A 2009 conference lamented this so-called immigrant paradox. Just as educational attainment begins to decline with future generations, unwed motherhood increases and incarceration rates rise dramatically. Reflecting on the circumstances of later generations, the conference organizer, Cynthia Garcia Coll, suggested that "as kids acculturate . . . they lose the protectiveness of their home"; although they speak better English, they do less homework. Once they begin to do poorly in school, Coll argued, these young men and women become fatalistic about their futures, with many drifting into behaviors—gang membership, early sexual experimentation—that put their futures at risk.[42]

Mexican gang involvement did increase during the 1990s. Rather than acculturation, it reflected a response to the violence inflicted on Mexican youth by black and Puerto Rican gangs. One of the leaders of a Puerto Rican gangs told researchers, "Everybody be ripping them off; they easy prey 'cause they illegal, most of them. . . . Everybody takes Mexicans like a joke."[43]

Gangs also grew in the 1990s in New York City as a result of family unification provisions that allowed many Mexicans to bring their teenage children to the United States. These children had difficulty adjusting. When they lived in Mexico, their absent parents would periodically come and shower them with gifts and affection. In New York, however, they saw little of their parents, and strained relations often developed. For these disaffected youth, gangs provided "a social structure of belonging that youth want and need, but that their parents cannot readily provide."[44]

While gangs may have been initiated for self-defense, they often evolved into criminal enterprises. Criminal behavior among second-generation Latinos is substantially higher than among the first generation. These differences are explained in part by family relationships and school bonding, particularly parent-child conflicts and school troubles that increase with later immigration generations.[45]

The inability of many children of immigrants to move forward may also reflect the transnational attitudes of their parents and community elders. Community leaders are often centrally focused on their homeland. Ethnographic research emphasized this behavior among the tightly knit New York City immigrant community from Ticuani, Mexico. Through committees, the community elders give substantial funds for the maintenance of not only their Ticuani relatives but also the town's infrastructure: roads, schools, and public buildings. As ethnographer Robert Smith relates:

While the Committee imagines itself present in Ticuani politics despite its physical absence, its members are frequently absent from home: collecting funds for Ticuani public works projects places a heavy burden on them and their families. For several months or even years during a project, Committee members may spend all their weekends collecting funds, meaning they almost never spend an entire day with their families.[46]

Parents also invest heavily in their children's ability to maintain homeland ties by sending them during summers and at festival times to Ticuani. For many second-generation Mexican American youth, negotiating their gender roles is a real challenge. These trips create problems as Mexican American youth are encouraged to embrace the traditional machismo culture there.

What sustained the community elders was an adapted *ranchero* image— the hardworking immigrant who "legitimizes his masculinity through his enduring capacity to work and sacrifice for his family."[47] For their sons, however, this is not an attractive option because it lacks a notion of upward mobility. This next generation is unwilling to take their father's jobs, and if they cannot earn educational credentials that would enable them to gain more skilled and professional positions, they search for their masculinity among the *pandilleros*—Mexican gang members.

The trips to Ticuani increase the chances that young Mexican Americans will adopt masculine traits that will weaken their chances for success. Smith followed Tono, a Mexican American in his twenties who is enrolled in college. In Ticuani, Tono embraces the traditional macho image. He told the ethnographic team that being Ticuanense was about "wearing a cowboy hat, getting drunk every nite [and] listening to Ranchera music." The drinking and all-night partying during festival weeks created volatile situations that often ended up in fights. Tono's girlfriend, Julia, says she "hates the ways guys act when they come here [Ticuani] to drink. . . . They act 'macho,' they act stupid, then end up fighting."[48]

His father, Tomas Maestro, asserts tighter control over Tono in New York, giving him more freedom to "have fun" in Ticuani. Maestro worries, however, that "his son's lack of effort toward educational and professional success imperils the male authority to which his status as the oldest son entitles him."[49] If these behavior patterns endanger the advancement of those on the path for success, one can only imagine how the Mexican experience impacts on those more at-risk youth.

This limited upward mobility of second- and third-generation youth may also reflect the competition they face from even newer Latino immigrants, including the undocumented. Whatever the source of the problem, however, we cannot be confident that the children and grandchildren of less educated immigrants will experience the American success story: moving into the middle classes, owning their own home, and adding revenues to government coffers.[50]

Policy Implications

This literature surveyed in this chapter has provided some consistent findings: (1) less educated native-born workers have been harmed by immigration—lower wages and lower employment rates—especially in areas that have a high and growing concentration of immigrants and in areas with a weak economy; (2) government social welfare expenditures in high immigrant areas are substantial and long-lasting due to the large proportion of less educated and older immigrants; (3) there is substantial displacement of native-born blacks, especially from private-sector job niches; and (4) immigrants strain educational budgets and may adversely affect students, particularly less educated native-born blacks and Latinos.

The preponderance of evidence that immigrants harm less educated workers is minimized by most immigrant supporters, as are the tax burden concerns we have documented. Most of these supporters continue to claim that immigrants primarily take jobs that no one else will accept, so that these immigrant-black worker conflicts are overstated. These supporters articulate the position taken by former Mexican president Vicente Fox, who declared in 2006 that Mexican immigrants perform the jobs that "not even blacks want to do."

Despite President Fox's assertion, in 2008, all of the top six occupational sectors for undocumented immigrants employed hundreds of thousands of blacks. That year, almost 15 percent of meat-processing workers were black, as were more than 18 percent of janitors. And although blacks on the whole are not involved in agriculture at anywhere near the rates of undocumented immigrants—a quarter of whom work in farming—about 14 percent of fruit and vegetable sorters are African American.[51]

The modest crackdown on undocumented immigrants has provided additional evidence that immigrants and black workers are in competition for even the worst jobs. In 2008, a U.S. Immigration and Customs Enforcement raid nabbed 300 undocumented workers at a Columbia Farms poultry-processing plant. In response, another poultry company, House of Raeford Farms, quietly began replacing immigrants with native-born labor at all its plants. Less than a year later, House of Raeford's flagship production line in Raeford, North Carolina, had been transformed, going from more than 80 percent Latino to 70 percent African American.[52]

Weighing all these aspects, we believe the evidence strongly suggests some recommendations concerning the *distribution* of immigrants. A disproportionate increase in immigration of any educational category is likely to adversely impact on others in the same category. One way to moderate these adverse effects from our current disproportionately large supply of less educated workers is to move to a *proportional* scheme: new immigrants should be distributed among the various educational levels proportionate to their distribution in the native population. If one-third of the native labor force has four-year degrees, so should new immigrants.

We sympathize with those who believe that immigrant families can benefit from forming political ties to others, particularly labor unions and African American organizations. A united movement is more likely to shape public policy in the interest of working people, including raising the minimum wage and implementing union-friendly policies, better funding of educational institutions to reduce dropout rates, and "second chance" strategies that focus on adult education, job training, and prisoner reentry.[53] We believe, however, that the serious schisms that separate these groups would be much easier to surmount if the stream of low-wage immigrant labor is reduced substantially.

The case for moving to this more balanced immigration policy is strengthened by evidence of the substantial tax burden caused by less educated immigrants and their families. These higher social costs put a strain on state and local budgets that invariably adversely affect native-born workers either through higher taxes or a lowered quantity and quality of government services. This policy shift would reflect moving to a system similar to that of Canada, where points are awarded based in part on the educational attainment and labor market skills of the applicant.

The Comprehensive Reform Act of 2007 contained key provisions we endorse. It would have ended current faamily reunification policies that strain U.S. safety net programs and increase tax burdens. Under version S. 1639, only the spouse and children of a new citizen would be made eligible for green cards.

S. 1639 also would have eliminated the employer-sponsored component of the immigration system and replaced it with a point-based "merit" system. Points would be awarded for a combination of education, job skills, family connections, and English proficiency. Sponsorship of a U.S. employer would not be required, although additional points would be awarded if a U.S. job offer was available. The labor certification process would also be eliminated. Several family-based immigration categories would also be folded into the point system.

The bill contained within it the entirety of the DREAM Act, a bill that has been introduced unsuccessfully several times in the House and Senate by liberal Democrats. It provides a path to citizenship for illegal immigrants brought into the country as minors who either go to college or serve in the U.S. military. The DREAM Act would require the youth to (1) have entered the country before the age of sixteen; (2) graduate from high school or obtain a GED; (3) have no criminal record; and (4) at have least five years of continuous presence in the United States.

This Senate bill garnered significant Democratic support, including that of Harry Reid, Diane Feinstein, and the now deceased Ted Kennedy. Points-based systems are already used for admitting skilled immigrants in the United Kingdom, Australia, and Canada. The Canadian system has been effective in limiting the fiscal strains on provincial governments and the competition faced by Canadian-born workers.[54] Hopefully, a similar version could be enacted during the Obama administration.

10

Recasting Housing Subsidies

Being able to afford a safe, clean place to live has always been central to escaping poverty. President Franklin Roosevelt's famous description of hardship in America was of one-third of a nation "ill-fed, ill-housed, and ill-clothed." When a National Academy of Sciences panel came out with its definition of poverty, it viewed food, housing, and clothing as "essentials."[1] Homelessness is the most severe manifestation of what happens when people cannot obtain adequate housing. Many face other hardships, such as having to live in substandard or overcrowded conditions or in crime-ridden neighborhoods or having to spend so much on housing that they deprive themselves and their families of other essentials.

The housing crisis engulfing the country since 2007 has put the problem into sharp relief as many families have lost their homes to foreclosure. The scale of the displacement is enormous. By the end of 2009, more than 4 million families were subject to foreclosure or were more than ninety days late on their mortgage payments. The size of the debacle is so great that it has stimulated a worldwide economic crisis. For the first time, we are hearing loud, critical voices questioning whether low-income families should become homeowners—perhaps owning a home should not be viewed as critical to the American dream. Government policies aimed at helping low-income and middle-income families to buy homes have come under withering attacks.

Since the 1930s, the U.S. government and other governments have intervened extensively in the housing market with the goal of helping people find and afford adequate shelter. The federal government has provided tax subsidies to families buying homes. To help low-income families, the federal government has funded local housing authorities to build and manage public housing, as well as tax credits for building private-sector units that low-income families can afford and housing vouchers directly to families, enabling them to reduce their rental costs to 30 percent of their income.

Currently about 28 percent of renters with incomes low enough to qualify for government support are lucky enough to benefit from one of these housing programs. But many of these programs are ill conceived, wasteful, and inequitable. They often discourage work by low-income recipients, and obtaining assistance is too much like a lottery—some win a big subsidy while other equally deserving families receive nothing.

Before turning to analysis of government programs, however, let us examine the key patterns and trends in the nation's housing conditions. Most remarkable is the long-term increase in the quantity and quality of housing, even among low-income families. Today, low-income families in the United States live in units that average about 1,400 square feet; amazingly, these homes are about 40 percent bigger than the homes lived in by the average family in France, Germany, and the United Kingdom.[2] Moreover, since the 1950s the United States has witnessed large reductions in overcrowding, in units without full plumbing facilities, and in homes in dilapidated condition. Homeownership rates rose as well, from about 55 percent in 1950 to 66 percent in 2000. By 2007, about 40 percent of low-income families had become homeowners. Although the national homeownership rate rose further during the housing bubble, the figure fell back to about 66 percent as of 2009.

Alongside these marked improvements in housing have come worries over the affordability of adequate shelter. As of 2005, only 3 percent of renters lived in severely inadequate housing, but 45 percent had rent burdens that exceeded 30 percent of their incomes. A large share of the poorest families spent more than half of their incomes on housing: 54 percent among those with income less than 30 percent of the area median income; and 20 percent among those with incomes between 30 and 50 percent of the area median income.[3]

These figures would be worse if not for the government housing programs that limit what recipients pay to 30 percent of their incomes. But how well are these housing programs working for low-income families? Many recipients of housing assistance live in place-based subsidized housing, including public housing blocks, that have bad reputations and are often located in segregated, poor neighborhoods. Others are in private units built by contractors who received large tax credits in return for renting some of their units to low-income households. Beneficiaries of these below-market rentals may be happily living in a high-quality unit but at enormous cost per recipient. Moreover, nearly all the direct subsidies steer eligible families toward renting instead of buying their home. Such a policy might seem appropriate in the wake of the dramatic decline in house prices. On the other hand, millions of low-income families have accumulated a good deal of wealth through homeownership.

This chapter begins by considering current housing policies for low-income families and how they have evolved. In part, we look at housing programs in the context of broad income support strategies. We focus only on those programs that subsidize tenants or subsidize construction that will yield rents affordable to low-income families. We leave out of the discussion two very large government interventions linked to housing—the favorable tax treatment of owner-occupied housing primarily benefits better-off families; and mortgage policies aimed at providing credit to low-income home buyers. Next, we offer a critique of current policies and consider the key trade-offs in housing policies. We then turn to a set of new proposals that are particularly relevant in today's environment: a shift away from (1) place-based subsidized units to vouchers that can be used widely throughout urban areas; (2) private-sector subsidies for new construction of low and affordable income units; and (3) rent subsidies to subsidies for homeownership.

Housing Subsidies and Income Support

Some of the aid to poorer families is in the form of relatively unrestricted cash transfers, including welfare, EITC, child credit, and unemployment insurance. More often, aid is tied to specific categories of expenditures. Child care subsidies must be used for child care purposes, and food stamps must be spent on food. Similarly, for most policy makers, the favored way to help low-income families meet their housing needs is through targeted housing assistance.

Historically, housing-directed assistance has been dominated by *place-based* units produced, managed, or directed by government. From 1937 through 1974, nearly all government housing assistance came through public housing produced and operated by local housing authorities subsidized by the federal government. Later, the federal government provided subsidized units to households by establishing long-term contracts with private landlords as part of the Section 8 new construction/substantial rehabilitation program.[4] Under public housing and the privately contracted subsidized housing, the assistance is "place-based." Local housing authorities match recipient families with specific, subsidized units. The families benefit by paying less than the full rent but only in a restricted set of units; if the family moves, it loses its subsidy.

In 1974, starting with the Section 8 voucher program, government subsidies began a significant move away from place-based housing toward *tenant-based* assistance. The subsidies come in the form of vouchers that allow households to select rental units from the broad housing market so long as the units are deemed in safe and sanitary condition at the time of leasing and the lease contract was fair. Families with incomes below 50 percent of the area median are eligible; 75 percent of the vouchers must be given to families with income below 30 percent of the area median. By 1983, the government stopped authorizing new public housing construction and Section 8 private construction; instead, it directed most new housing subsidies toward vouchers.

Still, housing assistance has evolved in this direction far more slowly than did food assistance. Through the late 1960s, the government provided food assistance in the form of specific commodities. By the mid-1970s, the dominant form of food assistance became food stamps, which allow people to make their own food choices. In housing, most assistance remains restricted to units owned or directed by government entities. As of 2007, about 1 million households lived in public housing units, 1.3 million received place-based assistance in private subsidized units, and 1.5 million live in privately developed housing funded through tax credits. By contrast, only 2 million households receive tenant-based assistance. Moreover, most new federal housing aid since 1990 has come in the form of place-based assistance.[5]

There are several reasons for the slow phase-out of place-based assistance. One is simply that housing units are durable. Public and private housing that is already built provides available units that can house low-income families, especially because federal funds pay for their operating and modernization costs. Second, various Section 8 projects were in the pipeline when the program terminated and were built and remain as subsidized units. Third, although the federal government has been supporting the effort to have local housing agencies demolish the worst public housing units, it has also provided funds to build some alternate projects. Fourth, the Low-Income Housing Tax Credit (LIHTC), established by Congress in 1986 and extended in 1993, has led to the construction of more than 700,000 subsidized units. In fact, from 1986 to 2003, 28 percent of all multifamily housing built in the United States received tax credits from the LIHTC program. Moreover, the LIHTC is connected to a broader network of programs that provide support for construction of housing units geared toward low-income households. Among these are the Community Development Block Grants (CDBGs) and the HOME investment partnership grants to states.[6]

Housing programs for low-income families resemble some aspects and depart from other aspects of cash and food assistance programs. As in other programs, the subsidies embedded in housing programs are income-related.

For housing vouchers, this maximum is the fair market rent (FMR), or the expected rent required to lease a safe and clean unit in adequate condition. This FMR is set at the 40th percentile of the rent distribution in the local area. The maximum benefit is available only to those with no countable income.

As income increases, the net benefit to recipients begins phasing out at about a 30 percent rate. For example, consider a family that qualifies for a housing voucher for a two-bedroom unit in an area where the FMR is $1,000 per month. If the family's income is $1,400 per month, the family would pay about $420 per month (30 percent of $1,400). The family's net benefit would equal $580 per month.

This 30 percent phase-out rate applies to public housing and place-based Section 8 units as well. It reflects a widely accepted affordability criterion, namely, that families should not have to pay more than 30 percent of their income for shelter.

As with other benefit programs, the phase-out rate acts like a tax rate. Each added $100 of income that the family earns raises their housing cost by $30. When combined with other tax rates on income and benefit reductions linked to other phase-outs, families can face serious disincentives to increase earnings or at least to increase reported earnings. For example, families with subsidized housing who receive food stamps keep less than 40 percent of their added earnings; each $100 of added earnings means a rent increase of $30, a decline in food stamps worth $24, payroll taxes of about $7, and other possible phase-outs related to child care and health care. The evidence suggests that the housing disincentives matter—that housing subsidy recipients lower their earnings in response to the high work disincentives and to the reduced urgency of income when the government is subsidizing rents.[7] The estimated impacts vary, but recent results from a quasi-experimental design indicate that households lower their earnings by about 10 percent. As a result, the cost of helping a family obtain better housing is not simply what the taxpayer has to spend on the benefits but the induced impact of lost earnings on the part of the recipients.[8]

Several differences between housing assistance and other income support programs are worth noting. In many programs, such as food stamps and Supplementary Security Income (SSI), the benefits are an entitlement; every eligible family that applies can receive benefits according to the program's formula for determining benefits. If the number of eligibles claiming benefits increases, Congress increases the money available for the program. By contrast, similar to child care subsidies, housing assistance programs do not cover most eligible households because funding is fixed at a level unlinked to demand and eligibility. As a result, housing programs have long waiting lists that can persist for years.

A second distinction is that the benefits in housing programs vary widely. Unlike food stamp and SSI levels that are constant across the country, housing programs provide benefits that differ dramatically across metropolitan areas (at least in money terms). A family qualifying for a two-bedroom unit will have access to a rent voucher worth $1,758 in San Francisco and $746 in Memphis.

Third, there are a number of reasons why subsidized housing in place-based units may have less value to tenants than the taxpayer cost of providing them. The land might have substantial market value for commercial or upper-income residential uses but not for lower-income tenants. This is a real cost to government when it forgoes selling the land for other uses to sustain public housing. In addition, tenants might place a lower value on the unit than comparable Section 8 housing because of the additional government regulations placed on tenants, including the various ways in which they can be evicted. There also might be a mismatch between the apartment size available and the family's needs. Finally, there may be negative neighborhood effects associated with living in public housing—for example, the bias employers may have in hiring or its weaker networking value.

Table 10.1 compares the economic cost and value of the tenant-based Section 8 housing unit previously discussed with a place-based public housing unit of equal economic cost. While they both cost $1,000, the value of place-based housing to the tenant is only $650. Its value is still above its rental cost to tenants of $420 [(0.3)$1,400]. Because there are net benefits, there would still be substantial demand for these public housing units. However, public housing would not be a very cost-efficient use of government funds. Net benefits ($230) to tenants are just 40 percent of the net costs ($580) to government. By contrast, rents in Section 8 housing are based on fair-market value so that tenants obtain net benefits equal to the net costs to government. This numerical example is consistent with one well-cited estimate that suggests that the efficiency of public housing expenditures is about 37 percent.[9]

LIHTC subsidizes the development costs of private housing through tax credits awarded mainly by state authorities in a competitive process. The federal government allocates the credits based on a formula, and then state governmental units select from among applications by developers. In return for the tax credits, developers agree to lease some units to low-income families and to charge them below-market rents. Developers typically sell the tax

TABLE 10.1
Cost and Value of Rental Units

Line		Tenant-Based Section 8	Place-Based Public Housing
1	Economic cost	$1,000	$1,000
2	Economic value to tenant	1,000	650
3	Rent paid by tenant	420	420
4	Net benefit to tenant = line 2 – line 3	580	230
5	Net cost to government = line 1 – line 3	580	580
6	Efficiency = (line 4)/(line 5)	1.00	0.40

credits to investors, thereby reimbursing them for a large share of the development costs. For the costs of units that developers reserve for low-income families, they earn annual credits for ten years equal to 9 percent of construction costs.

The maximum income for tenants qualifying for LIHTC-subsidized units equals 60 percent of the area median income. Applicants who take advantage of the program need not interact with the government, since the owners of the subsidized dwellings select qualified tenants and measure income. Rents are fixed at 30 percent of the area eligible income (60 percent of the median), or 18 percent of median income. In 2009, the median income of a St. Louis four-person family was $56,833. As a result, monthly rent was fixed at $1,018, and all four-person families with monthly incomes up to $3,395 qualify.

For families with monthly incomes below $3,395, their fixed rent payment will be more than 30 percent of their income. For example, for families with monthly incomes of $2,036, the fixed rent represents 50 percent of their income. As a result, this program best serves near-poor rather than poor households. Still, the approach has the advantage of not penalizing work, since rents do not rise with increased income.

Housing subsidies can potentially generate a broad range of external benefits beyond the shelter provided to beneficiaries.[10] By increasing the housing quality available to low-income recipients, subsidies may also provide nonhousing benefits. For example, it may increase residential stability, which improves overall family welfare, or it may allow families to move to better neighborhoods with lower crime rates and improved school options. As a result of these outcomes, housing subsidies might lead to increased school achievement among children.

Researchers have attempted to quantify these benefits. For example, the Moving to Opportunity (MTO) demonstration project examined how vouchers might affect recipients of public or private placed-based housing assistance. The experiment, which took place in Baltimore, Boston, Chicago, Los Angeles, and New York, randomly assigned participating families into three groups: (1) families receiving only place-based subsidies; (2) families offered standard Section 8 housing vouchers that they could use to move anywhere; and (3) families offered conditional vouchers with counseling but available only to those that move to areas with poverty rates below 10 percent.[11]

At the start of the demonstration, all eligible families who applied for the program (about 4,600) were living in subsidized housing in areas of the cities with poverty rates of 40 percent or higher. More than 90 percent of these families were Hispanic or African American, and about 92 percent were headed by females. Nearly three-quarters were randomly assigned to receive a voucher offer; the others served as the control group. More than 60 percent with the standard Section 8 voucher and nearly 50 percent of those offered the conditional voucher found a new place to rent and moved. The evaluators collected data on how well each of the groups was doing about four to seven years after the voucher offers. The results provide compelling evidence about how well vouchers or conditional vouchers perform relative to place-based subsidies.[12]

The first question is: Did conditional vouchers help beneficiaries to end up in better neighborhoods? The answer is a clear yes. Of those not offered a voucher, nearly half (48 percent) were still living in high-poverty areas (40 percent or higher) four to seven years after the demonstration began. In contrast, the figure was only about 30 to 32 percent for those offered vouchers. Over the full four- to seven-year period, families that used vouchers were 35 to 47 percent less likely to live in high-poverty areas than the control group. Both groups of voucher recipients were more likely to feel safe in their current neighborhood, less likely to have a household member victimized by crime, and less likely to have litter or abandoned buildings in the neighborhood.

A second question is: To what extent did conditioning the voucher on moves to nonpoor neighborhoods generate better family outcomes? Here, the answer is mixed. For a large number of health outcomes, vouchers exerted no discernible effects. However, psychological distress and anxiety among twelve- to nineteen-year-old girls did decline sharply among those offered vouchers. Girls from families offered conditional vouchers were less likely to smoke than girls in other groups. On the other hand, vouchers were associated with higher smoking and worse behavioral and delinquency problems among twelve- to nineteen-year-old males. Although vouchers did apparently lead to enrollment in better schools, gains in educational and test score outcomes were not statistically significant in nearly all cases. One might have expected or hoped that living in a less poor neighborhood and/or a location chosen by the recipients would lead to improved employment and earnings, but in fact, levels of job holding and earnings did not improve at all.[13]

A third question is: Did families that were offered the standard voucher fare better or worse than families offered the conditional vouchers plus training? In general, the conditional vouchers yield somewhat better outcomes than the standard vouchers. However, the conditional vouchers required additional services and led to fewer people finding apartments. And, if all vouchers were conditional on moving to low-poverty areas, many recipients would have even more trouble locating the limited supply of moderate-cost housing. Fortunately, standard vouchers worked reasonably well and yielded markedly better housing outcomes than those limited to place-based housing. Though not emphasized in the evaluation of Moving to Opportunity, the demonstration offers considerable support for continuing the shift from place-based programs to vouchers.

Key Flaws in the Nation's Rental Housing Programs

Direct subsidy programs for low-income families are already almost entirely focused on rental housing. Unfortunately, these programs are subject to serious structural flaws. Before expanding these programs, it is important to assess and remedy their shortcomings

Place-Based versus Tenant-Based Subsidies

One problem already cited is the inefficiency of place-based subsidies, including not only public housing but also other construction-based programs such as the LIHTC. Despite the consensus that vouchers generally work better than place-based subsidies, spending on place-based subsidies accounts for about 70 percent of all housing subsidized by the federal government and nearly 60 percent of the spending. Outlays in 2008 on public housing ($7.5 billion), on Section 8 place-based subsidies ($8.7 billion), and on the LIHTC (about $5.4 billion) still exceed the $15.7 billion spent on vouchers.[14] Moreover, these figures understate the resources put toward place-based subsidies, since they do not account for the forgone income that housing authorities could earn by using public housing (or the land it occupies) for other purposes. These programs are inefficient in that their subsidy cost per recipient is higher and their quality is no better and often worse than voucher-based programs. At least in the cities involved in the MTO demonstration mentioned earlier, residents subsidized through place-based programs live in more racially segregated and lower-income neighborhoods than families that started out in poor neighborhoods but were offered standard vouchers. Nationally, the share of subsidized dwellings in high-poverty neighborhoods was 54 percent for public housing, 22 percent for privately subsidized dwellings, and 15 percent for voucher recipients.

In 1996, Henry Cisneros, secretary of the Department of Housing and Urban Development (HUD), explored the idea of "vouchering out" all tenants in public housing. Current tenants would receive a voucher that they could use to pay the full rent in a public housing dwelling or to lease an alternative unit. Housing authorities could use the units to rent to the open market or to sell the properties. Unfortunately, not only did this proposal fail to materialize but also new expenditures have since gone mainly toward place-based subsidies. Moreover, the political consensus has shifted back to a construction-oriented approach. In 2002, the congressionally mandated Bipartisan Millennial Housing Commission issued its final report, endorsing both the preservation of existing subsidized projects and the construction of many more projects.

The inefficiency of production subsidies extends to the LIHTC program. It is popular politically, partly because credits generally support new construction projects under the approval of local planning processes. Still, the program is less efficient than vouchers. By some estimates, a substantial share of the LIHTC subsidy flows to the suppliers of housing under the program. Moreover, some of the added low-income housing stimulated by the credit crowds out housing that would have been built in the absence of the subsidy. Given the combination of a crowd-out effect and the substantial subsidy linked to LIHTC housing, some researchers estimate a long-term cost of $100,000 per added subsidized unit.[15]

A substantial portion of government subsidies to LIHTC housing does not reach tenants because of the profits developers obtain. Consider a development with a construction cost of $90,000 per unit and a land cost of $10,000 per unit. If all the units were available for rent only, the developer would gain credits worth about $60,000 per unit. Financing the remaining $40,000, the monthly interest costs would be $233 per month. If taxes, insurance, maintenance, and utilities added another $350, the total monthly costs would be $583. We have seen that in St. Louis, the developer could charge $1,018 per month, thus earning more than $400 per month in profits. Moreover, owners of LIHTC units often receive additional subsidies through community block grants. This example indicates why the LIHTC program is so popular with developers that they are willing to spend a good deal of effort qualifying for the scarce tax credits. It also indicates why developers are in a long queue for the credits.[16]

Despite these problems, supply-side housing subsidies might be worthwhile if they markedly increase the supply of dwellings, thereby lowering rents for the market as a whole. The evidence suggests that they actually displace other dwellings. For every two units added by supply-side programs, 1 to 1.3 unsubsidized units do not get built or rehabilitated.[17] Still, supply-side programs might generate some increases in the stock of housing, especially in areas where prices are high and regulations and other factors are constraining supplies. But the LIHTC program does not allocate funds on the basis of their supply impact. In addition, in many areas, demand-side subsidies would stimulate supplies as well.

Advocates of expanding "low-income" housing seem to disregard the high costs of place-based subsidies, their inevitable inequities and inefficiencies, and the locking-in effect that results from requiring subsidized families to take a specific dwelling or lose their subsidy. Instead, they apparently are most concerned with remaking neighborhoods, moving toward "mixed-income" developments, and reducing the concentration of minorities and the poor. But even on this count, place-based measures generally fall short, including new LIHTC projects.

Inequities in the Distribution of Housing Subsidies

A fundamental problem with all the subsidy programs is their unfair distribution. Equity in part means that equals are treated equally. In the housing subsidy world, families with the same incomes and family size can receive vastly different amounts, and poorer families often obtain less assistance than better-off families. The differentials are often stunningly high. Consider two families in San Francisco with incomes sufficiently low (say, $1,000 per month) that they qualify for a voucher linked to the ability to rent a two-bedroom unit.[18] The payment standard for the voucher is set at the fair market rent, designated as the 40th percentile of area rents, or $1,658 in 2009. Because vouchers are scarce, consider an example in which only one of the two families receives a Section 8 voucher. The lucky recipients could rent a unit at $1,658 but pay only $300 per month, for a net subsidy of $1,358. This subsidy would more than double the recipient's implicit monthly income from $1,000 to $2,358. The unlucky family would receive no subsidy at all. Thus, housing subsidy programs increase inequality within the low-income population.

The average gap between recipients and nonrecipients is much smaller in the average community than in San Francisco. Still, with an average FMR of about $1,000 per month, the winning family would see a 70 percent increase in income with the subsidy and a 70 percent advantage over families not receiving housing subsidies.

The magnitude of the inequity is enormous. Of the 9.7 million renter families with children and with incomes at or below 30 percent of the area median income, only 3.3 million receive either a voucher or assistance through public housing or place-based Section 8 housing.[19] Other low-income families live in dwellings subsidized through tax credits and other government grants (mostly the LIHTC), but almost all of these families have incomes between 30 and 50 of the area median income, and the size of the rent savings is unclear.

Providing high housing subsidies but only to a minority of low-income families came about because it has never been feasible to build sufficient units to meet the demand by all eligible low-income families. Moreover, because place-based subsidies provide access to specific dwelling units, the benefits vary greatly, depending on the quality, size, and condition of the unit. As housing policies shift away from place-based subsidies toward vouchers, offering the same subsidies to all families with the same income becomes feasible. However, the barriers to making this shift are significant. First, place-based subsidies remain widespread, and the transition toward vouchers has been slow; a faster phase-out of place-based subsidies would have to take place. Second, to provide the same access to housing subsidies to all low-income families would involve a tripling of the housing budget, a cut in the size of the subsidies per family, or some combination of the two.

The enormous variations in subsidy levels by geographic area constitute another inequity that can be quite wasteful as well. Compare two families in cities with differing housing markets but with $1,000 per month of income and with vouchers based on rents for a three-bedroom unit. For a family in Pittsburgh, for example, the voucher is worth $881 per month less 30 percent of income. For the comparable family living in San Diego, the voucher is worth $2,067 minus 30 percent of income. Thus, the subsidies for the two families with the same incomes are $581 and $1,767, a threefold difference.

In one sense, the large gaps reflect differences in housing costs between the two areas. Differences in rental levels are also linked to the relative attractiveness, the composition of local rental markets, and/or differences in incomes between the two areas. In 2008, San Diego's median family income was over $76,000, more than 50 percent higher than Pittsburgh's median of about $49,000. Assuming families in San Diego use some of their income advantage to buy more housing than in Pittsburgh, higher average San Diego rents reflect higher living standards, not just higher costs. By compensating for these area differences, the federal government ends up supporting a much more favorable living standard for some subsidy holders than for others. The voucher program may also be wasteful by encouraging people to stay in high-cost areas, either because of the subsidy itself or because those on the waiting list hope they will eventually qualify for a very substantial benefit.

The Biases against Homeownership

The tax system is well known for encouraging homeownership over renting, especially among high-income taxpayers. Two examples are allowing homeowners to deduct interest from mortgages and home equity loans, and providing favorable treatment of capital gains from selling one's home. In sharp contrast, nearly all subsidies to low-income families are only for rental housing. Except for a very small number using the homeownership voucher, low-income families gain access to a subsidy only if they choose to rent instead of buy.

A common question raised about this type of program is: Should low-income to lower-middle-income families be homeowners? Is it not too risky for low-income families to own homes? Can they maintain their homes properly? Because homes represent a high share of net worth and prices vary, many see purchasing a home as a particularly risky investment, one that low-income families can ill afford. But this approach fails to recognize the importance of homeownership as a hedge against increases in area housing costs, as indicated by rent levels.[20] Owning a home with a fixed-rate mortgages locks in the price of housing services for a long period, whereas prices for housing services in rental units can be highly variable. Although capital losses are possible, they are damaging only when one moves to another location where home prices are not correlated with prices in one's existing location.

Long time horizons lower the risks of homeownership relative to renting. Although many low-income households have short time horizons and move often, they tend to stay in the same geographic area. Moreover, the government should have a long time horizon and thereby favor locking in the cost of their subsidies. A second point is that households who apply a high share of their incomes to renting are particularly sensitive to rent risks, making homeownership a more attractive option for those with high rent-to-income ratios.

One interesting nonfinancial rationale for helping many low-income families own homes through this approach relates to marriage and family structure. As Kathryn Edin and Maria Kefalas point out, unmarried couples with children often choose to delay marriage until they can afford to live in their own home.[21] Helping these couples make their way to owning homes can stabilize the relationship and encourage marriage.[22]

In addition, other noneconomic benefits of homeownership have been found in various empirical studies.[23] Benefits have been detected for child outcomes, satisfaction, wealth accumulation, and political activity. Still, questions remain about whether the government can promote this goal at a reasonable cost and without creating additional financial problems in the future.

Finally, the focus on rentals generally disqualifies poor homeowners from receiving a housing subsidy. Given renter and owner families with the same incomes and housing expenses (say, at 40 percent of income), only the renter will generally be able to obtain a subsidy. Another problematic aspect of the exclusive emphasis on rentals is that some areas have very thin rental markets and very affordable markets for purchase. But can homeownership subsidies offer a substitute for rent vouchers? The next section shows why the answer is yes and how homeownership vouchers can play a positive role in the housing subsidy system.

Directions for Reform

What steps can be taken to make housing assistance more fair and less wasteful? Before embarking on reforms, we should not lose sight of the primary goal of helping low-income families afford decent housing. In addition, we must recognize that nearly all programs that transfer resources from taxpayers to low-income families involve costs beyond the taxes paid to finance the program. Finally, many reforms are likely to have unintended consequences, just as do the existing programs. While caution is appropriate, inaction will leave several problems unaddressed, including the inequities and inefficiencies that leave many families without housing assistance. We propose three reforms: (1) move quickly away from place-based programs toward tenant-based assistance; (2) gradually reduce differentials by geographic areas and some benefit levels as ways to widen coverage to all eligibles; and (3) create 1 million new homeownership vouchers to increase the demand for owner-occupied housing and to save the amount the government must spend per subsidized household.

Shifting Away from Place-Based Subsidies

Federal policy makers have too slowly shifted housing subsidies toward tenant-based subsidies for more than two decades. Most resources still go to place-based subsidies, including public housing. Most people, including local housing authorities, have long recognized the dysfunctional, dilapidated, and quite dangerous nature of some public housing projects.[24] Until recently, housing authorities could not demolish even distressed projects without replacing them with the same number of public housing units. They could not, for example, simply offer vouchers to families displaced by the demolition. After a 1998 law eliminated this restriction, housing authorities tore down some of the worst public housing projects and provided vouchers to some former residents, but built more public housing, albeit in smaller and more dispersed projects.[25]

A 2010 transaction between Citigroup and New York City highlighted the difficulty many politicians face when trying to shift away from place-based housing. At the time, there were twenty-one state-run public housing projects that had substantial maintenance problems making them too costly to be sustained given the gap between their economic costs to government and their value to tenants. These projects were bailed out by Citigroup's willingness to spend more than $200 million to purchase low-interest government bonds to provide the necessary maintenance. Citibank was motivated not by profits but by its ability to qualify for federal tax write-offs through the LIHTC program. Mayor Michael Bloomberg, generally a defender of market-based solutions to urban problems, strongly defended this politically driven transaction. "Let me just remind you: Other cities, you see on television, they're blowing up public housing. Here, we're investing in public housing," Bloomberg said.[26] Thus, problematic place-based public housing was sustained rather than shifting funding to more efficient and effective housing strategies.

It is time to recognize that continuing current policies will waste precious resources that could otherwise be used to help some of the millions of low-income families who face enormous housing costs and receive no subsidy at all. One sensible reform approach, advocated by Secretary Cisneros, would offer rent vouchers to current occupants of public housing units, avoid extending contracts with owners of privately subsidized units, and stop additional funding for the LIHTC and other new construction. The vouchers received by current public housing tenants could be used to remain in their existing units but also could be used elsewhere.

Local authorities operating public housing would have to compete for tenants and attract sufficient rents to pay for operating costs and capital improvements. Alternatively, they could sell the projects and use the annual proceeds from the sale to fund additional vouchers. Phasing out the LIHTC would ultimately save nearly $6 billion per year or more if related subsidies are included, enough to fund about 850,000 added vouchers per year. The number of households in LIHTC-subsidized units is higher than the number of vouchers that could be provided with the same funds. The benefits to voucher recipients are much higher than to tenants in LIHTC units because developers and others reap much of the gain.

Reducing Area Differentials and Helping More Families

Shifting away from place-based subsidies is only one way of expanding coverage of vouchers. Another obvious approach is to spend more money. However, expansions can also occur within existing budgets, when spending is adjusted annually for rising rental prices. One incremental reform would be to shift resources from existing voucher holders by freezing voucher levels and using the saved proceeds to increase the number of vouchers. Another possibility is lower voucher levels, especially in very high-rent areas, for newly issued vouchers that materialize when one family leaves the program and opens up a voucher slot for another. A third approach would be to expand the number of vouchers but set the maximum benefit well below the current fair market rent levels. Over time, the aim should be to provide sufficient vouchers to reach all eligible families.

However commendable, reducing vouchers will be painful. One can cite the reaction in New York City to changes in a rent subsidy program that affects the homeless. As more families had gone to homeless shelters, advocates were successful in obtaining funding so that some of these families could move into subsidized rental housing. This program was expensive, since families were required to pay only $50 monthly so that they, on average were receiving rent subsidies of about $1,000 monthly. Facing budgetary problems, New York City legislated a change whereby these families would have to pay 30 percent of their incomes during the first year and 40 percent the following year. "It's to build good behavior because ultimately they are going to have to assume the full burden of the rent," said new Homeless Department commissioner Seth Diamond, noting the new higher fees are similar to those paid by folks in federal housing. Predictably, homeless advocates and the NYC public advocate Bill de Blasio fear the plan will backfire, leaving more families stuck in homeless shelters.[27] Thus, there will be a political struggle to forestall its implementation as would be the case with any federal voucher reduction.

One way to mitigate the impact of lower voucher levels is to reduce the work disincentives built into the voucher program. The program could reduce the rate at which benefits phase out from 30 percent to, say, 20 percent. Another alternative would be to apply some of the tenant's 30 percent contribution toward an escrow account that would become available to tenants when they exit the program.[28]

Plan for Expanding Homeownership Vouchers

We should expand and add flexibility to the existing homeownership voucher program to take advantage of recent home price declines relative to rent levels. Between December 2007 and December 2008, the median price of houses sold declined by 15 percent while the Bureau of Labor Statistics shelter index (which measures rents or the rental value of an owner-occupied home) actually increased by 3 percent. As a result, homes in an increasing share of metropolitan areas have become affordable to low-income families receiving rent vouchers.

The plan is to expand dramatically homeowner vouchers that allow families to use their rent vouchers for the carrying costs of an existing home or a home purchase. We propose to add 1 million new homeownership vouchers (HVs) and to offer the homeowner option directly to holders of existing rent vouchers. The annual economic terms of the program would be identical to existing vouchers, though the new vouchers might include time limits. Currently, HVs are available as a local option, and some local housing authorities have used the approach and the wide discretion allowed over the terms of HV subsidies. The expanded program would operate at a much larger scale and involve some changes in federal guidelines.

Participants in the HV program would qualify for the FMR for their household size and would pay 30 percent of their income to offset the subsidy. As in the case of rent vouchers, families would contribute more toward housing costs as their incomes rose and would contribute less when their incomes fell. The program would follow current practice in requiring homeowners to complete a preassistance homeownership counseling program, which includes topics such as home maintenance, budgeting, credit counseling, and how to find a home.

A key question about the plan is whether vouchers at current subsidy levels would be enough to support the carrying costs of a home. Central to the issue of affordability is quality of the home. The average incomes of people who own homes at the 25th percentile are about twice as high as the incomes of renters at the FMR on which the rent vouchers are based. Thus a move from renting at the 40th percentile of rents to owning at the 25th percentile of home values would very likely improve living standards.

Let us now judge the financial viability of using current rental vouchers to purchase and maintain homes at the 25th percentile. After all, recent critiques of housing policy have highlighted the role of the federal government and financial institutions in lending to low-income households on terms that they could not afford.[29] We certainly do not want to reproduce situations in which low-income families will be burdened with housing costs that will lead to foreclosures.

Carrying costs include interest on a thirty-year mortgage that finances the *full* purchase price of the home, plus taxes and interest payments. Inclusion of principal would mean that the government is not only providing a subsidy for shelter each month but providing a capital transfer as well. Using data on FMR and home values in nearly all of the largest 108 counties,[30] we find that in more than 80 percent of the top 100 metro areas current vouchers would allow recipient families to pay the interest, tax, and insurance costs of a home purchase in their areas. In fact, either the government or the family would actually save money, since the FMR exceeds the homeownership costs by about $400 per month.

Consider the case of the provision of homeowner vouchers in a particular area—Allegheny County, Pennsylvania, which is part of the Pittsburgh metro area. The area's population in 2000 was 1.3 million. As of the first quarter of 2010, the price of a home at the 25th percentile stood at $76,664. The FMR for a three-bedroom apartment was $883 per month. If a current renter borrowed the full $76,664 at 5 percent interest for thirty years, the full monthly mortgage payment would be only about $411 per month, about $495 less per month than the FMR. Of course, taxes and insurance add to the monthly costs; the repayment of principal involves the accumulation of wealth. Not including principal by making it an "interest-only" loan but adding in taxes and insurance, the costs would amount to $486 per month, still nearly $420 less than the current FMR allowance, more than enough to pay for the maintenance of the property.

What about the riskiness of these loans and future foreclosures? In fact, lending through the HV program would be less risky than normal because the monthly voucher (an amount more than enough to pay the mortgage) would go to the bank independently of the family's income. Wouldn't the new policy repeat past mistakes in encouraging homeownership? Because the loans have relatively low risks, they could be provided at low interest rates. The low-income owners would not lose their home because of unemployment, since the income loss would lower the participant's contribution while the government maintained the subsidy payment. Of course, even where rents and home values are favorable for the homeowner voucher, not all families will be ready to assume the upkeep and other responsibilities.

From the federal government's perspective, the fixed-rate, long-term mortgage will lock in the bulk of housing costs at today's levels. Instead of continuing to finance rentals at the FMR, which is likely to rise over time, the federal government would be less subject to the risks of rising rents. These risks are real—the monthly principal and interest payment on a median-priced existing home rose by 79 percent between 1983 and 2007, much less than the rental equivalence increase of 140 percent.[31] Thus, savings could be substantial.

Government programs that subsidize homeownership of lower-income households are proving effective in a variety of contexts. The Michigan State Housing Development Authority runs active homeownership voucher programs that require training on mortgage loans, budgeting, basic home maintenance, and how to avoid foreclosure. Although the program has so far generated purchases by modest numbers of people, there have been no foreclosures.[32] Similar programs are operating successfully in many parts of the country, but only about 1,600 vouchers per year have been used for home purchases.

Collaborative programs that have some of the homeownership voucher components are promising as well. Today, many homes in less wealthy neighborhoods are in foreclosure. By contrast, of the more than 60,000 New York homes built or rehabilitated by the city in partnership with nonprofit groups, less than 1 percent have fallen into foreclosure. The Department of Housing Preservation and Development and nonprofit groups screened credit histories and required that applicants attend ownership classes, put cash down, and obtain prime-loan mortgages. "If you didn't have good credit, you were out—it was old-fashioned," recalled Zandra Brockman, fifty-two, who bought one of the Nehemiah homes in East New York for $68,500 in 1999. "They didn't want to sell you a home and have you lose everything."

In these New York neighborhoods, both liberal and some conservative analysts see a model for bringing low- and middle-income workers, many of them black and Latino, back into the housing market. "They have recapitulated the elements of healthy, working-class neighborhoods—it's back to the future," said Howard Husock, a vice president for social research at the conservative Manhattan Institute. "Learning to save and building up credit is a prelude to becoming a good homeowner."[33]

For the existing 2 million rent voucher recipients, encouraging the HV approach could expand demand for owner-occupied housing as well as modest administrative expenses. If 25 percent of voucher holders moved to the HV program and government also scaled up the program with funding for an additional 1 million households, the nation would have 1.5 million new buyers—enough to make a dent in home inventories.

What about the impact on the deficit? We estimate the annual costs of the 1 million homeownership voucher plan at about $2.5 to 2.75 billion per year. To offset this cost, we could reduce or eliminate the LIHTC. In today's housing market, where there is a glut of housing in many areas, spending funds on the LIHTC to expand the supply of housing does not make sense. Morever, the LIHTC is highly inefficient. Replacing the LIHTC with the homeownership voucher plan will more than offset the costs of the homeownership vouchers—it will reduce the deficit by about $5 billion per year by 2020.

Conclusions

Housing is a necessity, but millions of families face enormous financial burdens in obtaining housing. As of 2005, millions of low-income renters without housing assistance were paying more than 50 percent of their incomes on rent or living in severely substandard housing. These severe housing needs are taking place despite a federal budget for low-income housing assistance of about $45 billion per year and tens of billions of dollars in foreclosure relief. For the same expenditures, the government could reach 6 million families—including the current 3.3 to 3.5 million *plus* another 2.5 to 2.7 million— with vouchers costing about $7,500 per year.

Given the serious unmet needs facing many families, using housing assistance as efficiently as possible is an urgent priority. There are risks with any dramatic policy change that will be seized upon by those who fear moving away from the status quo: government housing authority administrators and workers whose positions are at risk; private developers who reap generous profits from LIHTC programs; and government officials who are sensitive to community groups that are more comfortable with the present set of policies. It is time, however, to realize that the housing problems faced by working families cannot be solved by tinkering at the margins with current programs. It is the policy transformation we propose that has a chance to succeed.

11

The Politics of Reform

Having formulated policies that are based on sound assessments is one thing; to legislate them is another. In the November 2010 election, the outcome created a divided government. In one sense, it makes the recommended centrist policies more likely. This is what happened after the Republican victory in 1994. After the Gingrich-led Congress overreached, centrist policies were enacted. One difference this time has been the increased partisanship among elected officials. Moderate Republicans and moderate Democrats have become a reduced share of Congress and are less likely to form an effective bridge for centrist legislation.

Partisan politics often lead legislators to emphasize issues that will help them with their political base rather than form bipartisan alliances around sound policy initiatives. To go against the political base may serve the nation but not necessarily political ambitions. This was the sacrifice Lyndon Johnson and other southern Democrats had to make when they supported civil rights legislation.

More often, politicians must determine their priorities. While sympathetic to a number of policies, they may fail to support some that conflict with their ability to pursue the ones that have a higher priority. This was certainly one of the reasons why, a decade ago, supporters of the Simplified Family Credit were unable to mount a successful legislative campaign. While there was broad bipartisan sympathy for this policy initiative, no legislator saw it as a priority. For Democrats, there was no group in the core constituency that lobbied for it; among Republicans, it was not something President George W. Bush sought when he took office.

Financing new initiatives can also be an obstacle, especially during a period of large deficits. In order to pass the Bush-era income tax policies, Congress had to label them "temporary" reductions to be rescinded in 2011. In December 2010, President Obama and Congress extended all of the tax cuts for another two years. Hopefully, when Congress revisits this issue, it will consider more comprehensive tax reforms. If this occurs, it is more likely that the recommendations made here could be considered as substitutes for a portion of the Bush tax cuts.

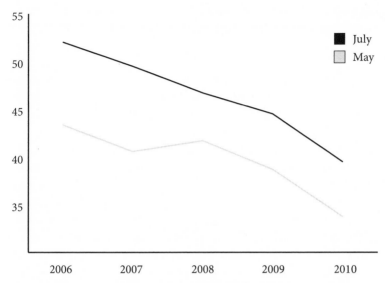

Figure 11.1. Seasonal employment ratio for school-aged workers, 2006–2010

Teenage Employment

This book has documented the dramatic drop in teen employment over the last decades. Between 1978 and 2007—two years of low national unemployment—teenage males saw their job-holding rate fall from 56 to 37 percent. The current economic slowdown has intensified these downward trends.

The grim situation teenagers currently face is reflected by changes in the ratio of employment rates of teenagers to those of young adults aged twenty to twenty-four. While the employment rate of young adults has deteriorated, the continued decline of this employment ratio (figure 11.1) indicates that it has deteriorated far more for teenagers. Looking at (presummer) May rates, the ratio has declined each year, from about 42 percent in 2006 to 34 percent in 2010. Even summer employment has given less of a stimulus to teen employment. The July employment ratio has declined continuously from 52 percent in 2006 to 39 percent in 2010.[1]

In June 2010, only about one in four sixteen- to nineteen-year-olds held jobs, down from 38 percent in June 2007. This collapse of teen employment is a symptom of the more general problem teenagers face. This book has highlighted the particularly devastating collapse of black teen employment rates and the fear that it will re-create the disconnectedness that led to such bleak outcomes during the 1980s. This concern has led many analysts to demand that the government do more for young black men, and we join them.

The lack of jobs not only harms earnings and work experience of young people but also can affect family formation. Conversely, rising female employment rates have been linked to the reduction of black teenage pregnancy rates. Employment seems to give these women the financial independence that enables them to withstand pressure to engage in risky sexual behavior.

This concern for improving teen employment within the black community should not lead us to ignore the plight of white teenagers. By some measures they have been at least as harmed by the employment collapse as their black counterparts. In June 2007, the black and white teen unemployment rates were 31.0 and 14.2 percent, respectively, yielding a ratio equal to 2.18. While both official rates increased, the black rate increased by a smaller percentage than the white rate so that by June 2010, the ratio fell to 1.72.

Unemployment rates can understate the employment difficulties faced, since economic slowdowns cause workers to withdraw from the labor force. Between June 2007 and June 2008, black labor force withdrawals were more substantial than white withdrawals. This could certainly have been anticipated as the employment situation initially deteriorated more for black than for white teens.

As the employment slowdown progressed, however, it was white youth who were disproportionately adversely affected. By June 2010, white withdrawals were so substantial that there would have been more than 1 million more white teens in the labor force if their June 2007 labor force participation rate had been maintained. Inclusion of these withdrawals almost doubled the number of individuals counted as being unemployed. Thus, white teens have also been substantially harmed, and aiding their employment efforts should be part of a comprehensive government initiative.

The reasons for the long-term decline in teen employment rates are not clear. As mentioned, increased schooling can explain only a fraction of this decline. Moreover, for many youth, employment is necessary to afford college so we cannot expect increased educational attainment to reduce the need for teen employment. A second explanation offered was the presence of less educated immigrants. This potential link provides one more reason why U.S. immigration policies should shift to more educated and occupationally skilled workers. Is it so far-fetched to anticipate a return to teenagers working for landscaping companies and cleanup staff at restaurants?

But before one blames the problem on immigration, the last few years have offered another explanation: older workers. The bursting of the housing bubble resulted in the loss of around $5 trillion in residential wealth. With plummeting home values and shrinking 401(k)s, many people lost a significant portion of their planned retirement funds. In the face of such a loss, many older workers chose to delay retirement and either continue working or go back to work because they could not afford to retire. These growing numbers also reflect the large number of so-called baby boomers who are aging. As a result, between 2007 and 2010, the size of the labor force declined by 6.3 percent for young workers, but it increased by 8.5 percent for workers fifty-five and older. As any trip to the mall indicates, these older workers have taken many of the jobs that otherwise would have been given to teenagers.[2]

Certainly there should be more government-funded summer employment opportunities for young people. However, to put a real dent in the disconnectedness requires more sustained programs that link education and employment. Earlier, a New York City program that partnered vocational high school students with community college occupational programs was discussed. It is an example of tech-prep programs that link high school education with community college training programs.

Career Academies (CAs) are another variation on this theme. They provide career and technical education in which a sector-specific "academy" is part of a broader high school. Academy students take courses in career development and supplement their classroom education with summer and year-round employment. CAs establish partnerships with local employers to provide work-based learning opportunities to improve student preparation for the workforce as well as college attendance. The programs have been shown to be the most effective intervention for at-risk youth. Evaluation of participants at nine urban high schools found a significant reduction in the number of high school dropouts among at-risk students compared with a control group. In addition, during an eight-year follow-up, participants realized an 11 percent increase in monthly earnings over the control group, or an additional $2,088 in earnings per year. Importantly, CA youth were just as likely to attend college as the control group.[3] Thus, government funding should be substantially increased in support of these endeavors.

Evidence from other countries reinforces the importance of career-focused options for young people. Countries in which high proportions of young people participate in apprenticeship and other work-based, occupational training have much lower youth unemployment rates than do countries that rely on school-based, academic systems with weak school-to-career transitions. Compare the recent experience in Germany and Switzerland, countries with extensive apprenticeship and work-based learning, with Belgium and France, where work-based occupational education is far less developed. In 2009, fifteen- to twenty-four-year-old men faced unemployment rates of more than 20 percent in Belgium and France but less than 12 percent in Germany and Switzerland.[4]

Less Educated Black Workers

This book has highlighted the employment problems faced by less educated black adult workers. The debilitating effects of negative stereotypes, discriminatory behavior, and structural impediments have been well documented. Recently, Algernon Austin looked at measures of good jobs by education and race, defining a good job as one that would pay at least $30,000 annually and would provide health coverage and a pension (figure 11.2). Among workers with four-year degrees, the share of black workers with good jobs (43.0 percent) was virtually the same as the share of white workers (47.0 percent). However, at each successively lower level of educational attainment, the *ratio* of the share of black workers to the share of white workers with good jobs declined dramatically. Among those with less than a high school degree, the share of black workers with good jobs (3.7 percent) was less than one-half the share of white workers with good jobs (8.9 percent).[5]

Why is it more difficult for less educated black workers to gain good jobs than for comparably educated white workers? Working-class white workers are somewhat more skilled than black workers as measured by the job requirements they meet. In addition, interviews during in the hiring process lead firms to perceive that white workers more than black applicants possess desirable soft skills. These results suggest that more emphasis should be placed on educational programs that develop the occupational skills necessary for attainment of good jobs and that firms should become much more sensitive to the unconscious biases in the interview process and sometimes shift to objective tests of the measurable skills they desire.

The book has also noted that the use of educational credentials or criminal records to make an *initial* hiring decision can result in less than optimal decisions. Studies found that black workers hired through affirmative action programs tended to have less formal credentials, like educational attainment or test scores, but were able to perform as well as their white counterparts. This suggests that while educational attainment and test scores are important, other characteristics of the applicant *may* compensate. Thus, particularly when employers are seeking a qualified but diverse workforce, they should not eliminate too quickly minority candidates who have somewhat lower formal credentials.

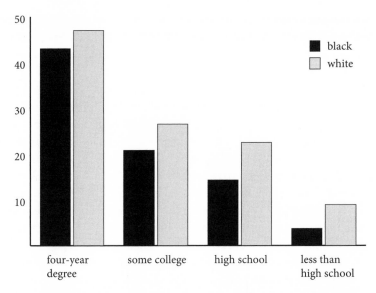

Figure 11.2. Share of workers with good jobs by race and by educational attainment, 2009

Similarly, evidence indicates that firms do best if they do not prejudge applicants with criminal records. Using "ban the box" policies," government agencies hired more qualified workers with criminal records and reduced screening costs by eliminating unnecessary background checks. As a *New York Times* editorial stated, "Boston, Chicago and San Francisco set a welcome example earlier in the decade when they abandoned counterproductive policies that often barred former offenders from municipal jobs, no matter how minor their crime nor how distant in the past. Connecticut, New Mexico and Minnesota have recently passed laws protecting the employment rights of former offenders. Other states should quickly follow."[6]

Unfortunately, "ban the box" procedures are never going to be a panacea for solving the reentry problem. They will not enhance the hiring of recently paroled felons who have weak or nonexistent work histories, low skill levels, and behavioral problems. For these young men, training programs run by agencies like STRIVE are the only way to improve their employability. It would be a shame if too much energy is spent on expanding the agencies and vendors that use "ban the box" procedures while neglecting the funding of programs that attempt to transform ex-convicts, giving them first the soft and then the hard skills necessary for sustainable employment. These programs should have *permanent* government funding that will enable them to plan long-term services for the most at-risk young men.

More generally, EEO officials should monitor more closely firms that employ workers with less than four-year degrees. When firms fall short of diverse hiring, the screening and evaluation process should be evaluated. As we have seen, the role of formal credentials, interviews, and job testing can influence the diversity of workers who reach the final stages of the hiring process. EEO officials should be more proactive in promoting best practices in the hiring process, especially among smaller firms. As "ban the box" policies have demonstrated, moving to best practices expands the hiring pool, enabling firms to hire a more productive as well as a more diverse workforce.

Given EEO staffing issues, it is unlikely that increased monitoring will have much of an impact on hiring practices. Instead, local EEO offices could organize through trade associations and/or human resource college programs and organizations informational seminars to help firms move to these more effective hiring procedures. EEO offices or other local agencies could also initiate newsletters that are electronically sent to individual employers and/or human resource personnel, providing the latest information on best practices hiring policies, reports from organizations seeking internships and/or employment for participants in their programs, and testimonials from employers citing the impact that changing hiring policies had on their workforce. We recommend government funding of a pilot program to assess the efficacy of these locally based seminars and newsletters.

Working-Class Women

Over the last twenty years, women have made substantial advancements, especially within professional labor markets. While glass ceilings have been broken and gender wage gaps have been reduced, glaring problems remain. Occupational segregation persists and remains linked to gender wage disparities: female-dominated occupations are lower paying than male-dominated occupations.

As noted in chapter 5, since the 1980s, occupational dissimilarity indices have declined modestly. This decline, however, has not been across all occupational groupings. While there has been some lessening of gender segregation among four-year college graduates, since the 1980s there has been virtually no change among those with less education (figure 11.3). In particular, in 1989, among women with less than a four-year college degree, almost 60 percent would have had to change jobs to bring about gender employment equity. There was a small movement toward equality in the 1990s, but more recently the dissimilarity index has moved back to where it was twenty years earlier.[7]

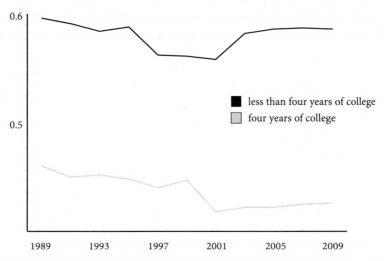

Figure 11.3. Trends in occupational segregation of men and women, aged 25–64 years old, 1989–2009

While personal inclinations and choice may play a role, workforce development policies and access to affordable child care can influence career decisions. Reviewing training programs administered through the Workforce Investment Act (WIA), a 2009 study found that "women who entered employment after receiving WIA services earned almost $1,500 less per quarter than their male counterparts and women who received services as dislocated workers earned over $2,000 less than their male counterparts—about 20 to 25 percent less."[8]

The study's coauthor Ariana Hegewisch suggested, "The intensity of service didn't seem to explain it, but there was a big difference in the type of training. Women typically got trained for jobs which are more likely to be done by women and men got trained for jobs that were more likely to be done by men."[9] Thus, training programs have reinforced occupational segregation, funneling more women into lower-paying occupations.

Government funding for child care has increased sharply over the years but is still not sufficient. While some advocacy groups place a priority on expanding targeted programs to the most needy, universal programs should be given priority. Efforts to have more states fund pre-K programs and full-day kindergartens with after-school programs are crucial for many working mothers. In particular, they need these services to seek employment in many male-dominated occupations and to enroll in educational and training programs to advance in the workplace.

For many mothers, government child care slots are often inaccessible or inconvenient or have substantial co-payments. As a result, tax benefits to pay these co-payments or private-sector nonsubsidized programs are important. Because the federal child and dependent care tax credit is nonrefundable, it has little value to poor and many near-poor working mothers. As a result, DC accounts can offer more federal tax benefits. The problem, however, is that except for a few states, child care expenses paid through DC accounts do not qualify for state CADC tax credits. Thus, we recommend that more states adjust their tax regulations so that these working mothers are not penalized.

Community Colleges

The pressure to minimize the occupational reach within urban community colleges cannot be overstated. Entrenched forces are unwilling to move away from the vision that four-year degrees should be the goal for all those who enroll at community colleges. Even when these community college administrators and faculty are forced to develop occupational programs, they demand that students still have an equal opportunity to seek four-year degrees as those students who enroll in academic courses geared to the transfer function.

As mentioned, my college, the City University of New York, was successful in securing approval for a new community college that offered twelve occupation programs. The administration, however, was so sensitive to critics that it required all members of the first group of founding faculty to have traditional academic credentials. This signaled that faculty with industry expertise would have secondary status. In addition, funding for job placement officers is still pending.

This de-emphasizing and downgrading of occupational skills has had a harmful impact on the manufacturing sector. During the current economic slowdown, domestic manufacturers increasingly have sought U.S. workers who can operate sophisticated computerized machinery, provide expert welding, follow complex blueprints, and demonstrate higher math proficiency than was previously required of the typical assembly-line worker. Makers of innovative products like advanced medical devices and wind turbines are among those growing quickly and looking to hire, and they too need higher skills. "It's not just what is being made," said MIT economist David Autor, "but to the degree that you make it at all, you make it differently."[10]

Unfortunately, laid-off blue-collar workers generally do not have the necessary skills. In a survey of 779 industrial companies, 32 percent reported "moderate to serious" skills shortages. Sixty-three percent of life science companies and 45 percent of energy firms cited such shortages. It is only training and occupational programs that can prepare workers with the necessary skills. "That's where you're seeing the pain point," said Baiju R. Shah, chief executive of BioEnterprise, a nonprofit group in Cleveland trying to turn the region into a center for medical innovation. "The people that are out of work just don't match the types of jobs that are here, open and growing."[11]

At the same time that occupational programs at community colleges should be expanded, there needs to be a tightening up of standards at the for-profit proprietary schools. The for-profit sector has mushroomed in the last decade. While overall postsecondary enrollment increased 31 percent from 1998 to 2008, the for-profits' enrollment grew by 225 percent. Although for-profit colleges enroll less than 10 percent of the nation's higher-education students, they receive almost a quarter of the federal aid. In 2008–9, for-profit colleges received $4.3 billion in Pell Grants and $19.6 billion in Stafford Loans.[12]

As already documented, minority students are disproportionately represented in the for-profit schools. Most striking, the for-profit University of Phoenix reported that in 2009, African Americans constituted 30 percent of all university enrollments, up from 23 percent in 2007. As a result, more than 130,000 African Americans are students at the University of Phoenix—6 percent of *all* African Americans enrolled in higher education nationwide.[13]

While many for-profits have improved, others still prey on desperate and ill-informed students. There is proposed legislation intended to protect students who enroll in the for-profit sector, with new regulations that assess for-profits based on students' debt levels and repayment records. To be fully eligible for federal aid, for-profit programs must either have at least 45 percent of their former students paying down the principal on their federal loans or graduates with debt-to-earnings ratios of less than 8 percent of their total income.[14] Schools that do not meet these standards would be subject to restrictions on their enrollment growth and/or federal financial aid available to their incoming students.

One viable option for improving occupational skills and for diversifying routes to rewarding careers is to expand the nation's apprenticeship program. Western European countries that are highly successful in retaining manufacturing sectors, often in advanced and specialized niches, have large-scale apprenticeship programs. These offer in-depth, largely work-based training along with some academic courses, so that workers gain mastery of an occupation within three to four years. Because apprentices earn money while learning-by-doing, they do not bear one of the largest costs of postsecondary education—the earnings forgone by attending school. And, while many postsecondary students work and go to school at the same time, most jobs they hold are unrelated to their course of study. In quality apprenticeships, the work and academics are intertwined.

Currently, the United States has about 480,000 apprentices in programs registered with the U.S. Department of Labor. More apprentices are learning advanced skills in unregistered programs. Although this is a high absolute number, it pales in comparison to the number of labor force entrants and college students. The evidence about the relative effectiveness of apprenticeship is minimal, but we do have some evidence that going through an apprenticeship yields gains that far outpace the returns to community college.[15] Jumpstarting an expansion of apprenticeship training would require increased federal funding beyond the current tiny budget of the Office of Apprenticeship of $20 million for the nation as a whole. In addition, we should provide subsidies to firms that are willing to expand registered apprenticeships.

Apprenticeship's appeal is especially great in today's cash-poor environment. Government costs—for marketing and oversight—are low, since employers pay most training costs. The skills learned are what the market demands, bolstering the worker's career prospects. Unlike full-time students, apprentices earn wages that increase as skills increase. And many apprentices earn credit toward a college degree, which still matters in many jobs workers-in-training hope to land.

Strengthening Partnerships

The sharp rise in nonmarital births, along with high divorce rates, continues to raise serious concerns about the future of children. The declining share of children growing up with both biological or adoptive parents not only has increased poverty and inequality but also has been linked to widening gaps in future opportunities. For example, recent data show clear intergenerational associations between growing up in a single-parent family and women having a nonmarital child by age twenty-one. Among women from one-parent families, 30 percent had a nonmarital birth by age twenty-one, and 40 percent by age twenty-five; in comparison, only 12 percent of women from families with two biological parents had a nonmarital birth by age twenty-five.[16]

Thanks to the Fragile Families and Child Wellbeing Study, we have learned a great deal about parents with nonmarital births. At the time of the birth, the glass is mostly full, since about half of unmarried parents are cohabiting and 31 percent are in close romantic relationships. Moreover, more than 70 percent of unmarried mothers and a striking 90 percent of unmarried fathers report their chances of marrying the other parent are fifty-fifty or better. On the other side of the ledger, even at the point of birth, one in ten fathers are already disengaged, with little or no contact. By the child's fifth birthday, only 16 percent of the unmarried parents had actually married. Moreover, fathers were disengaging. By the time the child reached age five, more than one-third of fathers had not visited the child within the previous month.

The dynamics of nonmarital childbearing and parenting suggest that the time of the birth was a "magic moment" when unmarried parents are thrilled with their newborn, have a close romantic relationship, and expect to marry.[17] If all goes well at this critical phase of life—with at least one parent finding a good job and the parents remaining in a close relationship—many will marry and raise their children in a good environment. Marriages often end in divorce, but parents are much more likely to remain together and do better in the job market if they marry than if they cohabit or maintain another type of relationship. If at the magic moment they stumble in the job market or in their relationship, many fathers will gradually disengage from the children, and the couple will face increasingly difficult financial problems. A natural policy implication is to concentrate services near the time of a nonmarital birth. So far, as chapter 7 reports, the results are at best mixed.

How best to help couples, especially parents, stay together in fulfilling relationships is unclear. Teaching people the skills for healthy relationships and healthy marriages makes sense and has achieved some successes for middle- and upper-class families, but the situation is less clear for low-income, cohabiting couples, especially in light of the weak early results from the Building Strong Families demonstration.

We support continued research into relationship skills/marriage education programs but favor strengthening the jobs and training components of services provided to couples. Family-strengthening activities can complement skill development because the high motivation of workers (especially men) to provide for their families spills over into diligence in learning job skills, seeking new jobs, and retaining existing jobs. Conversely, holding a good job reduces the tensions that arise when parents are frustrated with their lack of success in the labor market.

Finally, federal policies should enact targeted policies to reduce the substantial marriage penalty faced by working single mothers. We suggested a number of policies targeted to newly married couples. In particular, we recommended that the federal government institute income averaging for purposes of calculating EITC and child tax credits (or the Simplified Tax Credit if implemented). This would enable families to avoid a sharp drop in federal tax benefits when they marry, eliminating an important disincentive.

Federal Income Taxes

This book has highlighted the value of recasting federal child-related tax benefits for working families. Foremost was the desire to reduce the work and marriage disincentives faced by near-poor families. As family income grows, through either increased salaries or marriage, mean-tested benefits decline. Moreover, by combining benefits received into one credit, the tax system becomes simplified and more transparent, enabling more rational decisions to be made. This is why we support moving to a Simplified Family Credit or a similar program.

The main stumbling block is the budgetary cost of reducing the phase-out rate. Millions of near-poor families would receive additional tax savings. One place to obtain the necessary funds is rescinding a portion of the Bush-era tax cuts. During his presidential campaign, candidate Obama pledged that the tax rates would be returned to their higher Clinton-era levels only for families with taxable incomes above $250,000. Even if President Obama is successful at fulfilling this pledge, it will leave in place the tax benefits gained by upper-middle-class families during the Bush era. For those with taxable incomes between $137,000 and $250,000, tax rates would remain at least 3 percentage points lower than their Clinton-era rates.

President Obama's unwillingness to touch the income of these upper-middle-class families was front and center during the health care deliberations. These families benefit substantially from the current tax policies related to health care in two ways. First, the majority have company-paid health care benefits that are exempt from taxation. Second, funds they put into flexible spending health care accounts are also exempt from taxation. For example, suppose that a company pays $6,000 toward a family's health care policy and the family pays for other health care expenses through a $4,000 flexible spending account. If the family is in the 28 percent federal tax bracket, exempting this $10,000 reduces its federal income taxes by $2,800 (0.28 times $10,000), and any state income tax savings increase the benefits still further. In addition, many private-sector executives and some government professionals have much more generous health care benefits—the so-called Cadillac plans—and obtain even more tax savings.

By contrast, near-poor and lower-middle-class families are much less likely to have company-funded health care policies and the ability to use flexible health care accounts. Moreover, even if they did, they are in the 15 percent tax bracket, so the tax savings would be considerably less. For example, if they could shield $4,000 health expenditures from taxation, it would yield a federal income tax reduction of only $600 (0.15 × $4,000). Thus, similar to federal child care–related tax policies, there is a "middle-class penalty": families have too much income to benefit from health care programs for the poor and too little income to benefit as much as upper-middle-class families from federal health care tax policies.

A simple solution, one that presidential candidate John McCain proposed, would have been to make at least some if not *all* health care expenditures subject to taxation but to give families a flat 15 percent tax credit on these taxed outlays. In this case, lower-income families would obtain the same tax credit on these nonexempt expenditures as upper-middle-class families. In addition, the 15 percent credit would enable lower-income families to receive at least as much tax benefits as they were currently receiving from health care expenditures that were paid by their companies or through flexible spending accounts. Unfortunately, because there were some union members who would face higher taxes, pressure was put on President Obama, who then eviscerated legislation to tax the so-called Cadillac health plans.

Hopefully, when the Bush tax cuts are revisited, Democrats will stand firm on rejecting their extension to not only those with incomes over $250,000 but also to upper-middle-class families. In 2001, the Democratic tactic was to claim that the Bush tax cuts were fiscally irresponsible because they would threaten the ability to balance future federal budgets. This strategy was not politically successful, since the public was more impressed with the tax benefits they would obtain, not the potential future problems that might be caused.

Democrats should learn from this experience that any attempt to fight for the rescinding of tax breaks for wealthy (and upper-middle-class) families without offering something to working families will again be doomed. By putting the Simplified Tax Credit into the mix, President Obama can argue that, yes, the economy needs more consumer spending to boost a weak economy, but it would be more efficient and more equitable if tax cuts were given to working families, not better-off families who gained disproportionately from the Bush tax cuts. This strategy, moreover, would strengthen his position with working families, a group that is increasingly disconnected from the Democratic Party.

President Obama could also highlight the disparate tax benefits from many universal programs. Upper-middle-class families have more discretionary income and so are much more able to take advantage of tax savings than working-class families. Over the last two decades, health care, child care, and savings programs have enabled upper-middle-income families to shield substantially more income from federal taxation than middle-class and lower-middle-class families. In addition, for each dollar allocated to these qualifying programs, the tax savings are much greater to upper-middle-class families because they are in higher tax brackets than the vast majority of working families.

Immigration Policies

The politics of immigration reform are complicated. We have documented that the emphasis on less educated immigrants has had a harmful impact on the wages and employment of less educated native-born workers, especially young black men. Even the liberal Economic Policy Institute found this adverse consequence in high-immigrant states; focusing on the impact of unauthorized immigration, it concluded, "A larger inflow of unauthorized immigrant workers, who are easily exploited by employers, may put downward pressure on the wages of similar native workers in these states, a pressure that is largely masked in estimates at the national level."[18] Teenage employment may also be a victim as well. Though these less educated immigrants work, their low wages enable them to qualify for many of the means-tested programs, increasing state and federal expenditures. Generous family unification policies further tax social services, including educational services and social security payments. These concerns, however, appear to hold little sway with the forces aligned in support expanding immigration.

Historically, the main supporters of less educated immigrants were industrial firms that willingly exploited these workers. During the 1970s and 1980s, low-wage immigrants enabled some manufacturers to survive, providing complementary employment for native-born professionals. There are still examples of egregious behavior by some manufacturers. On August 25, 2008, 592 illegal workers were arrested at the Howard Industries electrical transformer plant in Laurel, Mississippi, in the biggest workplace immigration raid in U.S. history. In a 2011 settlement, the company paid fines of $2.5

million and admitted knowingly accepting false documentation even after federal authorities notified it of document irregularities. Howard still has pending a lawsuit filed by a group of black workers who documented their repeated unsuccessful attempts to secure employment at its Laurel plant. "We want Howard Industries to pay for the blatant discrimination it allowed to exist in this plant," the women's attorney, Lisa Ross, said Friday after the lawsuit was filed in U.S. District Court in Hattiesburg.[19]

Notwithstanding Howard Industries' behavior, the vast majority of manufacturers no longer have a significant stake in immigration. It is only meatpackers and other food-processing firms that rely on unskilled workers who may benefit from the lax enforcement of immigration laws.

During this earlier period, not surprisingly, industrial unions opposed immigration as a threat to their jobs and wages. Increasingly, this stance has conflicted with left liberals who embraced expansive immigration in the name of multiculturalism. As the union movement among professionals working for the government grew, and industrial unionism waned, it became impossible for the AFL-CIO to continue its anti-immigrant stance. Thus, one of the main barriers to expanded immigration fell.

Indeed, public-sector universities have become a major force in the movement to expand immigration. In many communities, ethnic studies and social science faculty members have been the primary spokespersons for weakening immigration laws and their enforcement. In addition, they often see immigration as the best way to generate a diverse faculty. Many Latino and African American faculty members did their undergraduate studies abroad, often also obtaining their doctorates outside the United States. Perhaps most important, a large number of public and private universities have a financial stake in recruiting foreign students for their undergraduate and graduate programs, many of whom are able to shift from student visas to permanent residency. For example, 57 percent of all postdoctoral fellows in the United States are here on temporary visas.[20]

The evidence of the crucial role of foreign students in the viability of schools was illustrated by the Times Square bomber, Faisal Shahzad. Coming from an elite Pakistani family, Shahzad was able to gain enrollment at Southeastern University, a private college in Washington, D.C., that recently lost its accreditation. After five semesters there, he transferred to Bridgeport University, another school that was having accreditation problems. At both colleges, foreign students made up a sizable share of the student populations.

Theoretically, foreign students like Shahzad must leave the United States within one year after completing their studies. Many, however, find their way into the H1-B visa program. This program grew in the 1990s when high-tech firms complained that they could not find qualified Americans with the necessary technical skills. However, the requirements for the program have been written so broadly that all kinds of firms seeking all kinds of workers can obtain H-1B slots. Again, the history of the Times Square bomber is illustrative. After graduating from Bridgeport with a less than sterling record, he was able to obtain an H1-B visa to work as an entry-level financial analyst in the accounting department at Elizabeth Arden. It is hard to believe he had any skill set that was in scarcity, particularly since his undergraduate degree was not in the financial field.

Similarly, a recent Israeli woman I know had just completed her four-year degree in sociology on a student visa. Through an immigration lawyer, she was able to obtain an H1-B visa to teach Hebrew in a Jewish day school. Given the tens of thousands of New Yorkers who graduated from Jewish day schools and who have spent substantial time in Israel, it is ludicrous to justify giving an H1-B visa to this school on the grounds that it would not be able to fulfill the position without it.

Employers have a clear financial interest in hiring workers under the H-1B visa program: having a captive workforce that can be underpaid. Shahzad complained that during the three years he worked at Elizabeth Arden, he did not receive one raise. It was only after marrying an American citizen that Shahzad was able to get a green card, freeing him to work for another firm. Similarly, the Jewish day school that is employing my friend benefits financially. She is only guaranteed twenty-nine hours weekly and thus does not qualify for the benefits available to full-time workers. Thus, universities and white-collar employers have replaced manufacturers as the main proponents of expanded immigration that circumvents national quotas. In a more comprehensive study of the H-1B visa program, Ron Hira found that "many employers use guest work visa programs simply for temporary labor mobility and reduced labor costs."[21]

In some ways, the generous interpretations that have allowed foreign students to enroll at U.S. colleges and work under H1-B visas have provided the balance that our recommendations seek: a movement away from legal immigration policies that unduly favor less educated immigrants. These students and workers shift immigration toward those with professional skills. The problem is that these backdoor mechanisms accomplish this objective in a much less efficient manner than if it was part of a direct immigration policy.

The current bill proposed by New York senator Chuck Schumer holds open the possibility of improving the situation. It proposes to limit family unification and to improve the educational background of new legal immigrants. However, as a result of opposition from Latino and left-liberal organizations, the bill deleted any immediate changes in family unification or educational requirements. It only mandates that these issues be studied by a commission that would eventually make recommendations.

Moreover, left-liberal and Latino support was gained only with the inclusion of the DREAM Act, which gives pathways to citizenship to children illegally brought into the United States before they were sixteen years old. The act allows these youths—estimated to number between 2 and 3 million—to become legal residents if they either enroll in college for two years or join the military. While there are strong humanitarian grounds for these allowances, they would put further financial burdens on community colleges.[22]

With the weak academic skills of many high school graduates, community colleges are already flooded with ill-prepared students. In 2010, about one-quarter of all entering students in the New York City community college system required remediation in all three areas: reading, writing, and math. Their numbers are about one-third greater than a decade ago. Most troubling, in "the past five years, a subset of students deemed 'triple low remedial'—with the most severe deficits in all three subjects—has doubled," reported Lisa Foderaro.

Her report highlighted a student who points to the risks of a "college for all" vision. As a freshman at LaGuardia, Angel Payero, eighteen, took the necessary assessment tests and discovered that he was deficient in reading, writing, and math. "Throughout high school, I was a good math student, and to find out that it was my lowest grade of all three was really surprising," said Mr. Payero, who graduated from the High School for Arts, Imagination and Inquiry. Yet Mr. Payero yearns for a career in psychology. "I feel like I can really understand people and where they come from," he said.[23]

Already, administrators are worried that the growing budget for remediation will shift resources away from well-prepared students. "It takes a lot of our time and energy and money to figure out what to do with all of these students who need remediation," said Alexandra W. Logue, the university's executive vice chancellor and provost. "We are doing some really good things, but it's time that we're not thinking about our other wonderful students who are very highly prepared. We need to focus on them, too."[24] As a result, there are likely significant unintended consequences that would result from passage of the DREAM Act in its present form. Minimally, there should be some offset in the ability of those with student visas to enroll in public colleges. Specifically, each public college should have firm limits on the total number of foreign students—either those on student visas or those who qualify under the DREAM Act—who can enroll annually.

Housing Policies

In addition to battering the U.S. economy, the collapse of home prices, the subprime debacle, and record foreclosures have created a new conventional wisdom that encouraging homeownership for relatively low-income families is a bad idea. It is certainly true that the U.S. tax treatment of homeownership lowers the effective price of owning a home, especially for middle-income and high-income families who itemize their returns. But only 35 percent of all tax returns involve itemized deductions. At the same time, of the federal government spending of more than $35 billion on housing assistance for the low-income population, nearly all goes toward rental assistance and not homeownership. In fact, whatever their housing cost burden, low-income families receive no direct subsidy for owning instead of renting.

What, then, is the source of the view that the federal government tried to pay low-income people to invest in buying a home? Despite the fact that low-income and even most middle-income families benefit little from tax or direct subsidies to homeownership, government entities have played a central role in sustaining the broader long-term mortgage market. Since 1934, the federal government has created and monitored several housing finance enterprises (GSEs), including the Federal Housing Authority, Fannie Mae, and Freddie Mac. Although these financing giants have smoothed the way for potential homeowners to borrow more than 80 percent of the price of the home for up to thirty years, they were not meant to embody a subsidy. Of course, after the fact, these government-sponsored entities have experienced massive losses when homeowners experienced dramatic drops in their home values and had more debt than the value of the home, but this unexpected capital loss to the lender is not the same as a direct subsidy. True, in promoting an ownership society, Presidents Clinton and Bush and the Congress encouraged banks and GSEs to increase the accessibility of mortgage credit to low-income families. Yet, the federal government has provided virtually no direct subsidies for low-income families to buy homes.

Today, advocates for low-income families are turning away from homeownership as a policy objective. Because many families (including low-income families) who borrowed on their own experienced a large, nearly unprecedented drop in home values and, in some cases, lost their homes to foreclosure, homeownership is increasingly viewed as an investment that is too risky for low-income families to pursue. In February 2010, Congressman Barney Frank argued, "We should be focused on affordable rental housing, not in pushing low income people into owning homes that they can't afford."[25]

From our perspective, many are misinformed about current federal subsidies and about the riskiness of renting versus owning. In addition, current analyses are backward-looking, fighting the last war, when government leaders and some policies did encourage home buying when home prices were extraordinarily high relative to rental properties.

As we noted in chapter 10, viewed properly, owning a home can be a hedge against the rising and variable costs of rental housing. By combining a cash down payment with a fixed-rate, long-term mortgage to buy a home, families essentially lock in the level of most monthly costs to stay in their dwelling. In contrast, people who rent have no control over their housing costs from one year to the next. As a result, rents generate far more variable housing costs. For low-income families, sudden rent increases associated with neighborhood improvements often lead to major economic distortions, such as rent controls or regulations that keep neighborhoods stagnant. Insurance against rapid rent increases is one way to deal with the problem,[26] but in the absence of such instruments, broad homeownership is the most viable way to insure that low-income families benefit from gentrification and other rent shocks. One further point is that in many towns, the rent market is quite thin relative to the market for owner-occupied dwellings.

This is not to excuse excesses in the mortgage market and government policies that led to unwise home purchases in 2003 through 2007. By unwise, we mean having families undertake monthly homeownership costs that were too high relative to rents on equivalent-quality housing and relative to income.

Still, past mistakes in excessively promoting homeownership in one economic context are no reason to discourage it under market conditions highly favorable to homeownership. In chapter 10, we presented a viable path to homeownership for many low-income families, one that takes advantage of today's low home prices. Under the plan, the government would create 1 million homeownership vouchers that low-income families could use to cover the monthly carrying costs of buying a home. Like the existing rent voucher program, participants would pay 30 percent of their income to offset the costs of the voucher. The homeownership voucher levels in each community would be set equal to current rent vouchers. At these levels, participants in well over 80 percent of communities would be able to cover the monthly interest, taxes, and insurance costs of buying a home at the 25th percentile of home values or lower. There would even be money left over that the government could recoup or put aside for maintenance and repairs. The cost of the plan—about $7 billion per year—could be paid for by zeroing out the Low Income Housing Tax Credit, an initiative aimed at expanding the supply of housing at a time when the main market problem is one of effective demand.

This plan is a winner on several counts. It would provide a welcome increase in the demand for owner-occupied housing. It would substantially reduce the waiting list for subsidized housing. It would target funds to low-income families with chronic affordability problems instead of scattering foreclosure relief funds to families at various income levels who may unwisely have taken second mortgages or committed themselves to monthly housing costs beyond their means. And it could be achieved by shifting funds from an inefficient supply-side program to a sensible and well-targeted demand-side initiative.

Strengthening our nation's housing assistance effort could go a long way toward reducing the material hardship of poor and near-poor families. We have long provided food assistance to assure families will avoid hunger and food insecurity. Expanding housing assistance will move the country closer to ensuring that virtually no families are ill-housed.

Summing Up

This book has detailed the legislative initiatives that can move working families forward. Liberals might argue that they do not go far enough in combating the race and gender inequities found in employment areas, that they do not support the higher educational aspirations that many working-class families have for their children, and that they shift focus away from helping poverty-stricken families. For far too long, however, the needs of struggling working families have been ignored, have not been a political priority, and have led many of them to conclude government policies do not serve their interests. For far too long, idealism has clouded liberal thinking, leading them to ignore the potential ineffectiveness and unintended consequences of the policies they recommend. A fear of blaming the victim, of holding individuals accountable for their behavior has paralyzed their ability to make sound policy choices. While these Third Way policy recommendations will not solve all the problems working families face, they can be part of the solution.

Hopefully, the Republican-led House of Representatives will not be held captive by Tea Party rhetoric and maintain its posture as the "party of no" in the hopes of regaining the presidency in 2012. In addition, the most liberal wing of the Democratic Party should be suitably chastened by its defeat to accept the centrist policies that can be legislated. Much of this will depend on the leadership provided by President Obama, who should learn from the Clinton experience. This book can provide a blueprint for his legislative efforts.

Notes

NOTES TO CHAPTER 1

1. Heidi Shierholz, "Job Seekers Still Face Intolerable Odds" (Economic Policy Institute press release, July 13, 2010).

2. Quoted in Jason DeParle, "Welfare Aid Isn't Growing as Economy Falls Off," *New York Times*, February 2, 2009, A1.

3. Editorial, "Food Stamps in Hard Times," *New York Times*, February 25, 2009, A26.

4. David Brooks, "The Long Voyage Home," *New York Times*, May 5, 2009, A27.

5. Thresholds are slightly higher for Alaska and Hawaii. U.S. Department of Health and Human Services, *The HHS Poverty Guidelines, 2007*, http://aspe.hhs.gov/poverty/07poverty.shtml.

6. For alternative poverty measures, see U.S. Census Bureau, *Poverty Measure Studies and Alternative Measures, 2007*, http://www.census.gov/hhes/www/povmeas/tables.html. For the impact of the shift from money income to disposable income, see U.S. Census Bureau, *Impact of Taxes and Transfers on Income and Poverty in the United States, 2005*, http://www.census.gov/prod/2007pubs/p60-232.pdf.

7. Heather Boushey et al., *Hardships in America* (Washington, DC: Economic Policy Institute, 2001), table 7.

8. U.S. Census Bureau, Current Population Survey, Table FINC-01, Selected Characteristics of Families by Total Money Income in 2007, http://pubdb3.census.gov/macro/032008/faminc/new01_000.htm

9. U.S. Census Bureau, Current Population Survey, Table FINC-01, Selected Characteristics of Families by Total Money Income in 2007, http://pubdb3.census.gov/macro/032008/faminc/new01_000.htm

10. Elaine Kamark and Will Marshall, *Mandate for Change* (Washington, DC: Progressive Policy Institute, 1988)..

11. Kathryn Edin and Laura Lein, *Making Ends Meet: How Single Mothers Survive Welfare and Low Wage Work* (New York: Russell Sage, 1997).

12. David Mills, "Sister Souljah's Call to Arms," *Washington Post*, May 13, 1992, B1.

13. Anthony Lewis, "Abroad at Home; Black and White," *New York Times*, June 18, 1992, A27.

14. Katha Pollitt, "About Race: Can We Talk?" *Nation*, July 7, 1997, 183.

15. Marianne Wright Edelman, "Protect Children from Unjust Policies," Children's Defense Fund letter published in *Washington Post*, November 3, 1995, http://econ161.berkeley.edu/Politics/edelman_open_letter.html.

16. Quoted in Judith Havermann, "Chief of HHS Objects to Governor's Proposal," *Washington Post*, February 29, 1996, A6.

17. Press release, Children's Defense Fund (August 22, 1996).

18. Hannah Matthews and Danielle Ewen, "Child Care Assistance in 2005; State Cuts Continue" (Center for Law and Social Policy, November 1, 2006).

19. According to William Darity and Samuel Myers (*The Underclass* [Hamden, CT: Garland, 1994], 50): "Groups like Planned Parenthood Federation explicitly advocate reduction in the number of children born out of wedlock via family planning measures, including abortion. Such measures, Planned Parenthood Federation spokespersons have argued, will be a crucial step in reducing the supply of welfare-eligible persons. ... [We] have referred to this outlook as the doctrine of *preemptive extermination of the unborn*, who are anticipated to become part of the permanent poverty population."

20. Arlene Geronimus and Sanders Korenman, "The Socioeconomic Consequences of Teen Childrearing Reconsidered," *Quarterly Journal of Economics* 107 (1992): 1187–1214. For a different evaluation of the data, see Saul Hoffman, "Teenage Childbearing Is Not So Bad after All . . . or Is It?" *Family Planning Perspectives* 30 (1998): 236–39.

21. For early criticism, see Christopher Jencks, "Introduction," in Edin and Lein, *Making Ends Meet.*

22. Scott Winship and Christopher Jencks, "Understanding Welfare Reform," *Harvard Magazine*, November–December 2004, 1–7. Of interest, in 2000 Jencks was still pessimistic about reform and, like other critics, emphasized the adverse consequences to the poorest single mothers and the limited economic benefits to many others. Christopher Jencks and Joseph Swingle, "Without a Net." *American Prospect* 11 (January 3, 2000): 37–41.

23. Robert Lerman and Caroline Ratcliffe, "Did Metropolitan Areas Absorb Welfare Recipients without Displacing Other Workers?" (Washington, DC: Urban Institute, 2000). For white never-married women the rate increased from 52 to 67 percent. Arloc Sherman, Shawn Fremstad, and Sharon Parrott, "Employment Rates for Single Mothers Fell Substantially during Recent Period of Labor Market Weakness," Center on Budget and Policy Priorities (June 22, 2004).

24. June O'Neill and M. Anne Hill ("Gaining Ground, Moving Up," Manhattan Institute Civic Report No. 35 [March 2003]) estimate that 44 percent of the employment gains were the result of welfare legislation, while less than 10 percent were the result of a stronger economy. Clinton's Council of Economic Advisors ("Economic Expansion, Welfare Reform, and the Decline in Caseloads: An Update" [Washington, DC: Executive Office of the President, 1999]) estimated that 35 percent of the change in caseloads was due to welfare reform, while only 9 percent was due to a stronger economy. For a full set of estimates, see Rebecca Blank, "Evaluating Welfare Reform in the United States," *Journal of Economic Literature* 90 (December 2002), table 6.

25. See Karen Christopher, "Welfare as We [Don't] Know It: A Review and Feminist Critique of Welfare Reform Research in the United States," *Feminist Economics* 10 (July 2004): 143–71; Avis Jones-DeWeever, Janice Peterson, and Xue Song, *Before and after Welfare Reform* (Washington, DC: Institute for Women's Policy Research, 2003); and Sharon Parrott and Arloc Sherman, "TANF at 10: Program Results Are More Mixed Than Often Understood," Center for Budget Policies and Priorities (August 17, 2006).

26. Randy Albelda and Ann Withorn, eds., *Lost Ground: Welfare Reform, Poverty, and Beyond* (Cambridge, MA: South End Press, 2002); Kenneth J. Neubeck and Noel A. Cazenave, *Welfare Racism: Playing the Race Card against America's Poor* (New York: Routledge, 2001); and Mimi Abramovitz, "A Triple Whammy for the Poor: The Combined Impact of

Welfare Reform, the Recession, and the World Trade Center Attack," National Association of Social Work, NYC Chapter, http://www.naswnyc.org/w21.html.

27. See Eduardo Bonilla-Silva, *Racism without Racists: Color-Blind Racism and the Persistence of Racial Inequality in the United States* (Lanham, MD: Rowman and Littlefield, 2006); and Eduardo Bonilla-Silva, *White Supremacy and Racism in the Post–Civil Rights Era* (Boulder, CO: Lynne Rienner, 2001).

28. See Robert Cherry, *Who Gets the Good Jobs? Combating Race and Gender Disparities* (New Brunswick, NJ: Rutgers University Press, 2001), chaps. 7 and 8. For the impact of class rank, see William Bowen and Derek Bok, *The Shape of the River: Long-Term Consequences of Considering Race in College and University Admissions* (Princeton, NJ: Princeton University Press, 1998); and Stacy Berg Dale and Alan Krueger, "Estimating the Payoff to Attending a More Selective College: An Application of Selection on Observable and Unobservables" (NBER Working Paper No. 7322, August 1999), 1–54.

29. Philip Moss and Chris Tilly, "How Labor-Market Tightness Affects Employer Attitudes and Actions toward Black Job Applicants: Evidence from Employer Surveys," in *Prosperity for All? The Economic Boom and African Americans*, ed. Robert Cherry and William Rodgers (New York: Russell Sage, 2000), 123–59.

30. Between 1955 and 1967, employment in durable goods industries increased by 74 percent in the South but by less than 5 percent in the Midwest. Robert Cherry, "Race and Gender in Radical Macroeconomic Models: The Case of the Social Structure of Accumulation Model." *Science and Society* 55 (1990): 60–78.

31. Joleen Kirschenman and Kathryn Neckerman, "'We'd Love to Hire Them, But . . . ': The Meaning of Race for Employers," in *The Urban Underclass*, ed. Christopher Jencks and Paul Peterson (Washington, DC: Brookings Institution, 1991), 202–32.

32. John Bound and Richard Freeman. "What Went Wrong? The Erosion of the Relative Earnings of Young Black Men during the 1980s," *Quarterly Journal of Economics* 107 (1992): 201–32. Bound and Freeman note that the decline among young white men was only 10 percentage points.

33. Becky Pettit and Bruce Weston, "Mass Imprisonment and the Life Course," *American Sociological Review* 69 (2004): 151–69.

34. R. Barri Flowers, *Domestic Crimes, Family Violence and Child Abuse* (Jefferson, NC: McFarland, 2000), table 3.1.

35. Among the teen mothers who were currently experiencing a severe level of domestic violence, 57 percent reported some form of sabotage of their employment and school efforts. In contrast, only 17 and 7 percent of those who experienced low levels of domestic violence or no violence, respectively, reported employment or educational sabotage. Jody Raphael and Richard Tolman, *Trapped by Poverty, Trapped by Abuse* (Chicago: Taylor Institute, 1997).

36. Joan Meier, "Domestic Violence, Character, and Social Change in the Welfare Reform Debate," *Law and Policy* 19 (April 1997): 223, 228. In *Dubious Conceptions* (Cambridge, MA: Harvard University Press, 1995), Kristin Luker dismisses the coercive behavior black teenage women experience when explaining their high birthrates and instead focuses on the broader systemic forces that constrain poor women: "The increase in the number of teenage and unwed mothers is an indirect measure of the toll that a bifurcating economy is taking on Americans, especially women of poor and minority backgrounds. It would be better to see early childbearing as a symptom, like infant mortality—not a cause

but a marker of events, an indicator of the extent to which many young people have been excluded from the American dream" (182).

37. For one left liberal who did support stronger enforcement, see Katha Pollitt, "Deadbeat Dads: A Modest Proposal," *Nation*, January 30, 1995.

38. Irwin Garfinkel, Theresa Heintze, and Chien-Chung Huang, "The Effects of Child Support Payments on Mothers' Income," *Poverty Research News* 5 (May–June 2001): 5–8; see also Center for Law and Social Policy, "Child Support Payments Benefit Children in Non-economic as Well as Economic Ways" (Research Fact Sheet, 2005).

39. For the initial reaction of Gates's defenders, see Lawrence Bobo, "What Do You Call a Black Man with a Ph.D?" *The Root*, July 21, 2009, http://www.theroot.com/views/what-do-you-call-black-man-phd; Charles Bow, "Welcome to the 'Club,'" *New York Times*, July 25, 2009; Maureen Dowd, "Bite Your Tongue," *New York Times*, July 25, 2009; and Stanley Fish, "Henry Louis Gates: Déjà vu All Over Again," *New York Times* blog, July 24, 2009. For one left liberal who rejected the view that the arrest was racially motivated, see Eric Alterman, "Class Not Race," *Nation*, August 17, 2009, http://www.thenation.com/article/class-not-race. For an article that claimed the race-motivated charge was a diversion from the real racism inflicted on black men, see Glenn Loury, "Obama, Gates, and the American Black Man," *New York Times*, July 25, 2009.

40. Pew Charitable Trusts, "Obama's Ratings Slide across the Board," Pew Foundation (July 30), http://www.pewtrusts.org/our_work_report_detail.aspx?id=54374.

41. Katha Pollitt, "The Politics of Personal Responsibility," *Nation*, August 21/28, 2000, 12.

42. Institute for Research on Poverty, "Expectations of Marriage among Unmarried Couples: New Evidence from Fragile Families Study," *Focus* 22 (Summer 2002): 13–17; Kathryn Edin, Paula England, and Kathryn Linnenberg, "Love and Distrust among Unmarried Parents" (paper presented at the National Poverty Center Conference on Marriage and Family Formation among Low-Income Couples, Washington, DC, September 4–5, 2003).

43. Rebekah Levine Coley and Lindsay Chase-Landsdale, "Fathers' Involvement with Their Children over Time," *Poverty Research News* 4 (March–April 2000): 12–15; and David Ellwood and Christopher Jencks, "The Uneven Spread of Single Parent Families," in *Social Inequality*, ed. Kathryn Neckerman (New York: Russell Sage, 2004), 3–78.

NOTES TO CHAPTER 2

1. Robert Cherry, "African Americans and the Social Benefits of Tight Labor Markets," *WorkingUSA* 5 (Fall 2001): 106–18.

2. Barry Bluestone and Mary Stevenson, "Racial and Ethnic Gaps in Male Earnings in a Booming Urban Economy," *Eastern Economic Journal* 25 (Spring 1999): 209–38.

3. W. Norton Grubb and Marvin Lazerson, *The Educational Gospel* (Cambridge, MA: Harvard University Press, 2004), 112.

4. Barbara Ehrenreich, *Nickel and Dimed: On (Not) Getting By in America* (New York: Metropolitan, 2000).

5. Interview, May 2006; see Liza Featherstone, *Selling Women Short: The Landmark Battle for Workers' Rights at Wal-Mart* (New York: Basic Books, 2004).

6. Thomas Li-Ping Tang and Vancie Smith-Brandon, "From Welfare to Work," *Public Personnel Management* 30 (Summer 2001): 241–60.

7. Jason DeParle, *American Dream: Three Women, Ten Kids, and the Nation's Drive to End Welfare* (New York: Viking, 2004), 177.

8. David Shipler, *The Working Poor: Invisible in America* (New York: Knopf, 2004), 261.

9. Robert Cherry, *Welfare Transformed: Universalizing Family Policies That Work* (New York: Oxford University Press, 2007), 48.

10. Katherine Newman, *No Shame in My Game* (New York: Russell Sage, 1999).

11. Katherine Newman and Chauncy Lennon, "Working Poor, Working Hard: The Trajectories of the Bottom of the American Labor Market," in *Social Inequalities in Comparative Perspective*, ed. Fiona Devine and Mary Waters (Boston: Blackwell, 2004), 128.

12. Elizabeth Scott, "Welfare Recipients Struggle to Balance Work and Family," *Poverty Research News* 4 (July–August, 2002): 12–15.

13. Anu Rangarajan and Robert Wood, "Current and Former WFNJ Clients" (Princeton, NJ: Mathematica, 2000), www.mathematica-mpr.com/.

14. Erin Burchfield and Sarah Yatsko, *From Welfare Check to Pay Check* (Seattle, WA: Seattle Economic Opportunity Institute, 2002).

15. Richard Freeman and William Rodgers, "Area Economic Conditions and the Labor Market Outcomes of Young Men in the 1990s Expansion," in *Prosperity for All? The Economic Boom and African Americans*, ed. Robert Cherry and William Rodgers (New York: Russell Sage, 2000), 50–87.

16. Sylvia Nasar and Kirsten Mitchell, "Booming Job Market Draws Young Black Men into Fold," *New York Times*, May 23, 1999, A1.

17. Ibid.

18. Ron Haskins, "The Rise of the Bottom Fifth," *Washington Post*, May 29, 2007, A13.

19. Newman and Lennon, "Working Poor, Working Hard."

20. Peter Edelman, Harry Holzer, and Paul Offner, *Reconnecting Disadvantaged Young Men* (Washington, DC: Urban Institute, 2006), tables 2.1 and 2.2.

21. Greg DeFreitas. "Urban Racial Employment Differentials: The New York Case," in *Prosperity for All? The Economic Boom and African Americans*, ed. Robert Cherry and William Rodgers (New York: Russell Sage, 2000), 110–26.

22. Harry Holzer and Paul Offner, "Trends in the Employment Outcomes of Young Black Men, 1979–2000," in *Black Men Left Behind*, ed. Ron Mincy (Washington, DC: Urban Institute, 2006), table 2.1.

23. John Foster-Bey, "Did Spatial Mismatch Affect Male Labor Force Participation during the 1990s Expansion?" in *Black Men Left Behind*, ed. Ron Mincy (Washington, DC: Urban Institute, 2006), 121–46.

24. Devah Pager, "The Mark of a Criminal Record," *American Journal of Sociology* 108 (March 2004): 937–75.

25. Harry Holzer, Steven Raphael, and Michael Stoll, "How Do Employer Perceptions of Crime and Incarceration Affect the Employment Prospects of Less-Educated Young Black Men?" in *Black Men Left Behind*, ed. Ron Mincy (Washington, DC: Urban Institute, 2006), 67–86.

26. Richard Freeman and William Rodgers, "The Fragility of the 1990s Economic Gains," Allied Social Science Association, Philadelphia (January 8, 2005).

27. Heather Boushey, "Last Hired, First Fired: Job Losses Plague Former TANF Recipients," *Economic Policy Institute Brief* 171 (December 12, 2001): 1–4. Between February and November 2001, employment in personal supply services fell from 3.73 to 3.28 million; in the hotel and lodging sector, from 1.95 to 1.85 million. From August to October 2001, employment in restaurants and bars fell from 8.28 to 8.19 million; and in general merchandise stores, from 2.80 to 2.76 million.

28. U.S. Bureau of Labor Statistics, Household Data: Annual Averages, table 2, http://www.bls.gov/cps/cpsaat2.pdf.

29. In 2000, the share of welfare leavers employed in each of these industries was non-eating retail (17.6 percent), eating places (14.4 percent), manufacturing (7.4 percent), personnel supply services (4.6 percent), hotels and lodgings (3.7 percent), labs and home care (3.6 percent), nursing and personal care facilities (3.5 percent), elementary and primary schools (3.5 percent), and child care services (3.3 percent). Heather Boushey and David Rosnick, "For Welfare Reform to Work, Jobs Must Be Available" (issue brief, Center for Economic and Policy Brief, April 1, 2004).

30. To judge the impact of the economic slowdown on welfare leavers, I assumed that their share of total employment in each of these nine sectors remained constant.

31. The lack of improvement during the mid-1990s is probably related to the substantial labor-market entry of welfare leavers. These mothers were overwhelmingly employed at low-waged jobs so that they would have dampened the upward trend in *average* female wages. The decline in 2001 was undoubtedly related to the harsh experience of female workers in the initial stages of the economic slowdown. See Heather Boushey and Robert Cherry, "The Severe Implications of the Economic Downturn on Working Families." *WorkingUSA* (Winter 2002/2003): 35–54.

32. Sandi Nelson, "Trends in Economic Hardship," Urban Institute (March 18, 2004). Consumption studies among the poor are consistently more favorable than income studies. For example, see Bruce Meyer and James Sullivan, "The Well-Being of Single-Mother Families after Welfare Reform" (Policy Brief No. 33, Brookings Institution, 2005).

33. Between 2000 and 2004 the poverty rate for female householders rose from 28.59 percent to 30.51 percent, while for the nation, it rose from 11.25 percent to 12.75 percent.

34. Mary Daly and Joyce Kwok, "Did Welfare Reform Work for Everyone?" *FRSSF Newsletter*, August 3, 2009.

35. U.S. Bureau of Labor Statistics, *Labor Force Statistics*, table A-2, http://www.bls.gov/webapps/legacy/cpsatab2.htm.

36. Phillip Moss and Chris Tilly, *Stories Employers Tell: Race, Skill, and Hiring in America* (New York: Russell Sage, 2000).

37. Gregory Acs and Pamela Loprest, "Job Differences by Race and Ethnicity in the Low-Skill Job Market." *Urban Institute Brief* 4 (February 2009): 1–11.

38. Mickey Meece, "Job Outlook for Teenagers Worsens," *New York Times*, June 1, 2010, B1.

39. Ibid.

40. Ibid.

41. Heather Boushey and Robert Cherry, "Exclusionary Practices and Glass Ceiling Effects across Regions," in *Prosperity for All? The Economic Boom and African Americans*, ed. Robert Cherry and William Rodgers (New York: Russell Sage, 2000), 153–81.

42. "A Year of Unbalanced Growth" (National Employment Law Project Data Brief, February 2011).

1. For a summary of a benefit-cost approach to marriage, see Robert Cherry, "Rational Choice and the Price of Marriage." *Feminist Economics* 4 (Spring 1998): 27–49

2. Charles Sheldon, *Charles Sheldon: His Life Story* (New York: Doran, 1925), 81.

3. Nicholas D. Kristof, "Good Deeds for Profit," *New York Times*, November 25, 2008; and Dan Pallotta, *Uncharitable* (Medford, MA: Tufts University Press, 2008).

4. Richard Margolis, "Cost Per Life: $22,000," *New York Times*, March 8, 1991, A29.

5. John Iglehart, "The American Health Care System: The End-Stage Renal Disease System." *New England Journal of Medicine* 328 (February 4, 1993): 367; and Tom Koch, *Scarce Goods: Justice, Fairness, and Organ Transplantation* (Westport, CT: Praeger, 2001), 56–57.

6. For a summary of the Oregon program, see Daniel Fox and Howard Leichter, "Rationing Care in Oregon," *Health Affairs* 10 (Summer 1991): 7–27, http://content. healthaffairs.org/cgi/reprint/10/2/7.pdf. For subsequent evidence that restricting access substantially lowered medical costs, see Jonathan Oberlander, Theodore Marmor, and Lawrence Jacobs, "Rationing Medical Care: Rhetoric and Reality in the Oregon Health Plan," *Canadian Medical Association Journal* 164 (May 2001): 1583–87.

7. Jackie Calmes, "Obama Plans Major Shifts in Spending," *New York Times*, February 27, 2009, A1.

8. David Card and Alan Krueger, *Myth and Measurement: The New Economics of the Minimum Wage* (Princeton, NJ: Princeton University Press, 1995).

9. Timothy Egan, "For $7.93 an Hour, It's Worth a Trip across a State Line," *New York Times*, January 11, 2007.

10. For a response to the conservative claim, see Jennette Wicks Lim, "EITC and the Minimum Wage," Spotlight on Poverty (February 15, 2011), http://www.spotlightonpoverty.org/ExclusiveCommentary.aspx?id=4d121305-1d95-41c3-802f-b6a91330d247.

11. Robert Cherry, "Race-Based Affirmative Action Policies: Why University of Michigan Supporters Were Wrong," Georgetown University Journal of Law and Public Policy 3 (Summer 2005): 501–21; "University Race-Sensitive Admissions Programs Are Not Helping Black Students Who Most Need Assistance," *Journal of Blacks in Higher Education* 56 (Summer 2007), http://www.jbhe.com/news_views/56_race_sensitive_not_helping.html.

12. Gavin Wright, *Old South, New South* (New York: Basic Books, 1986), 230.

13. The Roosevelt administration was consistently insensitive to the needs of black Americans. Roosevelt resolutely refused to support national antilynching legislation while supporting the National Recovery Act (NRA) that caused the loss of probably 500,000 jobs for black workers and was cynically called the "Negro Removal Act" by black newspapers throughout the country. For evidence, see Robert Cherry, *Who Gets the Good Jobs?* (New Brunswick, NJ: Rutgers University Press, 2001), chap. 4.

14. Up until recently, ethanol had little impact on clean air. With newer, more energy-efficient ethanol plants and their more energy-efficient locations, there is now a significant reduction in greenhouse gases (GHG) by shifting from gasoline to ethanol. See "Study Finds Recent Improvements in Corn Ethanol Production Result in 48–59% Less Direct-Effect GHG Than Gasoline" (Green Car Congress, January 24, 2009), http://www.GREENCARCONGRESS.COM/2009/01/STUDY-FINDS-REC.HTML.

15. Richard Perrin, "Ethanol and Food Prices—Preliminary Assessment" (Agricultural Economics Department, University of Nebraska), http://www.ethanol.org/pdf/content-mgmt/Ethanol_and_food_prices_UNL_Perrin_08.pdf.

16. Lester R. Brown, "Why Ethanol Production Will Drive World Food Prices Even Higher in 2008," Earth Policy Institute (January 8, 2008), http://www.earth-policy.org/Updates/2008/Update69.htm; Brittany Sauser, "Ethanol Demand Threatens Food Prices," *Technology Review*, February 13, 2007, http://www.technologyreview.com/Energy/18173.

17. Harry Holzer, Paul Offner, and Elaine Sorensen, "Declining Employment among Young Black Less-Educated Men: The Role of Incarceration and Child Support" (Urban Institute Research Paper, April 2004), http://www.urban.org/publications/411035.html.

18. Nicholas Kristof, "Where Sweatshops Are a Dream," *New York Times*, January 15, 2009; and Paul Krugman, "In Praise of Cheap Labor," *Slate Magazine*, March 21, 1997.

19. Mary Jo Bane and David Ellwood, *Welfare Realities* (Cambridge, MA: Harvard University Press, 1994), table 2.3.

20. For Baltimore, see Robert Moffitt and David Stevens, "Changing Caseloads" (conference paper, Federal Reserve Bank of New York, November 17, 2000). In Milwaukee, in 1995, 65 percent of recipients had been on welfare continuously for more than two years, 77 percent for at least nineteen of the previous twenty-four months: Maria Cancian et al., "Before and after TANF" (Special Report No. 77, Institute for Research on Poverty, University of Wisconsin, May 2000).

21. It still could have been the case that factors other than the entitlement aspect of prereform cash assistance could explain the rise in dependency In particular, Kathryn Edin and Laura Lein (*Making Ends Meet* [New York: Russell Sage, 2007]) contend that it was the low wages that recipients faced that led them to remain on welfare rather than seek employment.

22. Michael Tanner, "On the Dole Again," *New York Post*, February 13, 2009, 26. Also, see Mickey Kaus, "The Welfare Issue Is Alive, Alive!" *Slate*, kausfiles.com, February 15, 2009; and Robert Rector and Katherine Bradley, "Stimulus Bill Abolishes Welfare Reform and Adds New Welfare Spending" (Web Memo No. 2287, the Heritage Foundation, February 11, 2009), http://www.heritage.org/Research/Welfare/wm2287.cfm.

23. Robert Cherry, *Who Gets the Good Jobs?* (New Brunswick, NJ: Rutgers University Press, 2001), chap. 10.

24. Whether in recognition of these disastrous results, the University of Michigan began to reduce substantially its admission of black students from about 500 in 1999 to 350 in 2004 with a resulting reduction in the number of black students with very low GPAs. Althea Nagai, "Racial and Ethnic Preferences in Undergraduate Admissions at the University of Michigan," Center for Equal Opportunity (October 17, 2006), figure 7, http://www.ceousa.org/index.php?option=com_content&task=blogcategory&id=78&Itemid=100.

25. Patricia Gurin, "The Compelling Need for Diversity in Education," *Michigan Journal of Race and Law* 5 (1999): 363–425.

26. John Robertson, "Norplant and Irresponsible Reproduction," in *Coerced Contraception: Political and Moral Challenges of Long-Acting Birth Control*, ed. Ellen H. Moskowitz and Bruce Jennings (Washington, DC: Georgetown University Press, 1996); Editorial, "Norplant and the Poor," *Philadelphia Inquirer*, December 12, 1990, A18.

27. "Editorial Retraction," *Philadelphia Inquirer*, December 23, 1990, C4.

28. Spencer Hsu, "Marriage Fund for Poor Proposed," *Washington Post*, July 22, 2005, B5; Wade Horn, "Wedding Bell Blues: Marriage and Welfare Reform," *Brookings Review* 19 (Summer 2001): 39–42; and Robert Rector and Melissa Pardue, "Understanding the President's Health Marriage Initiative" (Report No. 1741, Heritage Foundation, March 26, 2004).

29. Jennifer Medina, "Next Question: Can Students Be Paid to Excel?" *New York Times*, March 5, 2008.

30. Barbara Dwyer Gunn, "On-the-Ground Lessons from a Landmark Anti-poverty Initiative in New York City," *Spotlight on Poverty*, April 28, 2010; and Julie Bosman, "City Will Stop Paying the Poor for Good Behavior," *New York Times*, March 31, 2010, A1.

NOTES TO CHAPTER 4

1. Among men twenty-five to sixty-four years old, the racial employment rate gaps are 8.1 and 4.1 percentage points, respectively, for those with less than a high school degree and those with at least a four-year degree.

2. James Heckman and Peter Siegelman, "The Urban Institute Audit Studies: Their Methods and Findings," in *Clear and Convincing Evidence: Measurement of Discrimination in America*, ed. Michael Fix and Raymond Struyk (Washington, DC: Urban Institute, 1992), table 5.1.

3. Gregory Acs and Pamela Loprest, "Working for Cents on the Dollar: Race and Ethnic Wage Gaps in the Noncollege Labor Market," Urban Institute, March 2009.

4. Philip Moss and Chris Tilly, *Stories Employers Tell: Race, Skill, and Hiring in America* (New York: Russell Sage, 2002), table 1.1.

5. Ibid., 79.

6. Acs and Loprest, "Working for Cents on the Dollar."

7. June O'Neill and David O'Neill, "What Do Wage Differentials Tell Us about Labor Market Discrimination?" in *The Economics of Immigration and Social Diversity*, ed. Solomon Polachek, Carmel Chiswick, and Hillel Rapoport (Greenwich, CT: JAI Press, 2006), table 3.

8. Patrick Bayer, Stephen L. Ross, and Giorgio Topa, "Place of Work and Place of Residence: Informal Hiring Networks and Labor Market Outcomes," *Journal of Political Economy* 116 (December 2008): 1150–96.

9. Laura Giuliano, David I. Levin, and Jonathan Leonard, "Manager Race and the Race of News Hires," *Journal of Labor Economics* 27 (October 2009): 589–631.

10. Harry Holzer, *What Employers Want: Job Prospects for Less-Educated Workers* (New York: Russell Sage, 1996).

11. Moss and Tilly, *Stories Employers Tell*, table 4.7.

12. William Julius Wilson, *When Work Disappears* (New York: Vintage, 1996), 134.

13. Ibid., 36–37.

14. Harry Holzer, "Statement," U.S. Equal Employment Opportunity Commission (April 19, 2006), http://www.eeoc.gov/abouteeoc/meetings/4-19-06/holzer.html.

15. Holzer, *What Employers Want*; Joleen Kirschenman and Kathryn Neckerman, "'We'd Love to Hire Them But ...': The Meaning of Race for Employers," in *The Urban Underclass*, ed. Christopher Jencks and Paul Peterson (Washington, DC: Brookings Institution, 1991), 203–34.

16. Wilson, *When Work Disappears*.

17. Harry Holzer, Steven Raphael, and Michael A. Stoll, "Perceived Criminality, Criminal Background Checks, and the Racial Hiring Practices of Employers," *Journal of Law and Economics* 49 (2006): 451–80.

18. National League of Cities, "Cities Pave the Way: Promising Prison Reentry Policies That Promote Local Hiring of People with Criminal Records," National Law Employment Project (June 29, 2010), www.nelp.org/page/-/SCLP/2010/PromisingLocalHireReentry-Policies.pdf.

19. Ibid.

20. Moss and Tilly, *Stories Employers Tell*, 211.

21. Achieve, Inc., *An Action Agenda for Improving America's High Schools* (Washington, DC: National Governors Association, 2005), http://www.achieve.org/files/actionagenda2005.pdf.

22. James Heckman, Jora Stixrud, and Sergio Urzoe, "The Effect of Cognitive and Non-cognitive Abilities on Labor Market Outcomes and Social Behavior," *Journal of Labor Economics* 24 (2006): 411–82; John Deke and Joshua Haimson, *Valuing Student Competencies: Which Ones Predict Postsecondary Education and Earnings, and for Whom?* (Princeton, NJ: Mathematica Policy Research, 2006), http://www.mathematica-mpr.com/publications/PDFs/valuestudent.pdf.

23. Melinda Mechur Karp et al., "Dual Enrollment Students in Florida and New York City: Postsecondary Outcomes," *CCRC Brief* 37 (February 2008): 1–8.

24. For evidence that these tests are good predictors of job performance, see Alexandra Wigdor and Bert Green, eds., *Performance Assessments for the Workplace*, vol. 1 (Washington, DC: National Academies Press, 1991); Murray Barrick and Michael Mount, "The Big Five Personality Dimensions of Job Performance: A Meta-Analysis," *Personnel Psychology* 44 (1991): 1–26; Robert Tett, Douglas Jackson, and Mitchell Rothstein, "Personality Measures as Predictors of Job Performance: A Meta-analytic Review," *Personnel Psychology* 44 (1991): 703–42; and Richard Lanyon and Leonard Goodstein, *Personality and Assessment* (New York: Wiley, 1997).

25. David H. Autor and David Scarborough, "Will Job Testing Harm Minority Workers?" (NBER Working Paper No. 10763, September 2004, revised January 2007).

26. Adversity.net, "U.S. Supreme Court Rules against Racial Quotas in New Haven FD!" (June 29, 2009), http://adversity.net/newhavenfd/default.htm.

27. Georgia Kral, "City Responds to Firefighter Exam Complaints," *New Haven Independent*, July 24, 2007.

28. Nicole Allan and Emily Bazelo, "The Ladder," *Slate*, June 25, 2009, http://www.slate.com/id/2221250/entry/2221252/.

29. Ibid.

30. Harry Holzer and David Neumark, "Affirmative Action: What Do We Know?" *Journal of Policy Analysis and Management* 25 (Spring 2006): 18.

31. Charles Savage, "Report Examines Civil Rights during Bush Years," *New York Times*, December 3, 2009, A26.

32. Michael Luo, "In Job Hunt, College Degrees Can't Close the Racial Gap," *New York Times*, December 1, 2009, A1.

33. Holzer, "Statement."

1. Barack Obama, "Democratic Radio Address" (November 21, 2008), http://blogs. usatoday.com/onpolitics/2008/11/obama-well-put.html.

2. Randy Albelda, "The Macho Stimulus Plan," *Boston Globe* online, November 28, 2008, http://www.boston.com/news/nation/articles/2008/11/28/the_macho_stimulus_plan/.

3. "How the American Recovery and Reinvestment Act Addresses Women's Needs," National Women's Law Center (February 13, 2009).

4. William Darity, David Guilkey, and William Winfrey, "Explaining Differences in Economic Performance among Racial and Ethic Groups in the USA: The Data Examined," *American Journal of Economics and Sociology* 55 (1996): 411–25.

5. Marlene Kim, "Has the Race Penalty for Black Women Disappeared in the United States?" *Feminist Economics* 8 (2002): 115–24. She finds a racial gap of 7 percent after controlling for productivity-related individual characteristics but only a 3 percent gap after adding occupational controls. For measures of gender discrimination among college graduates, see Catherine Weinberger and Lois Joy, "Relative Earnings of Black College Graduates, 1980–2001," in *Race and Equal Opportunity in the Twenty-First Century*, ed. Marlene Kim (New York: Routledge, 2009), 50–72.

6. June O'Neill and Dave O'Neill, "What Do Wage Differentials Tell Us about Labor Market Discrimination?" in *The Economics of Immigration and Social Policy*, ed. Solomon Polachek, Carmel Chiswick, and Hillel Rapoport (Greenwich, CT: JAI Press, 2006), table 9. They find that after controlling for age, location, and education, Latino women, aged thirty-five to forty-three, make 97 percent as much as comparable white women.

7. Francine Blau and Laurence Kahn, "The US Gender Pay Gap in the 1990s: Slowing Convergence" (NBER Working Paper No. 10853, October 2004).

8. Ibid., table 3.

9. Stephen Rose and Heidi Hartmann, "Still a Man's Labor Market: The Long-Term Earnings Gap" (Institute for Women's Policy Research Brief No. C366, February 2008).

10. O'Neill and O'Neill, "What Do Wage Differentials Tell Us about Labor Market Discrimination?" table 9.

11. Suhwa Lee, *Keeping Moms on the Job* (Washington, DC: Institute for Women's Policy Research, 2007), tables 1 and 2.

12. Tuomas Kosonen, "The Effect of Child Care Prices on the Labour Supply of Parents," University of Helsinki (May 2009).

13. D. Lundin, E. Mork, and B. Ockert, "How Far Can Reduced Childcare Prices Push Female Labour Supply?" *Labour Economics* 15 (August 2008): 647–59; Tarjei Havnes and Magne Mogstad, "The Irrelevance of Subsidized Child Care for Maternal Employment" (University of Oslo, February 2009).

14. Heather Boushey, "Staying Employed after Welfare" (EPI Briefing Paper No. 128, June 2002). See also Erdal Tekin, "Child Care Subsidy Receipt, Employment, and Child Care Choices of Single Mothers," *Economic Letters* 89, no. 1 (2005): 1–6; Elizabeth Cascio, "Maternal Labor Supply and the Introduction of Kindergartens into American Public Schools," *Journal of Human Resources* 44 (2009): 140–70; David Blau, "Childcare Subsidy Programs" (NBER Working Paper No. 7806, July 2000); and Hannah Matthews, "Childcare Assistance Helps Families Work" (Center for Law and Social Policy, April 3, 2006).

15. Edward D. Lowe, Thomas S. Weisner, and Sonya Geis, "Instability in Child Care" (Working Paper No. 15, Manpower Development Research Corporation, April 2003).

16. Peter Goodman, "The New Poor: Cuts to Child Care Subsidy Thwart More Job Seekers," *New York Times*, May 23, 2010, A1.

17. Virginia W. Knox, Andrew S. London, and Ellen K. Scott, "Welfare Reform, Work, and Child Care" (policy brief, Manpower Development Research Corporation, October 2003).

18. Goodman, "The New Poor."

19. Albert Wat and Chrisanne Gayl, *Beyond the School Yard: Pre-K Collaborations with Community-Based Partners*, The Pew Center on the States (July 2009). http://preknow.org/documents/pkn_collaboration_rept_final.pdf.

20. Heidi Hartmann and Stephen Rose, "Still a Man's Market: The Long-Term Earning Gap" (Institute for Women's Policy Research Brief No. C355, June 2004).

21. Also see Barbara Wootton, "Gender Differences in Occupational Employment," *Monthly Labor Review* 120 (April 1997): 15–37; Paul Gabriel and Susanne Schmitz, "Gender Differences among Workers," *Monthly Labor Review* 130 (June 2007): 19–24.

22. Herve Quineau, "Is the Long-Term Reduction in Occupational Sex Segregation Still Continuing in the United States?" *Social Science Journal* 43 (2006): 681–88.

23. Karen Chapple, "Promising Futures: Workforce Development and Upward Mobility in Information Technology Institute for Research on Labor and Employment" (University of California at Berkeley Institute for Urban and Regional Development Working Paper No. 121-05, May 2005).

24. J. McGrath Cohoon and William Aspray, eds., *Women and Information Technology Research on Underrepresentation* (Cambridge, MA: MIT Press, 2008), figure I.1; and Women's Employment Institute, "Recruiting Low Income Women into Information Technology Careers" (Chicago, 2005), www.womenemployed.org/docs/Recruiting Lower-Income.pdf.

25. Quoted in Jane Margolis and Allan Fisher, *Unlocking the Clubhouse: Women in Computing* (Cambridge, MA: MIT Press, 2005), 5.

26. Manuel Castells, *The Power of Identity* (New York: Blackwell, 1996).

27. Chapple, "Promising Futures," 108.

28. Ibid., 110.

29. Ibid., 98.

30. Ibid., 113.

31. Vicky Lovell, Heidi Hartmann, and Jessica Koski, "Making the Right Call: Jobs and Diversity in the Communications and Media Sector" (Institute for Women's Policy Research Brief No. 364, July 2006).

32. Mary Gatta, "It's More Than Just Job Placement! Re-thinking Workforce Development Policy to Raise Single Mothers Out of Poverty," in *Advances in Gender Research*, vol. 14, ed. Marcia Texler Segal and Vasilikie Demos (Bingley, UK: Emerald, 2010), 213–31.

33. Ibid.

34. This rises to 21.71 percent if workers in social assistance industries are included. See U.S. Bureau of the Census, "American Community Survey, 2007," table S2403, http://factfinder.census.gov/servlet/STTable?_bm=y&-geo_id=01000US&-qr_name=ACS_2007_3YR_G00_S2403&-ds_name=ACS_2007_3YR_G00_&-_lang=en&-_caller=geoselect&-state=st&-format.

35. David Moberg, "Martha Jernegons's New Shoes," *American Prospect* 11 (June 19, 2000): 1–7.

36. "Women and Paid Sick Days" (Institute for Women's Policy Research Fact Sheet No. B254a, February 2007), table 3. Also see Vickey Lovell, "Valuing Good Health in California: The Costs and Benefits of the Health Families, Healthy Workplaces Act of 2008" (Institute for Women's Policy Research No. B259, April 2008).

37. Shelley Waters Boots, Karin Martinson, and Anna Danziger, "Employers' Perspectives on San Francisco's Paid Sick Leave Policy" (Urban Institute, March 2009).

38. Kids Count, *Reducing the Teen Birth Rate* (Baltimore: Ann E. Casey Foundation, July 2009). http://www.kidscount.org.

39. Kristin Luker, *Dubious Conceptions: The Politics of Teenage Pregnancy* (Cambridge, MA: Harvard University Press, 1995); Arline Geronimus and Sanders Korenman, "The Socioeconomic Consequences of Teen Childbearing Reconsidered," *Quarterly Journal of Economics* 107 (1992): 1187–1214; and Saul Hoffman, "Teenage Childbearing Is Not So Bad After All . . . or Is It?" *Family Planning Perspectives* 30 (1998): 236–39.

40. Cynthia Colen, Arline Geronimus, and Maureen Phipps, "Getting a Piece of the Pie: The Economic Boom of the 1990s and Declining Teen Birth Rates in the United States," *Social Science and Medicine* 63 (2006): 1533.

41. Katherine Newman, *No Shame in My Game: The Working Poor in the Innercity* (New York: Russell Sage, 1999); David Shipler, *The Working Poor: Invisible in America* (New York: Knopf, 2004).

42. Janet Rosenbaum et al., "Condom Use and Sugar Daddies: Sexual Bargains and Condom Use among Low SES Women" (Johns Hopkins Working Paper, June 2010).

NOTES TO CHAPTER 6

1. Katherine Shaw and Jerry Jacobs, eds., "Community Colleges: New Environments, New Directions," *Annals of the American Academy of Political and Social Sciences* 586 (March 2003); Katherine Shaw, Sara Goldrick-Rab, Christopher Mazzeo, and Jerry Jacobs, *Putting Poor People to Work: How the Work-First Idea Eroded College Access for the Poor* (New York: Russell Sage, 2006).

2. Shaw et al., *Putting Poor People to Work*, 7–8.

3. Ibid., 11, 150.4. Ibid.; Bureau of Labor Statistics, news releases, "Table 4: Usual Weekly Wages," first quarter, 2009, http://www.bls.gov/news.release/wkyeng.to4.htm; NCHEMS Information Center, "Data for 2007," http://www.higheredinfo.org/dbrowser/index.php?su bmeasure=366&year=2007&level=nation&mode=data&state=0.

5. Bureau of Labor Statistics, news releases, "Table 4. Quartiles and Selected Deciles of Usual Weekly Earnings of Full-Time Wage and Salary Workers by Selected Characteristics, First Quarter 2009 Averages, Not Seasonally Adjusted." Lower quartile of four-year graduates for men and women equals $823 and $633, respectively; median for those with some college or an associate degree for men and women equals $844 and $627, respectively.

6. For those completing an associate degree, it was $31,468. One explanation for the lower earnings was that one-half of those who completed associate degrees went on to complete four-year degrees. By contrast, "many students struggling in associate programs might be better off in certificate programs." Louis Jacobson and Christine Mokher, "Pathways to Boosting the Earnings of Low-Income Students by Increasing Their Educational Attainment" (New York: Hudson Institute, January 2009).

7. Nancy Ritze, "The Evolution of Developmental Education at the City University of New York and Bronx Community College," *Responding to the Challenges of Developmental Education* 129 (Spring 2005): 73–81.

8. Robert Cherry, "Study of Brooklyn College Graduates," 1994.

9. Robert Cherry, "Kaplan University and the Shortchanging of Minority Women," *Minding the Campus* (November 11, 2010), http://www.mindingthecampus.com/originals/2010/11/by_robert_cherry_the_education.html.

10. Kristin Luker, *Dubious Conceptions* (Cambridge, MA: Harvard University Press, 1995), 120.

11. LaDonna Pavetti, "Against the Odds," Urban Institute, July 1997; Gary Burtless, "Employment Prospects of Welfare Recipients," in *The Work Alternative: Welfare Reform and the Realities of the Job Market*, ed. Demetra Nightingale and Robert Haveman (Washington, DC: Urban Institute Press, 1995), 185–204.

12. Anita Mathur et al., "Credentials Count: How California's Community Colleges Help Parents Move from Welfare to Self-Sufficiency" (Center for Law and Social Policy, May 2002). The authors do not dwell on these failure rates but instead focus on earnings outcomes. The earnings growth of even those who completed zero credits was quite robust during the economic boom. While they infer that this wage growth was due to the college experience, it probably had much more to do with the robust job market.

13. Gayle Hamilton, *Moving People from Welfare to Work: Lessons from the National Evaluation of Welfare-to-Work Strategies* (New York: Manpower Demonstration Research Corporation, July 2002). For a critique of the MDRC evaluations, see Erika Kates, "Debunking the Myth of the Failure of Education and Training for Welfare Recipients," in *Shut Out: Low Income Mothers and Higher Education in Post-welfare America*, ed. Valerie Polakow et al. (Albany: State University of New York Press, 2004), 35–69.

14. Dave Dhaval, Nancy Reichman, and Hope Corman, "Effects of Welfare Reform on Educational Acquisition of Young Adult Women" (NBER Working Paper No. 14466, November 2008), 30.

15. For Chicago, see Melissa Roderick, Jenny Nagaoka, and Elaine Allensworth, *From High School to the Future* (Consortium on Chicago School Research, University of Chicago, 2006), http://ccsr.uchicago.edu/publications/Postsecondary.pdf. For national, see Schott Foundation, "Fifty State Report," tables 6 and 7, http://www.blackboysreport.org/node/111.

16. Jennifer Engle, "Postsecondary Access and Success for First-Generation College Students," *American Academic* 3 (January 2007): 25–48, www.aft.org/pubs-reports/american_academic/issues/january07.

17. Xianglei Chen, *First-Generation Students in Postsecondary Education* (Washington, DC: National Center for Educational Statistics, 2005), https://nces.ed.gov/pubs2005/2005171.pdf.

18. Ibid.

19. Thomas Bailey, Davis Jenkins, and D. Timothy Leinbach, "Is Student Success Labeled Institutional Failure? Student Goals and Graduation Rates in the Accountability Debate at Community Colleges" (Working Paper No. 1, September 2006). James Rosenbaum, Regina Deil-Amen, and Ann E. Person, *After Admissions* (New York: Russell Sage, 2006), cites evidence that after eight years, only 18.7 percent of black community college entrants obtain any degree.

20. Roderick, Nagaoka, and Allensworth, *From High School to the Future.*

21. Ibid.

22. Sharon Otterman, "Most New York Students Are Not College Ready," *New York Times*, February 7, 2011, A1.

23. Eric Bettinger and Bridget Long, "Remediation at the Community College: Student Participation and Outcomes," *New Directions for College Communities*, no. 129 (Spring 2005): 17–26. After five years, only 16 percent had completed an associate degree, and less than 7 percent were either enrolled in or had completed a four-year college degree program. Also see Thomas Bailey, Davis Jenkins, and Timothy Leinbach, "Is Student Success Labeled Institutional Failure?" (CCRC Working Paper No. 1, Community College Research Center, Columbia University, June 2005).

24. G. Norton Grubb and associates, *Honored but Invisible* (New York: Routledge, 1999), table 5.1.

25. Robert McCabe, *No One to Waste* (Washington, DC: Community College Press, 2000).

26. Thomas Bailey, "Challenge and Opportunity: Rethinking the Role and Function of Developmental Education in Community College" (CCRC Working Paper No. 14, Community College Research Center, Columbia University, November 2008).

27. Ritze, "The Evolution of Developmental Education."

28. It seems to be common practice in the education literature to quote Grubb on the growing earnings gap rather than any direct statistics. See Bailey, Jenkins, and Leinbach, "Is Student Success Labeled Institutional Failure?"; and Rosenbaum, Deil-Amen, and Person, *After Admissions.*

29. John Riley, "Silver Signals: Twenty-Five Years of Screening and Signals," *Journal of Economic Literature* 39 (June 2001): 474.

30. Philip Moss and Chris Tilly, *Stories Employers Tell: Race, Skill, and Hiring in America* (New York: Russell Sage, 2001) 46.

31. After adjusting for class rank, the 1995 racial earnings gap among 1976 Harvard matriculants was virtually eliminated. William Bowen and Derek Bok, *The Shape of the River* (Princeton, NJ: Princeton University Press, 1998).

32. Rosenbaum, Deil-Amen, and Person, *After Admissions*, 85.

33. Quoted in ibid., 62.

34. Ibid., table 3.4.

35. In 2008, the City University of New York (CUNY) was proposing to open a new community college that was advertised as having an innovative approach to occupational programs. The community college faculty caucus scheduled a meeting with the CUNY administrator in charge of developing the curriculum and programming for the new school. Among more than thirty community college faculty present, there was not one individual who was an occupational instructor in the many occupational programs CUNY offers. Every one of those present had traditional academic credentials and was uniformly antagonistic to the intentions of the new college. These faculty members were quieted only when the CUNY administrator stressed that the transfer function will be a core component of the school's approach.

36. McCabe, *No One to Waste*, 41.

37. Karen Arenson, "Speedy Growth in Career Schools Raises Questions." *New York Times*, July 12, 2005, A1.

38. At public two-year colleges, 21 percent of these students receive no financial aid, and another 47 percent receive grants but have no loans. By contrast, at proprietary schools, only 4 percent of students receive no financial aid, and only 14 percent receive grants and do not have student loans. National Center for Education Statistics, "National Postsecondary Student Aid: Tables 74 and 76" (U.S. Department of Education, 2004).

39. U.S. Department of Education, "Table P74: Number of Undergraduate Career Educational Credentials Awarded: United States, 1997 to 2006" (National Center for Educational Statistics, 2008).

40. U.S. congressional hearing, "Enforcement of Federal Anti-fraud Laws in For-Profit Education" (Committee on Education and Workforce, Serial No. 109-2, Government Printing Office, March 1, 2005).

41. Mary Gatta, *Not Just Getting By: The Era of Flexible Workforce Development* (Lanham, MD: Lexington Books, 2005), 7.

42. Karen Pagenette and Cheryl Korzell, "The Advanced Technology Program: A Welfare-to-Work Success Story," *New Directions for Community Colleges*, no. 116 (December 2001): 49–59.

43. W. Norton Grubb and Marvin Lazerson, *The Educational Gospel* (Cambridge, MA: Harvard University Press, 2004), 96.

44. Thomas Bailey, "Increasing Competition and Growth of the For-Profits," in *Defending the Community College Equity Agenda*, ed. Thomas Bailey (Baltimore: Johns Hopkins University Press, 2006), 100.

45. Ben Brown, "A Smart Path—That Isn't 'College,'" *USA Today*, January 11, 2005, 11A.

46. Tamar Lewin, "Scrutiny Taking Toll on For-Profit Company," *New York Times*, November 9, 2010.

47. Bailey, "Increasing Competition," 93.

48. Ibid., 95.

49. Regina Deil-Amen and James Rosenbaum, "The Social Prerequisites for Success," *Annals of the Academy of Political and Social Sciences* 586 (2003): 120–43.

50. Rosenbaum, Deil-Amen, and Person, *After Admissions*, 131.

NOTES TO CHAPTER 7

1. Phillip Cutwright, "Illegitimacy and Income Supplements," in *The Family, Poverty, and Welfare Programs: Factors Influencing Family Instability* (Paper No. 12, Part 1, Studies in Public Welfare, Joint Economic Committee, 1973); Joyce Martin et al., "Births: Final Data for 2006," *National Vital Statistics Reports* 57 (January 2009): 7.

2. U.S. Bureau of the Census website, http://www.census.gov/population/socdemo/child/sipp2004/tab02.xls.

3. U.S. Bureau of the Census website, http://www.census.gov/hhes/www/cpstables/032009/pov/new02_100_01.htm.

4. See http://www.census.gov/hhes/www/poverty/sipp96/table03.html.

5. Sara McLanahan, "Divergent Destinies: How Children Are Faring under the Second Demographic Transition," *Demography* 41 (2004): 607–27.

6. See, for example, Kevin Lang and Jay L. Zagorsky, "Does Growing Up with a Parent Absent Really Hurt?" *Journal of Human Resources* 36 (2000): 253–73; and Sara McLanahan and Gary D. Sandefur, *Growing Up with a Single Parent: What Hurts, What Helps* (Cambridge, MA: Harvard University Press, 2004).

7. Lee Rainwater and William Yancey, *The Moynihan Report and the Politics of Controversy* (Cambridge, MA: MIT Press, 1967).

8. William Ryan, *Blaming the Victim* (New York: Pantheon Books, 1971); William J. Wilson, *The Truly Disadvantaged: The Inner-City, the Underclass, and Public Policy* (Chicago: University of Chicago Press, 1987).

9. Editorial, "Heartless Marriage Plans," *New York Times*, January 17, 2004.

10. Robin Toner, "Welfare Chief Is Hoping to Promote Marriage." *New York Times*, February 19, 2002, A17.

11. See Theodora Ooms, "Marriage Plus," *American Prospect* 13 (Spring 2002): 4–9; and Kathryn Edin, "Few Good Men: Why Poor Mothers Don't Marry or Remarry," *American Prospect* 11 (January 2000): 26–31.

12. Adam Thomas and Isabel Sawhill, "For Richer or Poorer: Marriage as an Antipoverty Strategy," *Journal of Policy Analysis and Management* 21 (2002): 587–600.

13. Daniel Lichter, Deborah Graefe, and J. Brian Brown, "Is Marriage a Panacea? Union Formation among Economically-Disadvantaged Unwed Mothers," *Social Problems* 50 (2003): 60–86.

14. Robert Lerman, "Married and Unmarried Parenthood and the Economic Well-being of Families: A Dynamic Analysis of a Recent Cohort" (Washington, DC: Urban Institute, 2002).

15. Wendy D. Manning and Daniel T. Lichter, "Parental Cohabitation and Children's Economic Well-Being," *Journal of Marriage and the Family* 58 (November 1996): 998–1010.

16. McLanahan, "Diverging Destinies."

17. Authors' tabulations from the National Vital Statistics System, National Center for Health Statistics, Center for Disease Control and Prevention, http://209.217.72.34/VitalStats/ReportFolders/reportFolders.aspx.

18. These results come from unpublished tables available through the National Vital Statistics System, National Center for Health Statistics, http://209.217.72.34/VitalStats/TableViewer/tableView.aspx.

19. Sara McLanahan, Irwin Garfinkel, Nancy Reichman, Julian Teitler, Marcia Carlson, and Christina Nordland Audigier, *The Fragile Families and Child Well-Being Study: The Baseline Report* (Princeton University, Benheim-Thoman Center for Research on Child Well-Being, 2003); and Lenna Nepomnyaschy and Irwin Garfinkel, "Child Support, Fatherhood, and Marriage: Findings from the First 5 Years of the Fragile Families and Child Wellbeing Study," *Asian Social Work and Policy Review* 1 (2007): 1–20

20. Timothy Smeeding, Irwin Garfinkel, and Ronald Mincy, "Young Disadvantaged Men: Fathers, Families, Poverty, and Policy" (Discussion Paper No. 1383-10, Institute for Research on Poverty, June 2010).

21. See Robert Lerman with Gregory Acs and Anupa Bir, "An Economic Framework and Selected Proposals for Demonstrations Aimed at Strengthening Marriage, Employment, and Family Functioning Outcomes" (report to the Department of Health and Human Services, 2007), http://www.urban.org/publications/411655.html.

22. Indeed, married adults in the United States save more and are more likely to own a home than other adults, even after controlling for socioeconomic factors. See J. Lupton and J. P. Smith, "Marriage, Assets, and Savings" (Santa Monica, CA: RAND Labor and Population Program, 1999), 9–12; Lauren Joy Krivo and Robert L. Kaufman, "Housing and Wealth Inequality: Racial-Ethnic Differences in Home Equity in the United States," *Demography* 41 (2004): 585–605.

23. Julie Brines and Kara Joyner, "The Ties That Bind: Principles of Cohesion and Cohabitation and Marriage," *American Sociological Review* 64 (1999): 333–55; and Linda Waite and Maggie Gallagher, *The Case for Marriage: Why Married People Are Happier, Healthier, and Better Off Financially* (New York: Doubleday, 2000).

24. Kathryn Edin and Maria Kefalas, *Promises I Can Keep: Why Poor Women Put Motherhood Before Marriage* (Berkeley: University of California Press, 2005).

25. Tabulations by authors from the March 2006 Current Population Survey. Using cross-country data from the 1980s, Robert Schoeni finds a wage advantage of married over single men in all fourteen countries studied (Schoeni, "Marital Status and Earnings in Developed Countries," *Journal of Population Economic* 8 [1995]: 1432–75).

26. Avner Ahituv and Robert Lerman, "How Do Marital Status, Work Effort, and Wage Rates Interact?" *Demography* 44 (August 2007): 623–47.

27. Irwin Garfinkel, Sara McLanahan, Sarah Meadows, and Ronald Mincy, "Unmarried Fathers' Earnings Trajectories: Does Partnership Status Matter?" (Princeton, NJ: Princeton Center for Research on Child Wellbeing, 2009).

28. Lingxin Hao, "Family Structure, Private Transfers, and the Economic Well-Being of Families with Children," *Social Forces* 75 (September 1996): 269–92.

29. W. Bradford Wilcox et al., *Why Marriage Matters: Twenty-Six Conclusions from the Social Sciences* (New York: Institute for American Values, 2005).

30. Richard Rogers, "Marriage, Sex, and Mortality," *Journal of Marriage and Family* 57 (1995): 515–26.

31. H. Brockmann and T. Klein, "Love and Death in Germany: The Marital Biography and Its Effect on Mortality," *Journal of Marriage and the Family* 66 (2004): 567–81.

32. David Blanchflower and Andrew Oswald, "Well-Being over Time in Britain and the USA," *Journal of Public Economics* 88 (2004): 1359–86.

33. Liliana Winkelmann and Rainer Winkelmann, "Why Are the Unemployed So Unhappy? Evidence from Panel Data," *Economica* 68 (1998): 1–15.

34. Beth Hahn, "Marital Status and Women's Health," *Journal of Marriage and Family* 55 (1993): 495–504.

35. Chris Wilson and Andrew Oswald, "How Does Marriage Affect Physical and Psychological Health? A Review of the Longitudinal Evidence" (Discussion Paper No. 1619, Institute for the Study of Labor [Germany], 2005).

36. H. Prigerson, P. K. Maciejewski, and R. A. Rosenheck, "The Effects of Marital Dissolution and Marital Quality on Health and Human Service Use among Women," *Medical Care* 37(1999): 858–73; and K. A. Wickrama, F. O. Lorenz, R. D. Conger, and G. H. Elder Jr., "Marital Quality and Physical Illness: A Latent Growth Curve Analysis." *Journal of Marriage and the Family* 59 (1997): 143–55.

37. Michael Hannan and Nancy Brandon Tuma, "A Reassessment of the Effect of Income Maintenance on Marital Dissolution in the Seattle-Denver Experiment," *American Journal of Sociology* 95 (1990): 1270–99; also see G. G. Cain, and D. A. Wissoker, "A Reanalysis of Marital Stability in the Seattle-Denver Income-Maintenance Experiment," *American Journal of Sociology* 95 (1990): 1235–69.

38. Burgess et al. restate the economic capability of individuals to live independently as a result of high earnings or other outside income as a self-reliance effect. See S. Burgess, C. Propper, and A. Aassve, "The Role of Income in Marriage and Divorce Transitions among Young Americans," *Journal of Population Economics* 16 (2003): 455–75.

39. Robert Lerman and Elaine Sorensen, "Child Support: Interactions between Private and Public Transfers," in *Means-Tested Transfer Programs in the U.S.*, ed. Robert Moffitt (Chicago: University of Chicago Press, 2003).

40. Harry Holzer, Paul Offner, and Elaine Sorensen. "Declining Employment among Young Black Less-Educated Men: The Role of Incarceration and Child Support," *Journal of Policy Analysis and Management* 24 (2005): 329–50; and David Bloom, Cecilia Conrad, and Cynthia Miller, "Child Support and Fathers' Remarriage and Fertility," in *Under Fire: The Revolution in Child Support Enforcement*, ed. Irwin Garfinkel, Sara McLanahan, Daniel Meyer, and Judith Seltzer (New York: Russell Sage, 1988).

41. David Steib, ed., "Sex Education in Schools," *Georgetown Journal of Gender and the Law* 8 (2007): 447–64.

42. David Kirby, *Emerging Answers 2007: New Research Findings on Programs to Reduce Teen Pregnancy* (Washington, DC: National Campaign to Prevent Teen and Unplanned Pregnancy, 2007), http://www.thenationalcampaign.org/ea2007/.

43. John B. Jemmott III, Loretta S. Jemmott, and Geoffrey T. Fong, "Efficacy of a Theory-Based Abstinence-Only Intervention over 24 Months: A Randomized Controlled Trial with Young Adolescents," *Archives of Pediatric and Adolescent Medicine* 164 (2010): 152–59, http://archpedi.ama-assn.org/cgi/content/short/164/2/152?home.

44. James Kemple with Cynthia Willner, *Career Academies: Long-Term Impacts on Labor Market Outcomes, Educational Attainment, and Transitions to Adulthood* (New York: Manpower Demonstration Research Corporation, 2008).

45. Ahituv and Lerman, "How Do Marital Status, Work Effort, and Wage Rates Interact?"; Waite and Gallagher, *The Case for Marriage*; Burgess, Propper, and Aassve, "The Role of Income in Marriage and Divorce Transitions among Young Americans," 455–75.

46. Kerwin Charles and Melvin Stephens Jr., "Job Displacement, Disability, and Divorce," *Journal of Labor Economics* 22 (2004): 489–522.

47. Robert Wood, "Marriage Rates and Marriageable Men: A Test of the Wilson Hypothesis," *Journal of Human Resources* 30 (Winter 1995): 163–94.

48. Shannon Seitz, "Accounting for Racial Differences in Marriage and Employment," *Journal of Labor Economics* 27 (2009): 385–437.

49. For information on the scores of studies that have emerged from these survey data, see http://www.fragilefamilies.princeton.edu/.

50. Robert Rector and Kirk Johnson, "Roles of Couples' Relationship Skills and Fathers' Employment in Encouraging Marriage" (CDA0-14, Heritage Foundation, 2004), http://www.heritage.org/Research/Welfare/upload/73827_1.pdf.

51. Edin and Kefalas, *Promises I Can Keep*.

52. Waite and Gallagher, *The Case for Marriage*.

53. Rachel Gordon and Carolyn Heinrich. "The Potential of a Couples' Approach to Employment Assistance: Results of a Nonexperimental Evaluation," *Review of Economics of the Household* 7 (2009): 133–58.

54. Katherine Boo, "The Marriage Cure: Is Wedlock Really a Way out of Poverty? *New Yorker*, August 15, 2003, 108.

55. Ibid., 109.

56. Ibid., 109–110.

57. James S. Carroll and William J. Doherty, "Evaluating the Effectiveness of Premarital Prevention Programs: A Meta-analytic Review of Outcome Research," *Family Relations* 52 (2003): 105–18.

58. H. J. Markman, M. J. Renick, F. J. Floyd, S. M. Stanley, and M. Clements, "Preventing Marital Distress through Communication and Conflict Management Training: A 4- and 5-Year Follow-Up," *Journal of Consulting and Clinical Psychology* 61 (1993): 70–77.

59. A recent example is the proposal for a large-scale effort to fund locally operating relationship- and parenting-education programs throughout Great Britain. Social Justice Policy Group, *Breakthrough Britain: Ending the Costs of Social Breakdown*, vol. 1, *Family Breakdown* (London: Centre for Social Justice, 2007), http://www.centreforsocialjustice.org.uk/client/downloads/family%20breakdown.pdf.

60. Carolyn Cowan and Philip Cowan, "Supporting Father Involvement in Low-Income Couples: Interventions for Fathers and Couples" (presentation at tenth annual ACF/OPRE research conference, Arlington, Virginia, 2007).

61. Robert Wood, Sheena McConnell, Quinn Moore, Andrew Clarkwest, and JoAnn Hsueh, *Strengthening Unmarried Parents' Relationships: The Early Impacts of Building Strong Families* (Princeton, NJ: Mathematica Policy Research, 2010).

NOTES TO CHAPTER 8

1. For single mother with one qualifying child, the phase-in rate is 34 percent, with a maximum of $3,043 reached at $8,950. The phase-out range begins at $16,450, with a 16 percent phase-out rate and eligibility ending at $35,450.

2. Robert Greenstein and Isaac Shapiro, "New Research Findings on the Effects of the Earned Income Tax Credit (Report No. 98-022, Washington, DC: Center on Budget and Policy Priorities, 1998); John Karl Scholz. "The Earned Income Tax Credit: Participation, Compliance, and Antipoverty Effectiveness," *National Tax Journal* 47, no. 1 (1994): 59–81; For studies that measured the positive employment effect, see Jeffrey Liebman and Nadia Eissa, "Labor Supply Response to the Earned Income Tax Credit," *Quarterly Journal of Economics* 112 (May 1996): 605–37; Bruce Meyer and Daniel Rosenbaum. "Welfare, the Earned Income Tax Credit, and the Labor Supply of Single Mothers, *Quarterly Journal of Economics* 117 (August 2001): 1063–14.

3. These areas are the District of Columbia, Maryland, Michigan, Minnesota, New Jersey, New York, and Vermont. Wisconsin, Kansas, Nebraska, and Massachusetts offer refundable credits of 10 to 15 percent of the federal EITC; and Illinois, Iowa, Indiana, Louisiana, North Carolina, New Mexico, Oklahoma, Oregon, Rhode Island, and Washington offer refundable credits of 5 to 7 percent of the federal EITC. Virginia, Delaware, and Maine have nonrefundable programs. Jason Levitis and Jeremy Koulish, "State Earned Income Tax Credits: 2008 Legislative Update," Center on Budget and Policy Priorities (October 8, 2008).

4. Stephen Holt and Jennifer Romich, "Longitudinal Evidence on Combined Marginal Tax Rates Facing Low- and Moderate-Income Families" (paper presented at the meetings of the Association of Public Policy Analysis and Management [APPAM], Washington, DC, November 2009).

5. Adam Carasso and C. Eugene Steuerle, "The Hefty Penalty on Marriage Facing Many Households with Children," *Future of Children* 15 (Fall 2005): 157–75.

6. Liebman and Eissa, "Labor Supply Response to the Earned Income Tax Credit."

7. David Moberg, "Martha Jernegons's New Shoes," *American Prospect* 11 (June 19, 2000).

8. David Ellwood and Jeffrey Liebman, "Middle-Class Parent Penalty" (NBER Working Paper No. 8031, December 2000).

9. The enacted legislation put the 15 percent phase-in rate on the share of the child credit that was in excess of nonrefundable benefits. As a result, in the income range where the family faced a 10 percent tax rate on additional income, it would receive a nonrefundable child credit of 10 percent to offset these taxes, and an additional 15 percent as refundable credits.

10. Quoted in Jeff Frankel, "Effective Marginal Tax Rates on Lower-Income American Workers," February 8, 2008, http://content.ksg.harvard.edu/blog/jeff_frankels_weblog/2008/02/08/8/.

11. Kevin Lindsay, Lawrence Hassett, and Aparna Mathur, "Moving towards a Unified Credit for Low-Income Workers" (American Enterprise Institute Working Paper No. 150, August 10, 2009), http://www.aei.org/docLib/Moving-Towards-a-Unified-credit.pdf.

12. To match the current combined benefits, in the range $16,450 to $19,300, the phaseout rate is 11 percent and then 12 percent thereafter.

13. Owing to the full phasing in of the dependent allowance, the combined phase-out rate is 11 percent in the income range $16,450 to $19,300 and 16 percent in the income range $23,950 through $31,250.

14. With a 9 percent phase-out rate, the implicit tax rate would be 31.65 percent in the income range $40,250 to $54,633. With a 12 percent phase-out rate, the implicit tax rate would be 34.65 percent in the income range $40,250 to $47,033.

15. Karen Schulman and Helen Blank, "State Child Care Assistance Policies 2008" (National Women's Law Center Issue Brief, September 2008), tables 1A and 3A.

16. In 2008, in virtually every state the monthly charges of child care facilities at quality centers—those at the 75th percentile of market rates—were at least $500 for four-year-olds and at least $600 for a one-year-old. Ibid., table 4C.

17. Stacey Dicket-Conlin, Katie Fitzpatrick, and Andrew Hanson, "Utilization of Income Tax Credits by Low-Income Individuals," *National Tax Journal* 58 (December 2005): 743–75. http://student.maxwell.syr.edu/kefitzpa/Home/NTJ.pdf.

18. National Women's Law Center, "An Expanded and Refundable Child and Dependent Care Tax Credit . . . " (November 2009), http://www.nwlc.org/pdf/CDCTCFactsheet2009.pdf.

19. Elaine Maag, "State Tax Credits for Child Care," *Tax Notes*, July 11, 2005, 239; see also National Women's Law Center, "Making Care Less Taxing: Improving State Child and Dependent Care Tax Provisions," various years, http://www.nwlc.org/pdf/DCTCUp-date2005.pdf. The fifteen jurisdictions that had nonrefundable credits are District of Columbia, Delaware, Georgia, Idaho, Kansas, Kentucky, Maryland, Massachusetts, Montana, North Carolina, Ohio, Oklahoma, Rhode Island, South Carolina, and Virginia.

20. One potential benefit not explored is the possibility that by using a DCA, a family's adjust gross income falls to a low enough level that the family becomes eligible for subsidies at an approved government child care center.

21. If she had one child, the federal gains would be $1,079 plus $500 in additional state tax benefits. She would, however, be ineligible for $810 of state child credits so that the net gain from shifting to a DCA would be $679. For a further analysis of New York, see Robert Cherry, "Using Child Tax Benefits in New York State," *CPA Journal* 79 (March 9, 2009): 10–16.

22. http://www.tax.state.nm.us/forms/year07/2007pitrcforminternet.pdf.

23. http://www.taxes.state.mn.us/taxes/individ/forms/m1cd.pdf.

24. http://egov.oregon.gov/DOR/PERTAX/docs/2007Forms/101-170-07.pdf.

25. "Impact of 1997 Legislation" (Research Report No. 6-04, Oregon Legislative Revenue Office, December 2004), http://www.leg.state.or.us/comm/lro/rr6_04earnedincome_tax-credit.pdf.

26. For a full discussion of the New York case, see Robert Cherry, "Using Child Tax Benefits in New York State," 10–16.

27. E-mail correspondence, October 24, 2007.

28. See Cherry, "Using Child Tax Benefits in New York State."

29. Carasso and Steuerle, "The Hefty Penalty on Marriage Facing Many Households with Children."

30. Spencer Hsu, "Marriage Fund for Poor Proposed," *Washington Post*, July 22, 2005, B5; Wade Horn, "Wedding Bell Blues: Marriage and Welfare Reform," *Brookings Review* 19 (Summer 2001): 39–42.

31. Ron Haskins and Isabel Sawhill, *Creating an Opportunity Society* (Washington, DC: Brookings Institution, 2009).

32. Gregory Acs and Elaine Maag, "Irreconcilable Differences? The Conflict between Marriage Promotion Initiatives for Cohabiting Couples with Children and Marriage Penalties in Tax and Transfer Programs" (Urban Institute, April 2005), 4.

33. Schulman and Blank, "State Child Care Assistance Policies 2008," notes to table 1-B.

NOTES TO CHAPTER 9

1. Robert Lerman, "U.S. Inequality Trends and Recent Immigration," *Inequality, Welfare and Poverty* 9 (2003): 289–307.

2. See Louis Utichelle, *The Disposable American* (New York: Knopf, 2006); and Robert Cherry, "Review of Disposable American," *WorkingUSA* 10 (Spring 2007): 153–57. For a more rigorous verification of this pattern, see Peter Gottschalk and Robert Moffitt, "Changes in Job Instability and Insecurity Using Monthly SIPP Data," *Journal of Labor Economics* 17 (October 1999): S91–S126.

3. Center for American Progress, "Unionization Climbs for Two Straight Years, but Remains a Fraction of 1980s Rates" (January 2009), http://www.americanprogress.org/issues/2009/01/unions.html; Bureau of Labor Statistics, "Unionization Rates by Industry, 2004" (January 2005), http://www.bls.gov/opub/ted/2005/jan/wk4/art05.htm.

4. U.S. Census, "Table 4: Poverty Status of Families, 1958–2008," http://www.census.gov/hhes/www/poverty/histpov/hstpov4.xls.

5. Lerman, "U.S. Inequality Trends."

6. Michael Piore, *Birds of Passage: Migrant Labor in Industrial Societies* (New York: Cambridge University Press, 1979).

7. Thomas Muller, *Immigration and the American City* (New York: New York University Press, 1993), 137.

8. Ibid., 121.

9. George Vernez, "Surveying Immigrant Communities," *Focus* 18 (Fall 1996): 19–23.

10. "States Hire Foreign Teachers to Ease Shortages," *USA Today*, September 19, 2008, http://www.usatoday.com/news/education/2008-09-14-importing-teachers_N.htm.

11. Ibid.

12. The National Commission on Math and Science Teaching for the 21st Century, *Before It Is Too Late* (Washington, DC: U.S. Department of Education, 2000), 13, http://www.ed.gov/inits/Math/glenn/report.pdf.

13. Quoted in Vernon Briggs, *Immigrants and American Unionism* (Ithaca, NY: Cornell University Press, 2001), 153.

14. David Jaeger, "Skill Differences and the Effect of Immigrants on the Wages of Natives" (U.S. Bureau of Labor Statistics, Working Paper No. 273, December 1995). Also see George Borjas, Richard Freeman, and Lawrence Katz, "How Much Do Immigration and Trade Affect Labor Market Outcomes?" *Brookings Papers on Economic Activity* 1 (1997): 1–90.

15. George Borjas, "The Labor Demand *Is* Downward Sloping: Reexamining the Impact of Immigration on the Labor Market," *Quarterly Journal of Economics* 118 (November 2003): 1335–76.

16. Briggs, *Immigrants and American Unionism*, 175.

17. Christine Zlolniski, "Unskilled Immigrants in High-Tech Companies: The Case of Mexican Janitors in Silicon Valley," in *The International Migration of the Highly Skilled*, ed. Wayne Cornelius, Thomas Espenshade, and Idean Salehyan (San Diego: Center for Comparative Immigration Studies, 2001), 270.

18. Hannes Johannsson, Stephan Weiler, and Steve Shulman, "Immigration and Employment of Low-Skilled Workers," in *Research in Labor Economics*, ed. Solomon Polachek, vol. 22 (Cambridge, MA: Elsevier Science, 2003), 291–308.

19. Marc Frenette, "Immigrant Occupational Concentration and Native-Born Wages" (Statistics Canada, Analytical Studies Research Paper Series, 2005).

20. For racial housing segregation, see Douglass Massey, "The Residential Segregation of Blacks, Hispanics, and Asians, 1970–1990," in *Immigrants and Race: New Challenges for American Democracy*, ed. Gerald Jaynes (New York: Russell Sage, 2000), 44–73.

21. John Bound and Richard Freeman, "What Went Wrong? The Erosion of the Relative Earnings of Young Black Men during the 1980s," *Quarterly Journal of Economics* 107 (February 1992): 215n.

22. Marc Breslow, "The Racial Divide Widens," *Dollars & Sense*, no. 197 (January/February 1995): 4–7.

23. Marta Tienda, "Immigration and Native Minority Workers: Is There Bad News after All?" in *Help or Hindrance? The Economic Implications of Immigration for African Americans*, ed. Daniel Hamermesh and Frank Bean (New York: Russell Sage, 1998), 345–52.

24. Judith Hellerstein, Melissa McInerney, and David Neumark, "Spatial Mismatch, Immigrant Networks, and Hispanic Employment in the United States" (NBER Working Paper No. 15398, October 2009), 26.

25. Daniel Hamermesh, "Immigration and the Quality of Jobs," in Hamermesh and Bean, *Help or Hindrance?* 75–106. Also see Jaeger, "Skill Differences."

26. Frank Bean, Jennifer Van Hook, and Mark Fossett, "Immigration, Spatial and Economic Change, and African American Employment," in *Immigration and Opportunity*, ed. Frank Bean and Stephanie Bell-Rose (New York: Russell Sage, 1999), 31–63.

27. Frank Bean, Mark Fossett, and Kyung Tae Park, "Labor Market Dynamics and the Effects of Immigration on African Americans," in Jaynes, *Immigrants and Race*, 143–62.

28. Harry Holzer, "Immigration Policies and Less-Skilled Workers in the United States," (Washington, DC: Migration Policy Institute, 2011) www.policymigration.org

29. Mary Waters, "West Indian and African Americans at Work," in Bean and Bell-Rose, *Immigration and Opportunity*, 194–217.

30. Roger Waldinger, "Network, Bureaucracy, and Exclusion," in Bean and Bell-Rose, *Immigration and Opportunity*, 228–60.

31. David Howell and Elizabeth Mueller, "Immigration and Native-Born Male Earnings," *Journal of Ethnic and Migration Studies* 26 (July 2000): 469–93.

32. Ibid.

33. Michael Rosenfeld and Marta Tienda, "Mexican Immigration, Occupational Niches, and Labor-Market Competition," in Bean and Bell-Rose, *Immigration and Opportunity*, 97.

34. Christopher Decker, Jerry Deichert, and Lourdes Gouveia, *Nebraska's Immigrant Population: Economic and Fiscal Impacts* (Omaha, NE: Office of Latino/Latin American Studies, University of Nebraska, 2008).

35. James Smith and Barry Edmonston, eds., *The New Americans: Economic, Demographic, and Fiscal Effects of Immigration* (Washington, DC: National Academies Press, 1997); David Demslow and Carol Weissert, "Tough Choices: Shaping Florida's Future" (LeRoy Collins Institute, University of Florida, October 2005), www.bebr.ufl.edu/Archives/CBAReport/Tough_Choices.pdf.

36. Steve Camarota, "Immigration at Mid-Decade" (Center for Immigration Studies, December 2005), table 6, www.cis.org/articles/2005/back1405.pdf.

37. Alan Gustman and Thomas Steinmeier, "Social Security Benefits of Immigrants and U.S. Born" (NBER Working Paper No. 6478, September 1998).

38. Michael Fix and Wendy Zimmerman, *Educating Immigrant Children* (Washington, DC: Urban Institute, 1993).

39. Julian Betts, "Educational Crowding Out: Do Immigrants Affect the Educational Attainment of American Minorities?" in Hamermesh and Bean, *Help or Hindrance?* 255–56.

40. James McKinley, "Hispanic Immigrants' Children Fall Behind Peers Early, Study Finds," *New York Times*, October 21, 2009, A19.

41. Edward Telles and Vilma Ortiz, *Generations of Exclusion: Mexican Americans, Assimilation and Race* (New York: Russell Sage, 2008), 133.

42. Coll quoted in Mary Ann Zehr, "Scholars Mull the 'Paradox' of Immigrants: Academic Success Declines From 1st to 3rd Generation," *Education Week* 28 (March 18, 2009): 7. See the proceedings from the conference "The Immigrant Paradox in Education and Behavior," Brown University, March 6–7, 2009, http://www.brown.edu/Departments/Education/paradox/.

43. Robert Smith, *Mexican New York: Transnational Lives of New Immigrants* (Berkeley: University of California Press, 2006), 213.

44. Ibid., 215.

45. Hoan Bui, "Parent-Child Conflicts, School Troubles, and Differences in Delinquency across Immigration Generations," *Crime and Delinquency* 55 (2009): 412–41.

46. Smith, *Mexican New York*, 95.

47. Ibid., 131.

48. Ibid., 134.

49. Ibid., 146.

50. David North, "The Immigration Paradox: The Stalled Progress of Recent Immigrants' Children" (Center for Immigration Studies, September 2009).

51. Cord Jefferson, "How Illegal Immigration Hurts Black America," *The Root*, February 10, 2010, http://www.theroot.com/views/how-illegal-immigration-hurts-black-america.

52. Ibid.

53. Manuel Pastor and Vanessa Carter, "Conflict, Consensus, and Coalition: Economic and Workforce Development Strategies for African Americans and Latinos," *Race and Social Problems* 1 (2009): 143–56.

54. Lucia Lo, Valerie Preston, Shuguang Wang, Katherine Reil, Edward Harvey, and Bobby Siu, "Immigrants' Economic Status in Toronto: Rethinking Settlement and Integration Strategies," in *Integrating Diversity* (Working Paper No. 15, CERIS-Toronto, 2000).

NOTES TO CHAPTER 10

1. Connie Citro and Robert Michael, *Measuring Poverty: A New Approach* (Washington, DC: National Academy Press, 1995).

2. Edward Glaeser and Joseph Gyourko, *Rethinking Federal Housing Policy: How to Make Housing Plentiful and Affordable* (Washington, DC: AEI Press, 2008).

3. U.S. Department of Housing and Urban Development, *Affordable Housing Needs 2005: Report to Congress* (HUD Office of Policy Development, 2007).

4. Edgar Olsen, "The Cost-Effectiveness of Delivering Housing Subsidies" (paper presented at the Association for Public Policy and Management Research conference, Washington, DC, November 2009); Margery Austin Turner and G. Thomas Kingsley, "Federal Programs for Addressing Low-Income Housing Needs" (Urban Institute, 2008).

5. Turner and Kingsley, "Federal Programs for Addressing Low-Income Housing Needs"; Robert Ellickson, "The Mediocrity of Government Subsidies to Mixed Income Housing Project," *Yale Law and Economics Research Paper* (New Haven, CT: Yale Law School, 2008).

6. Glaeser and Gyourko, *Rethinking Federal Housing Policy*; David Erickson, *The Housing Policy Revolution: Networks and Neighborhood* (Washington, DC: Urban Institute Press, 2009); George Peterson, "Housing Vouchers: The U.S. Experience," in *Vouchers and the Provision of Public Services*, ed. C. Eugene Steuerle et al. (Washington, DC: Brookings Institution, 2000).

7. Brian Jacob and Jens Ludwig, "The Effects of Housing Assistance on Labor Supply: Evidence from a Voucher Lottery" (NBER Working Paper No. 14570, December 2008); and Edgar Olsen, Catherine Tyler, Jonathan King, and Paul Carillo, "The Effects of Different Types of Housing Assistance on Earnings and Employment," *Cityscape* 8 (2005): 163–87.

8. In addition, the effect of the higher income taxes required to finance the benefits will distort taxpayer decisions about working and other actions, raising the costs to taxpayers above the revenues paid to the government.

9. Richard Green and Stephen Malpeezi, *A Primer on U.S. Housing Market and Housing Policy* (Washington, DC: Urban Institute Press, 2003).

10. Deven Carlson, Robert Haveman, Thomas Kaplan, and Barbara Wolfe, "Benefits and Costs of the Section 8 Housing Subsidy Program" (Discussion Paper No. 1380-10, Institute for Research on Poverty, May 2010).

11. Larry Orr, Judith Feins, Robin Jacob, Erik Beecroft, Lisa Sambomatsu, Lawrence Katz, Jeffrey Liebman, and Jeffrey Kling, *Moving to Opportunity for Fair Housing Demonstration Program: Interim Effects Evaluation* (Washington, DC: U.S. Department of Housing and Urban Development, Office of Policy Development and Research, 2004).

12. Jens Ludwig, Jeffrey Liebman, Jeffrey Kling, Greg Duncan, Ronald Kessler, and Lisa Sambomatsu, "What Can We Learn about Neighborhood Effects from the Moving to Opportunity Experiment?" *American Journal of Sociology* 114 (2008): 144–88.

13. For a comprehensive evaluation of the economic and social benefits, see Carlson, Haveman, Kaplan, and Wolfe, "Benefits and Costs of the Section 8 Housing Subsidy Program."

14. Douglas Rice and Barbara Sard, "Decade of Neglect Has Weakened Federal Housing Programs" (Center for Budget and Policy Priorities, 2009), http://www.cbpp.org/files/2-24-09hous.pdf.

15. Glaeser and Gyorko, *Rethinking Federal Housing Policy.*

16. Edgar Olsen, "The Cost-Effectiveness of Delivering Housing Subsidies" (paper presented at the Association for Public Policy and Management Research conference, Washington, DC, November 2009).

17. Glaeser and Gyourko, *Rethinking Federal Housing Policy.*

18. The $1,000 per month figure is about the average income of families currently receiving subsidies.

19. Turner and Kingsley, "Federal Programs for Addressing Low-Income Housing Needs."

20. Todd Sinai and Nicholas Souleles, "Owner-Occupied Housing as a Hedge against Rent Risk," *Quarterly Journal of Economics* 120 (2005): 763–89.

21. Kathryn Edin and Maria Kefales, *Promises I Can Keep: Why Poor Women Put Motherhood before Marriage* (Berkeley: University of California Press, 2005).

22. Thanks to Andrew Cherlin, a well-known family sociologist, for making this point.

23. Robert Lerman and Signe-Mary McKernan, "The Benefits and Consequences of Holding Assets," in *Asset Building and Low-Income Families,* ed. Signe-Mary McKernan and Michael Sherraden (Washington, DC: Urban Institute Press 2008), 175–206.

24. Jane Jacobs, *The Death and Life of Great American Cities* (New York: Random House, 1961); Michael Schill, "Distressed Public Housing: Where Do We Go from Here?" *University of Chicago Law Review* 60 (Spring 1993): 497–554.

25. Rod Soloman, "Public Housing Reform and Voucher Success" (Metropolitan Policy Program, Brookings Institution, 2005).

26. Howard Husock, "A Perilous 'Rescue' for NYC Housing," *New York Post*, March 17, 2010., 27.

27. Kathleen Lucadamo, "New York's Neediest Will Have to Pitch In 30% of Their Paycheck to Cover Rent Aid," *New York Daily News,* May 21, 2010, 23.

28. Reid Cramer and Jeffrey Lubell, *Rental Assistance Asset Accounts* (Washington, DC: New America Foundation, 2009), http://assets.newamerica.net/sites/newamerica.net/files/policydocs/RentalAsssistanceAssetAccounts.pdf.

29. Yuliya Demyanyk and Otto Van Hemert, "Understanding the Subprime Mortgage Crisis," *Review of Financial Studies* (published online, May 2009). 30. I thank Katharina Moll for her excellent research assistance in compiling these data.

31. Bureau of Labor Statistics, http://www.bls.gov/cpi/cpiqa.htm#Question_2.

32. This information comes from a telephone interview in February 2009 with Lisa Lehman of the Michigan State Housing Authority.

33. Michael Powell, "Old-Fashioned Bulwark in a Tide of Foreclosures," *New York Times*, March 7, 2010, MB1.

NOTES TO CHAPTER 11

1. Casey Mulligan, "The Season Job Surge: The 2010 Edition," *New York Times Economix Blog*, August 11, 2010, http://economix.blogs.nytimes.com/2010/08/11/the-seasonal-job-surge-2010-edition/.

2. Kathryn Anne Edwards and Alexander Hertel-Fernandez, "The Kids Aren't All Right: A Labor Market Analysis of Young Workers," Economic Policy Institute Bulletin 258 (April 7, 2010).

3. James Kemple, *Career Academies: Long-Term Impacts on Labor Market Outcomes* (New York: Manpower Demonstration Research Corporation, 2008).

4. See Organization for Economic Cooperation and Development, *Employment Outlook, 2010: Moving beyond the Jobs Crisis* (Paris: OECD, 2010), table C, http://www.oecd.org/dataoecd/27/40/45591607.pdf.

5. Algernon Austin, "Getting Good Jobs for People of Color" (Economic Policy Institute Report No. 250, November 12, 2009).

6. "Hiring and Fairness," *New York Times*, July 20, 2010, A26.

7. Heidi Hartmann, Ariane Hegewisch, Hannah Liepmann, and Claudia Williams, "The Gender Wage Gap, 2009" (Institute for Women's Policy Research No. C350A, April 2010).

8. Quoted in Kathy Ruff, "Report: WIA-Trained Women Earn less Than Male Counterparts," *Northeast Pennsylvania Business Journal*, April 1, 2010. For report, see Ariane Hegewisch and Helen Luyri, "The Workforce Investment Act and Women's Progress: Does WIA Funded Training Reinforce Sex Segregation in the Labor Market and the Gender Wage Gap?" (Institute for Women's Policy Research No. C372, January 2010).

9. Ruff, "Report."

10. Motoko Rich, "Factory Jobs Return but Employers Find Skills Shortage," *New York Times*, July 1, 2010, A1.

11. Ibid.

12. Tamar Lewin, "U.S. Releases Rules on For-Profit Colleges," *New York Times*, July 23, 2010.

13. Journal of Blacks in Higher Education Weekly Online Bulletin, "The University of Phoenix Has Become a Major Bulwark of African-American Higher Education" (December 31, 2009), http://www.jbhe.com/latest/news/12-31-09/phoenix.html.

14. Lewin, "U.S. Releases Rules on For-Profit Colleges."

15. Kevin Hollenbeck, "State Use of Workforce System Net Impact Estimates and Rates of Return" (presented at the Association for Public Policy and Management Meetings, Los Angeles, November 2008).

16. Kathleen Harris, "Capturing Intergenerational Aspects of Change in Family Patterns" (paper presented at the National Research Council Workshop on the Science of Research on Families, Washington, DC, July 2010), http://www.bocyf.org/mullan_harris_presentation.pdf.

17. Sara McLanahan, Irwin Garfinkel, and Ronald Mincy, "Fragile Families, Welfare Reform, and Marriage," in Isabel V. Sawhill, Ron Haskins, and Kent Weaver, eds., *Welfare Reform and Beyond* (Washington, DC: Brookings Institution, 2003).

18. Heidi Shierholz, "Immigration and Wages—Methodological Advancements Confirm Modest Gains for Native Workers" (Economic Policy Institute Briefing Paper No. 255, February 4, 2010), 4.

19. James Gates, "Mississippi Company Pleads Guilty in Immigration Raid," *Clarion Ledger* (Jackson, MS), February 26, 2011, 1.

20. Ron Hira, "Bridge to Immigration or Cheap Temporary Labor" (Economic Policy Institute Briefing Paper No. 257, February 17, 2010), 1–17.

21. Ibid., 12.

22. Steve Camarota, "Estimating the Impact of the DREAM Act," Center for Immigration Studies memorandum, November 2010, http://www.cis.org/dream-act-costs.

23. Lisa Foderaro, "CUNY Adjusts amid Tide of Remediation Students," *New York Times,* March 4, 2011, A21.

24. Ibid.

25. Daniel Indiviglio, "Barney Frank: The Poor Should Rent, Not Own," *The Atlantic* (February 1, 2010). See also Dean Baker, "Owning Versus Renting," *Spotlight on Poverty* (August 24, 2009). http://www.spotlightonpoverty.org/ExclusiveCommentary.aspx?id=a8140bde-9499-4384-a603-ccef7af500fd.

26. See Robert Lerman and Signe-Mary McKernan, "Promoting Neighborhood Improvement While Protecting Low-Income Families" (Opportunity and Ownership Brief No. 8, Urban Institute, 2007), http://www.urban.org/UploadedPDF/311457_Promoting_Neighborhood.pdf.

Index

2010 Congressional elections, 192

Abramovitz, Mimi, 13
Acs, Gregory, 149
ACT scores, 103
Advanced Placement courses, 67, 103
affirmative action, 14–15, 74, 90
African Americans. *See* black Americans
Agricultural Adjustment Act (AAA), 49
Aid to Families with Dependent Children
   (AFDC), 124
Air Force Qualifying Test (AFQT), 61–62, 100
Albelda, Randy, 13, 78–79
ALF-CIO, 207
American Dream (DeParle), 24–25
American Enterprise Institute, 141
apprenticeship programs, 96, 130, 195–196,
   201–202
Austin, Algernon, 196
Autor, David, 72, 200

Baldwin County, Alabama, 157
"ban the box" hiring procedures, 66–67,
   197–198
Bane, Mary Jo, 11
Baptist Hospital (Beaumont, Texas), 101
Barreras, Ivonne, 76–77
Bennett, Brian, 26
Betts, Julian, 165
Bipartisan Millennial Housing Commission,
   180
black Americans: college graduates among,
   employment of, 75; employers' preference
   for Latino workers, 64, 160; employment
   in companies reporting to EEOC, 160; for-
   profit proprietary schools, 201; with good
   jobs, 196; high school graduation rate, 165;
   job testing, 72; less educated black workers, 196–198; Moynihan report, 116–117;

New Deal legislation, 48–49; nonmarital
   birthrate, 117; policies targeting, need for,
   19; underemployment, 64–65
black men: in cities, 15–16, 28; Clinton-
   era economic boom, 27–28, 39, 64–65;
   criminal justice system, interaction with,
   16; earnings, 62–65; employment, 15–16, 24,
   26–29, 32–35, 39–40, 60–65, 67; incarceration rate, 62; industrial restructuring, 154;
   manufacturing jobs, 15–16, 28, 160; negative stereotypes of, 28, 33, 62, 65–67, 72;
   "nickel-and-dime" jobs, 24; targeted policies
   for, need for, 40; tight labor markets, 29;
   unemployment, 27, 28–29, 32–33; wages, 162;
   withdrawal from labor force, 39–40, 194
black women, 16, 79, 99
Blank, Helen, 82
Bloomberg, Michael, 2, 104, 185
Bluestone, Barry, 24
Boo, Katherine, 130–131
Borjas, George, 158
Boushey, Heather, 30
Briber, Deandre, 36–37
Bridgeport University, 207
Briggs, Vernon, 158–159
Brockman, Zandra, 190
Bronx Community College, 106
Brookings Institute, 138–139
Brooklyn College, 105–106
Brooks, David, 3–4
Brownback, Sam, 56–57, 148
Building Strong Families (BSF) demonstra-
   tion project, 132, 203
Burtless, Gary, 100
Bush, George W., 18, 75, 141, 192, 210
Bush administration, George W.: discrimina-
   tion in employment, 75; Healthy Marriage
   Initiative, 21, 117, 123, 148; public school sex
   education, 92; tax cuts, 20, 192, 204, 205–206

community colleges, individual: Bronx
Community College, 106; Columbus State
Community College, 111; Hagerstown
Community College Advanced Technology
Center, 111; LaGuardia Community Col-
lege, 92, 109, 110; Miami-Dade Community
College, 105; Union Community College,
110–111
Community Development Block Grants
(CDBGs), 174
Community Service Society of New York, 28
Comprehensive Reform Act (2007), 169–170
Congressional Black Caucus, 17
conservatives: affirmative action, 14–15; Brooks
on, David, 3–4; child health care subsidies, 54; Equal Employment Opportunity
(EEO) enforcement, 4, 14–15; government,
rejection of, 3–4; government-funded
educational programs, 4; housing markets,
22; labor markets, 14; minimum wage, 20,
46; personal responsibility, importance of,
2; program effectiveness, concern with, 3;
State Children's Health Insurance Program
(S-CHIP), 54; unemployment, responses to,
2; wage differentials, 4; welfare as entitlement, opposition to, 20; welfare dependency, 51–53
construction, employment in, 35, 78
corn prices, 49–50
criminal background checks in employment,
65, 66–67, 72, 76, 197

Daly, Mary, 32
de Blasio, Bill, 187
Deil-Amen, Regina, 107–108, 113
Deke, John, 69
Democratic Leadership Council, 8
Democratic Party: Bush tax cuts, 205; Civil
Rights Act (1965), 59; government's role, 4;
liberal wing, 212; Simplified Family Credit,
192; unemployment insurance, 1; working
families, 206
DeParle, Jason, 13, 25
dependent care (DC) account, 143–146, 151,
152, 200
dependent care account (DCA), 83
DeVry University, 99
Diamond, Seth, 187
discrimination, 4, 10
domestic violence, 16–17

Drake Business School, 110
DREAM Act, 170, 209

earnings: apprenticeship training, 130; black
men, 62–65; black women, 79; Career
Academies, graduates of, 195; four-year
college graduates, 98–99; human capital
development (HCD) program graduates, 100–101; Latino women, 79; lifetime
earnings, class rank's influence on, 107;
low income mothers, 80–81; marriage,
121, 127–128, 129; men, 129, 130; multi-
wage-earning households, 47; occupational degree holders, 98; phase-outs, 175;
remarriage, 121; white women, 79; women,
80–84, 129; work experience, 79–80; Work
First program graduates, 100. *See also*
EITC (Earned Income Tax Credit); income
earnings disparities, 59–95; female-to-male
earnings ratio, 37–39, 47; gender disparities
in, 78–95; between holders of four-year
degrees and those who do not, 97; racial
disparities in, 13–14, 59–77
economic disparities, 13–14, 17, 60
Economic Policy Institute (EPI), 138, 206
Edelman, Peter, 11
Edin, Kathryn, 120, 184
education: adult training exiters, 90–91;
apprenticeship training, 96, 130, 195–196,
201–202; career and technical education
(CTE) programs, 70; federal aid for higher
education, 201; four-year degree programs,
emphasis on, 21, 76–77, 97; government-
funded educational programs, 4; GPAs, 53,
98–99, 103–104; IT certificate programs,
87–89; Pinellas Technical Education centers, 111; publicly funded early education,
83–84, 94; quantitative reasoning courses,
114; school-age population, 164; sex education in public schools, 92, 126; sex education *vs.* marriage education, advocates for,
123; share of workers with good jobs by
race and educational attainment, 197; single mothers, 90–91; tech-prep programs,
195; teen pregnancy, 100; Title 1 funding,
165; welfare leavers, 96–97; welfare recipients, 100. *See also* colleges; community
colleges; for-profit proprietary schools;
high schools; occupational training
Ehrenreich, Barbara, 24

EITC (Earned Income Tax Credit), 133–140,
150–152; benefits, annual, 133; child tax credit
(CTC), 139–141; Clinton and, Bill, 11; costs,
annual, 134; dependent care (DC) account's
impact on, 143; eligibility cutoff, 142; eligibility for, 47, 164; employment decisions, 137;
family income, government measure of, 6;
food stamp benefits, 135, 139; immigrants,
162–163; implicit tax rate, 135–137, 138–139;
improving, 134–137; income averaging, 204;
labor force participation, 81; low income
mothers, 147; marriage, 124; marriage penalties, 150; maximum credit cutoff points, 135;
Mexican-immigrant households, 164; minimum wage, as supplement to, 47; near-poor,
the, 50; officially poor, the, 11; participation
rates, 135; phase-in range, 134–135, 139,
140, 149; phase-out range, 134–135, 137, 139,
140, 142, 150; plateau region, 134–135, 139,
150; politics of, 137–140; poor families, 48;
poverty, 22, 135, 137; refundable EITC programs, 135; rent payments in public housing
projects, 135; Section 8 housing program,
135; single mothers, 56, 136; Third Way, 5, 18;
understanding of how it works, 152; unions,
137–138; work, rewards for, 125
Ellwood, David, 138
employment, 23–40, 59–77; 2000-2004, 30–31;
2007-2009 downturn, 34–35; 2008-2010, 40;
academic credentials, 74–75, 76; affirmative
action, 74; assessment centers, 74; "ban the
box" hiring procedures, 66–67, 197–198;
benefits of a high-employment economy,
23–26; of black Americans in companies
reporting to EEOC, 160; black college
graduates, 75; black men, 15–16, 24, 26–29,
32–35, 39–40, 60–65, 67; black teenagers,
71–72, 193–194; black workers with good
jobs, 196; blue-collar share of total, 28; career
and technical education (CTE) programs,
70; central city jobs, 16; child care arrangements, 94; childbearing decisions of young
women, 93; Clinton administration's first
five years (1993-1998), 19; Clinton-era
economic boom, 23–24, 27–28, 37–40, 64; in
construction, 35, 78; criminal background
checks, 65, 66–67, 72, 76, 197; discrimination
in labor markets, 60–62; displacement of
black workers by Latinos, 160–161, 168–169;
economic downturns, impact of, 29–37;

educational attainment and test scores, 196;
employed persons by occupation and sex,
85; ex-offenders, 63, 65–66; growth in, 23;
informal hiring practices, 63, 161–162; informal labor markets, 50, 62, 75–76; job growth,
beneficiaries of, 36; labor force participation rate of native-born dropouts, 159; labor
productivity, 29–30, 60; Latino immigrants,
16; left liberals, 24–25; in manufacturing, 35,
37; marriage, 121; married men, 121; math
and academic skills, 67–68; New Haven Fire
Department, 72–74; "nickel-and-dime" jobs,
24; occupational training, 69–70, 76–77;
older workers, 194–195; personal interview as
screening device, 67, 72, 76, 196; race, 15; sex
segregation indices, 85–86; share of workers
with good jobs by race and educational
attainment, 197; single mothers, 20, 30–31, 56,
81–82; skills shortages, 201; social networks,
60–61, 63; soft skills, 66, 67–68, 76; summer
employment, 36, 70–71; teen childbearing,
92–93, 95; teen pregnancy, 194; teenagers,
27–28, 35–37, 40, 69–72, 77, 206; test-based
worker screening, 72–75; tight labor markets,
15, 29, 37, 40; undesirable jobs, 160–161; weak
job markets, 29; welfare leavers, 25, 29, 101;
welfare-to-work programs, 65–66; white
men, 24, 32–35, 60–61; women workers, 30,
35, 37. *See also* labor markets; underemployment; unemployment
Equal Employment Opportunity Commission
(EEOC), 160
Equal Employment Opportunity (EEO)
enforcement: black college graduates,
75; in communications industry, 89–90;
conservatives, 4, 14–15; of firms employing
workers with less than four-year degrees,
198; gender disparities in earnings, reducing, 95; in professional employment, 75–76;
Third Way, 5
ethanol policies, 49–50˙
ex-offenders, employment of, 63, 65–66

fair market rent (FMR), 175, 182, 188–189
family income: calculating, 6; employment
of wives, 7; female-headed families, 6;
income distribution, 6–7; inequality in, 153;
married-couple families, 6; structure of the
family, 116; of working families, 5. *See also*
low income families

Family Tax Relief Act (2009), 143
farm aid, 45
"Farm Aid" concerts, 45
Featherstone, Liza, 24
Federal Communications Commission (FCC), 89, 90
Feinstein, Diane, 170
female-headed families: marriage, 50–51; material hardships, persistence of, 8; poverty, 6, 12, 31–32
feminism, left liberals and, 18
financial incentives, Third Way and, 2–3
Firebirds Society, 74
Fisher, Allan, 86
Fix, Michael, 165
Foderaro, Lisa, 209
food prices, 50
food stamps, 135, 139, 175
for-profit proprietary schools: associate degrees granted, 112; black Americans, 201; certificate programs, 109–110; certificates granted, 112; degree grantors for black women, 99; faculty, 112; federal aid, 201; job placement, 113; as model for community colleges, 115; occupational training at, 113; remediation courses, 113; standards for, 201; student debt, 112; student services, 113
Fox, Vincente, 168
Fragile Families and Child Wellbeing Study, 128, 203
Frank, Barney, 210
Freshman Initiative Program (FIT), 106
Friedman, Milton, 137
Fuller, Bruce, 165

Gandy, Kim, 117
Gates, Henry Louis, Jr., 17
Gatta, Mary, 110
GDP, 29–30, 37
gender: earnings disparities in, 78–95; employed persons by occupation and sex, 85; occupational segregation, 198–199
General Electric, 160
Geronimus, Arline, 93
Glenn, John, 158
government antidiscrimination efforts: Clinton and, Bill, 13–14, 17, 75; left liberals, 4, 10, 13–14
government spending to support working people, 2, 3

government-sponsored enterprises (GSEs), 210
GPAs, 53, 98–99, 103–104
Gran Torino (film), 59–60, 62, 67
Grubb, W. Norton, 24, 111
Gustman, Alan, 164

Hagerstown Community College Advanced Technology Center, 111
Haimson, Joshua, 69
Hamermesh, Daniel, 160
Hartke, Vance, 43
Haskins, Ron, 1–2
health industry, women workers in, 91–92
Healthy Families Act, 91
Healthy Marriage Initiative, 21, 117, 123, 148
Heckman, James, 68–69
Hegewisch, Ariana, 199
Hernandez, Nina, 31
high schools: Advanced Placement courses, 67; career and technical education (CTE) programs, 70; in Chicago, 102–104; college, readiness for, 103–104; College Now programs, 69–70; dropouts among at-risk students, 195; graduation rates, 102–104, 165; math and academic skills, 67–68; occupational training, 69–70; tech-prep programs, 195
Hilger, Marion, 43
Hira, Ron, 208
Historically Black Colleges (HBC), 99
Holy Temple Baptist Church (Oklahoma City), 130
Holzer, Harry, 64, 65, 74, 161
HOME investment partnership grants, 174
homelessness, 186–187
homeownership, 183–190; affordability, 188; biases against in housing subsidies, 183–184; carrying costs, 188; foreclosures, 171, 188, 189, 210; as hedge against variable costs of rental housing, 211; homeownership vouchers (HVs) substitute for rent vouchers, 184–185, 187–190, 211; low income families, 171, 172, 187–190, 210–211; marriage, 184; noneconomic benefits, 184; preassistance counseling programs, 188
Horn, Wade, 57, 148
House of Raeford Farms, 168–169
Housing and Community Development Act (1974), 44–45

individualized training account (ITA), 90

inequality: among recent immigrants, 155; in family income, 153; immigration, 153–155; marriage, 116, 118; nonmarital childrearing, 117; single parent families, 129

information technology (IT), 86–89

Jackson, Jesse, 9–10

Jacobs, Jerry, 96–97

Jaeger, David, 158

Jencks, Christopher, 13

Jim Crow, 55

Job Training Partnership Act (JTPA), 90

Johnson, Lyndon, 59, 192

Kaplan University, 112

Kefalas, Maria, 120, 184

Kennedy, Ted, 170

Kids Count, 92, 93

King, Rodney, 9

King Cullen supermarket chain, 68

Kirschenman, Joleen, 64

Kristof, Nicholas, 51

Krueger, Alan, 46

Krugman, Paul, 51

Kwok, Joyce, 32

labor markets: black men's withdrawal from labor force, 39–40, 194; child support payments from noncustodial fathers, collection of, 50; conservatives, 14; discrimination in, 60–62; informal labor markets, 50, 62, 75–76; low-wage labor markets, 47, 63; noncollege labor markets, gender discrimination in, 79–80; tight labor markets, 15, 29, 37, 40; weak job markets, 29; white withdrawals from labor force, 194

labor productivity, 29–30, 60

LaGuardia Community College, 92, 109, 110

Latino women, earnings of, 79

Latino workers, 61, 64, 160

Latinos, four-year graduates, 99

Lazerson, Marvin, 24, 111

left liberals: benefit-cost analyses, 42; "blaming the victim" philosophy, 2, 12, 14, 212; Bush's Healthy Marriage Initiative, 21; cash transfers, 137; child support payments from noncustodial fathers, collection of, 17, 18; Clinton and, Bill, 10–11, 13; discrimination,

4, 10; domestic violence, 16–17; economic disparities, 14, 17; employment, 24–25; feminism, 18; four-year degree programs, 21, 98; Gates, Henry Louis, Jr., arrest of, 17; government antidiscrimination efforts, 4, 10, 13–14; government efforts to encourage marriage, 148; government-funded educational programs, 4; government spending to support working people, 2; housing markets, 22; immigration, 207, 208–209; incomes of working families, raising, 5; individual behavior, government policies influencing, 2, 14, 133; information technology (IT), 87; markets, 2–3, 42; multiculturalism, 207; Norplant implants, 56; occupational training, 5, 21, 114; personal responsibility, importance of, 2; public school sex education, 92; racism, 14, 17; single mothers, 18; sweatshops, 51; teen pregnancy, 12; wage differentials, 4–5; welfare dependency, 51–52; welfare reform, 9–11, 13

Lennon, Chauncey, 25, 26–27

Levitan, Mark, 28

Lewin, Tamar, 112

Liebman, Jeffrey, 138, 139–140

LIHTC (Low-Income Housing Tax Credit): developers, popularity with, 181; federal tax write-offs through, 185–186; inefficiency of, 179–181, 190; maximum income for tenants qualifying for, 177; near-poor, the, 177; replacement by homeownership vouchers (HV), 190, 211; tax credits awarded by, 176–177; units constructed since 1993, 174

Logue, Alexandra W., 209

Lost Ground (Albelda and Withorn), 13

low income families: child and dependent care (CADC) tax credit, 83; dependent care account (DCA), 83; government housing programs, 172; government tax benefits, 48; homeownership, 171, 172, 187–190; housing subsidies, 174–175, 182, 210; implicit tax rates, 137, 151; size of houses, 172; time horizons of, 184

low income mothers, 80–81, 147, 149, 150

low income women, marriage and, 117, 120–121, 126–127, 128–129

lower middle class families, 6, 54

Luker, Kristin, 93, 100

Lutheran Church-Missouri Synod v. FCC, 90

Maag, Elaine, 149

"Make Work Pay" philosophy, 10, 11, 13, 52

Mandate for Change (Democratic Leadership Council), 8

Manpower Development Research Corporation (MDRC), 100

manufacturing: black men, 15–16, 28, 160; employment in, 35, 37; movement away from cities, 15–16

Margolis, Jane, 96

market failures, 42

markets, 2–3, 42. *See also* housing markets; labor markets

marriage, 116–132, 202–204; access to help, 121; child support payments from non-custodial fathers, collection of, 125–126; cohabitation compared to, 118, 120, 129, 152, 203; discouragement of, 124–126, 134, 146–151; earnings, 121, 127–128, 129; economic well-being, 118–122; economies of scale, 120; EITC (Earned Income Tax Credit), 124; employment, 121; family income, 6, 116; female-headed families, 50–51; government efforts to encourage, 148; government policies, 123–127; happiness, 122; health benefits, 122–123; healthy relationship programs, 130–132; homeownership, 184; income, 120–122; inequality, 116, 118; job markets, success in, 128; living standards, 120–122; low income women, 117, 120–121, 126–127, 128–129; material hardships, persistence of, 8; mortality, 122; multipartner fertility, 119; norms associated with, 120, 122, 128; penalties for, 124–126, 134, 146–151, 152, 204; politics of reform, 202–204; poverty, 116, 118; pro-marriage attitudes, 128; promotion policies, effectiveness of, 148; public interest in encouraging, 123; relationship skills, 128; remarriage, 121; risk diversification, 120; specialization, 120; women, college-educated, 119; working single mothers, 134

marriage bonuses, 56–57

"marriage premium," 121

married-couple families: Aid to Families with Dependent Children (AFDC), 124; material hardships, persistence of, 8; poverty, 6, 8, 155

material hardships: food hardships, 31; persistence of, 8; single mothers, 18; welfare leavers, 13; of women in low-paying jobs, 18

McCabe, Robert, 105, 108

McCain, John, 20, 59, 205

McKeon , Adele, 36

McLanaham, Sara, 119

Medicaid, 43–44, 136, 164

Medicare, 135

Mellencamp, John, 45

Mellow, Gail, 110

men: college, 129; earnings, 129, 130; industrial restructuring, 154; job prospects for, 129; labor force participation rates, 154. *See also* black men; child support payments from noncustodial fathers, collection of; white men, employment of

Mexican Americans, 164, 165–168

Miami-Dade Community College, 105

Michigan State Housing Development Authority, 189

Mills, David, 9

minimum wage: Clinton and, Bill, 11; conservatives, 20, 46; EITC (Earned Income Tax Credit) as supplement to, 47; enactment of, 49; layoffs, 46; poverty, 47; purchasing power of, 154; state-legislated, 133; women workers, 47

Mink, Gwendolyn, 13

Minneapolis, 66–67

Moss, Philip, 72

Moving to Opportunity (MTO) demonstration project, 178–179, 180

Moyniham, Patrick, 11

Moynihan, Daniel Patrick, 116–117

Muller, Thomas, 156

multiculturalism, 207

multipartner fertility, 119

National Academy of Science (NAS), 158, 163–164, 171

National Center for Educational Statistics, 102

National Commission on Math and Science Teaching, 158

National Educational Summit of High Schools, 67

National Research Council, 163, 165

native-born Hispanics, high school graduation rate, 165

public housing projects: 1937-174, 173; construction of, cessation of, 55; households living in (2007), 174; phase-out rate, 175; poor, the, 55; rent payments in, 135; "vouchering out of," 180, 186

Putting Poor People to Work (Shaw and Jacobs), 97

Quineau, Herve, 85

race, 59–77; employment, 15; race-based college admission policies, 47–48, 53, 55; racial disparities in earnings, 13–14, 59–77; racial wage differentials, 61; share of workers with good jobs by race and educational attainment, 197

racism: discrimination in labor markets, 60–62; economic disparities, 13–14, 17, 60; left liberals, 14, 17; racial disparities in earnings, 13–14; structural impediments to equitable treatment, 59–60

Rainbow Coalition, 9

Raphael, Steven, 65

Reagan Democrats, 14, 59

Rector, Robert, 57

Reed, Bruce, 8, 10

Reid, Harry, 170

Republican Party: in cities and suburbs, 3–4; Simplified Family Credit, 138, 192; "Southern Strategy," 59; Tea Party, 212; unemployment insurance, 1

Ricks, Wayne, 73–74

Riley, John, 107

Ritze, Nancy, 98

Roberts, Anthony, 36–37

Roosevelt, Franklin D., 171

Roosevelt administration, Franklin D., 49

Rosenbaum, James, 107–108, 113

Rosenfeld, Michael, 162

Rosnick, David, 30

Ross, Lisa, 207

Ryan, William, 13–14

Savage, Charles, 75

Scarborough, David, 72

Schumer, Chuck, 208

Sears, 160

Seattle-Denver Income Maintenance Experiment (SIME/DIME), 125

Section 8 housing program: cost and value of rental units, 177; creation, 44; EITC (Earned Income Tax Credit), 135; inequities in distributing assistance, 182; lower-middle-class families, 54; near-poor, the, 54; new construction/substantial rehabilitation program, 173–174; poor, the, 54; provisions, 44–45; public housing projects, 55; rents in, 176; value to tenants, 186; vouchers, 55, 56

sex education, 92, 123, 126

Shah, Baiju R., 201

Shahzad, Faisal, 207–208

Shaw, Katherine, 96–97

Sheldon, Charles, 42

Shipler, David, 25, 93

Simplified Family Credit, 140–142; Democratic Party, 192; dependent care (DC) accounts, benefits from, 146; Economic Policy Institute (EPI), 138; expected beneficiaries, 138; implicit tax rate, 141–142; left-of-center support, 138; marriage penalties, reduction in, 150; near-poor, the, 138; Obama and, Barack, 205; recommendation for, 204; Republican Party, 138, 192

single mothers: child care arrangements, 81–83, 142; child tax credit (CTC), 133; dependent care (DC) account, 143; EITC (Earned Income Tax Credit), 56, 136; employment, 20, 30–31, 56, 81–82; government benefits to working single mothers, 134; income, 32; individual behavior of, government policies influencing, 152; left liberals, 18; marriage penalties, 124, 147–148, 204; material hardships, 18; "nickel-and-dime" jobs, 24; Obama administration stimulus funds, 52; poverty, 31–32, 125; Seattle-Denver Income Maintenance Experiment (SIME/DIME), 125; support from fathers of their children, 18–19; Third Way, 18–19; training programs, 90–91; wages, 38–39; Workforce Investment Act (WIA), 90

single parent families: children in, 116; explanations of, 127; food hardships, 31; inequality, 129; "jobs hypothesis" about, 127; never-married single parents, 119; nonmarital births, 202; poverty, 129, 155; "skill-attitudes hypothesis" about, 127; teen pregnancy, 116

Title 1 funding, 165
Training, Inc., 87–88

underemployment, 47, 64–65
unemployment: apprenticeship training,
195–196; black men, 27, 28–29, 32–33;
Clinton-era economic boom, 19, 23, 37;
conservatives, 2; GDP, 30; low-wage labor
markets, 47; married men, 121; occupational
training, 195–196; official statistics for, 27;
states' response to, 1–2; teenagers, 194
unemployment insurance, 1
Union Community College, 110–111
unions, EITC (Earned Income Tax Credit)
and, 137–138
U. S. Immigration and Customs Enforcement,
168–169
University of Michigan, 53
University of Phoenix, 99, 201
unmarried couples, births to, 116
upward mobility, 86, 87, 167–168
Urquilla-Diaz, Carlos, 112

Vernez, George, 157

wage differentials: behavioral and structural
factors, 5; black-white earnings gap, 61–62;
conservatives, 4; discrimination, 4; high
school-college gap, 158; lack of sustained
employment, 20; Latino-white earnings
gap, 61; left liberals, 4–5; racial wage differentials, 61; Third Way, 4–5
wage growth, 25–26
wages, 155–161; during Clinton-era economic
boom, 26; female-dominated occupations,
pay in, 91–93; female-to-male earnings
ratio, 37–39, 47; multi-wage-earning
households, 47; native-born black men,
162; native-born workers, 155–161, 168, 206;
professional women, 38, 40; single mothers, 38–39; wage stagnation, 31; welfare
leavers, 31; women workers, 31; working-
class women, 40. See also minimum wage
Wal-Mart, 24
Waldinger, Roger, 161–162
Wallace, Alexandria, 83
Waters, Mary, 161
Waters, Maxine, 110
Watson, Sandra, 92
welfare dependency, 16, 51–53

welfare leavers: aid in transition to work, 11;
average income, 25; economic situation,
improvements in, 11–12; educational programs for, 96–97; employment, 25, 29, 101;
life decisions, 93; material hardships, 13;
poverty, 13; wage trajectories, 31
welfare recipients, educational attainments
of, 100
welfare reform: Clinton and, Bill, 8–11; left
liberals, 9–10, 13; "Make Work Pay" philosophy, 10, 11, 13, 52, 97; nonmarital births,
117; poverty, 12; school attendance, 101;
teen pregnancy, 12–13; Third Way, 11; wage
growth, 25–26
welfare-to-work programs, 65–66, 100
Wellstone, Paul, 17
white men, employment of, 24, 32–35, 60–61
white women, earnings of, 79
Wilkins, Roger, 10
Wilson, William Julius, 14, 64
women, college-educated, 119
women workers: balancing family and work,
80, 142; child care arrangements, 81; economic downturns, 37; employment, 30, 35,
37; female-dominated occupations, pay in,
91–93; female-to-male earnings ratio, 37–39,
47; in health industry, 91–92; in information
technology (IT), 86–89; job turnover, 81;
labor force participation, 81; male-dominated occupations, women in, 84–91, 94,
199–200; minimum wage, 47/; professional
women, 38, 40; tax rates and employment,
81; teen childbearing, 92–93; in telecommunications industry, 89–90, 95; wages, 31
work experience, earnings and, 79–80
Work First programs, 26, 100
Workforce Investment Act (WIA), 90, 94, 199
working-class women, 198–200; career decisions, 199; child care, access to affordable,
199; occupational segregation, 198; policies
targeting, need for, 19, 38–39, 40, 199; politics of reform, 198–200; wages, 40
working families, 5–6
Working Families Tax Credit (WFTC), 145
Wright Edelman, Marianne, 11

Young, George, 130–131

Zimmerman, Wendy, 165
Zlolniski, Christine, 159

About the Authors

ROBERT CHERRY is Brueklundian Professor in the Department of Economics at Brooklyn College of the City University of New York and author of many books, including *Who Gets the Good Jobs: Combating Race and Gender Disparities* and *Welfare Transformed: Universalizing Family Policies That Work*.

ROBERT LERMAN is Professor of Economics at American University, Senior Fellow at the Urban Institute, and author or editor of many books, including *Improving Career Outcomes for Youth: Lessons from the U.S. and OECD Experience* and *Young Unwed Fathers: Changing Roles and Emerging Policies*.